Strategies and Challenges of Sustainable Development in Eurasia

This book examines the main environmental challenges and their management in post-Soviet Eurasia and China. It uncovers international, national, and subnational dimensions in sustainable development and aims to facilitate the understanding of pressing environmental problems in the region.

While supporting the values and goals of sustainable development at the international level, states might employ very different strategies at the national, regional, and local levels. The goal of this edited book is twofold. First, it aims to advance our understanding of different strategies, paying special attention to China and Russia at global, national, and sub-national levels. Thus, analysis of their strategies across different levels presents a more rounded picture. The second goal is to identify at least a few of the most pressing challenges of sustainable development across post-Soviet Eurasia and China (e.g. nuclear supply chain, emissions, environmental conflict management) and to attempt to understand their triggers, outcomes, and potential solutions. This book reflects the state of the art before the invasion in Ukraine took place. It aspires to develop a better dialogue across different sets of literature in area studies, environmental politics, and international relations to improve our understanding of obstacles to sustainable development in Eurasia.

The chapters in this book were originally published as a special issue of *Post-Communist Economies*.

Anastassia Obydenkova is Research Scientist at The Institute for Economics Analysis of the Spanish National Research Council (IAE-CSIC), Spain. and Affiliated Professor at the Barcelona School of Economics (BSE), Spain. Her main areas of expertise are sustainable development, socio-economic and geopolitical transformations, global environmental politics, and area-focus on Eurasia and China. She is the author and editor of multiple books and articles on these topics. She was awarded research fellowships at Yale, Princeton, and Harvard Universities.

Strategies and Challenges of Sustainable Development in Eurasia

Edited by
Anastassia Obydenkova

LONDON AND NEW YORK

First published 2024
by Routledge
4 Park Square, Milton Park, Abingdon, Oxon, OX14 4RN

and by Routledge
605 Third Avenue, New York, NY 10158

Routledge is an imprint of the Taylor & Francis Group, an informa business

Introduction, Chapters 1,2 and 4–6 © 2024 Taylor & Francis
Chapter 3 © 2021 Marianna Poberezhskaya and Alina Bychkova. Originally published as Open Access.

With the exception of Chapters 3, no part of this book may be reprinted or reproduced or utilised in any form or by any electronic, mechanical, or other means, now known or hereafter invented, including photocopying and recording, or in any information storage or retrieval system, without permission in writing from the publishers. For details on the rights for Chapter 3, please see the chapter's Open Access footnote.

Trademark notice: Product or corporate names may be trademarks or registered trademarks, and are used only for identification and explanation without intent to infringe.

British Library Cataloguing-in-Publication Data
A catalogue record for this book is available from the British Library

ISBN13: 978-1-032-70407-4 (hbk)
ISBN13: 978-1-032-70408-1 (pbk)
ISBN13: 978-1-032-70409-8 (ebk)

DOI: 10.4324/9781032704098

Typeset in Myriad Pro
by codeMantra

Publisher's Note
The publisher accepts responsibility for any inconsistencies that may have arisen during the conversion of this book from journal articles to book chapters, namely the inclusion of journal terminology.

Disclaimer
Every effort has been made to contact copyright holders for their permission to reprint material in this book. The publishers would be grateful to hear from any copyright holder who is not here acknowledged and will undertake to rectify any errors or omissions in future editions of this book.

Contents

Citation Information		viii
Notes on Contributors		x
Introduction: Strategies and challenges of sustainable development in Eurasia *Anastassia Obydenkova*		1
1	Leadership in high-level forums on energy governance: China and Russia compared *Jale Tosun and Karina Shyrokykh*	13
2	Environmental conflict management: a comparative cross-cultural perspective of China and Russia *Arthur L. Demchuk, Mile Mišić, Anastassia Obydenkova and Jale Tosun*	37
3	Kazakhstan's climate change policy: reflecting national strength, green economy aspirations and international agenda *Marianna Poberezhskaya and Alina Bychkova*	60
4	Greenhouse gas emissions regulation in fossil fuels exporting countries: opportunities and challenges for Russia *Ilya A. Stepanov and Igor A. Makarov*	82
5	Post-Soviet states and CO_2 emissions: the role of foreign direct investment *Raufhon Salahodjaev and Arletta Isaeva*	110
6	Nuclear supply chain and environmental justice struggles in Soviet and Post-Soviet countries *Ksenija Hanaček and Joan Martinez-Alier*	132
Index		161

Citation Information

The chapters in this book were originally published in the journal *Post-Communist Economies*, volume 34, issue 7 (2022). When citing this material, please use the original page numbering for each article, as follows:

Introduction
Strategies and challenges of sustainable development in Eurasia
Anastassia Obydenkova
Post-Communist Economies, volume 34, issue 7 (2022), pp. 835–846

Chapter 1
Leadership in high-level forums on energy governance: China and Russia compared
Jale Tosun and Karina Shyrokykh
Post-Communist Economies, volume 34, issue 7 (2022), pp. 847–870

Chapter 2
Environmental conflict management: a comparative cross-cultural perspective of China and Russia
Arthur L. Demchuk, Mile Mišić, Anastassia Obydenkova and Jale Tosun
Post-Communist Economies, volume 34, issue 7 (2022), pp. 871–893

Chapter 3
Kazakhstan's climate change policy: reflecting national strength, green economy aspirations and international agenda
Marianna Poberezhskaya and Alina Bychkova
Post-Communist Economies, volume 34, issue 7 (2022), pp. 894–915

Chapter 4
Greenhouse gas emissions regulation in fossil fuels exporting countries: opportunities and challenges for Russia
Ilya A. Stepanov and Igor A. Makarov
Post-Communist Economies, volume 34, issue 7 (2022), pp. 916–943

Chapter 5
Post-Soviet states and CO2 emissions: the role of foreign direct investment
Raufhon Salahodjaev and Arletta Isaeva
Post-Communist Economies, volume 34, issue 7 (2022), pp. 944–965

Chapter 6

Nuclear supply chain and environmental justice struggles in Soviet and Post-Soviet countries
Ksenija Hanaček and Joan Martinez-Alier
Post-Communist Economies, volume 34, issue 7 (2022), pp. 966–994

For any permission-related enquiries please visit:
http://www.tandfonline.com/page/help/permissions

Notes on Contributors

Alina Bychkova, Department of Social and Political Sciences, Nottingham Trent University, UK.

Arthur L. Demchuk, Lomonosov Moscow State University, Russian Federation.

Ksenija Hanaček, Institute of Environmental Science and Technology (ICTA), Autonomous University of Barcelona (UAB), Spain.

Arletta Isaeva, Research Department, ERGO Analytics, Tashkent, Uzbekistan.

Igor A. Makarov, Laboratory for Climate Change Economics, National Research University Higher School of Economics, Moscow, Russia.

Joan Martinez-Alier, Institute of Environmental Science and Technology (ICTA), Autonomous University of Barcelona (UAB), Spain.

Mile Mišić, Institute for the U.S. and Canadian Studies, Russian Academy of Sciences, Moscow, Russian Federation.

Anastassia Obydenkova, The Institute for Economics Analysis of the Spanish National Research Council (IAE-CSIC), Spain.

Marianna Poberezhskaya, Department of Social and Political Sciences, Nottingham Trent University, UK.

Raufhon Salahodjaev, Economics Department, AKFA University, Tashkent, Uzbekistan; Economics Department, Tashkent State University of Economics, Uzbekistan.

Karina Shyrokykh, Department of Economic History and International Relations, Stockholm University, Sweden.

Ilya A. Stepanov, Laboratory for Climate Change Economics, National Research University Higher School of Economics, Moscow, Russia.

Jale Tosun, Institute of Political Science & Heidelberg Center for the Environment, Heidelberg University, Germany.

Introduction: Strategies and challenges of sustainable development in Eurasia

Anastassia Obydenkova

ABSTRACT
While supporting the values and goals of sustainable development at the international level, states might employ very different strategies at the national level. The goal of this Forward and of special issue is twofold. First, it aims to advance our understanding of different strategies, paying special attention to China and Russia at global, national, and sub-national levels. Thus, analysis of their strategies across different levels presents a more rounded picture. The second goal is to identify at least a few of the most pressing challenges of sustainable development across Eurasia (e.g. nuclear supply chain, emissions, environmental conflict management) and to attempt to understand their triggers, outcomes, and potential solutions. This Forward aspires to develop a better dialogue across different sets of literature in area studies, environmental politics, and international relations to improve our understanding of obstacles to sustainable development in Eurasia.

Introduction

Studies on democratisation and regime transition in Eurasia have flourished over the last two decades.[1] The literature has looked into a wide range of causal explanations of the consolidation of a variety of political regimes in Eurasia and in the European Union's (EU) neighbourhood, such as historical legacies of Communism, the impact of the EU, and (associated with it) the diffusion of democratic values and principles even beyond its enlargement, at national and sub-national levels.[2] Membership in international organisations (IOs) has usually been associated with promotion of human rights, democratisation, marketisation, and economic development.[3] Only recently have scholars made the next step to ask a question regarding the possibility of the opposite impact of regional IOs led by autocracies on the consolidation of non-democratic regimes across Eurasia.[4] Yet, this rich and fast-growing body of literature on the variety of political regimes emerged in Eurasia, their causes, and their consequences, has somehow been detached from studies looking into the problems, challenges, and strategies of sustainable development in Eurasia.[5] In

Table 1. Strategies and challenges of sustainable development in Eurasia.

Strategies: Nation-States as Global, Regional, and National Actors

States as Actors	Strategy employed:	Contributions by:
China and Russia	Global and International	Jale Tosun and Karina Shyrokykh
China and Russia	National	A. L. Demchuk, M. Mišić, A. Obydenkova, J. Tosun
Kazakhstan	National	Marianna Poberezhskaya and Alina Bychkova

Challenges: Emissions and Nuclear Chain

Challenges:	Hypothetical Causes/Solutions:	Contributions by:
GHG Emissions	Political Regimes/Diffusion of Practices (introduction of tariffs)	Ilya A. Stepanov and Igor A. Makarov
CO_2 Emissions	FDI, Economic Growth, Trade / Environmental Conditionality	Raufhon Salahodjaev and Arletta Isaeva
Nuclear Supply Chain	Historical Legacies and Modern Political Regimes/Diffusion	Ksenija Hanaček and Joan Martinez-Alier

aThe summary outlined in this table goes beyond the arguments of contributions.

economics, however, a few studies have emerged connecting political regimes to outcomes of environmental policies, among other issues (e.g. Fredriksson & Neumayer, 2013; Fredriksson & Wollscheid, 2007; Nazarov & Obydenkova, 2021b). Despite this, there seems to be space for further, more interdisciplinary analysis of specific case studies and actors in Eurasia. While two sets of studies have been developing fast, they seemed to exist in two parallel worlds without much engagement with each other. Yet, both bodies of literature exhibit some similarities and unique insights, and can certainly benefit from establishing a deeper dialogue with each other. This special issue aspires to build on both somewhat separate sets of studies (on political regimes and on sustainable development in Eurasia) and to develop further the dialogue between them.

The goal of this special issue is two-fold. First, it aims to advance our understanding of different strategies, paying special attention to China and Russia at global, national, and sub-national levels. Singling out levels of analysis is highly important in this context. As the articles discussed below argue, both Russia and China seem to care about their international image as benevolent, environmentally friendly actors in the global arena. Yet, while supporting the values and goals of sustainable development at the international level, they might employ very different strategies at the national level. A certain degree of isolation and a lack of information and transparency allow for a generous interpretation of their actions within their own borders, which does not always come to the attention of international community. Thus, analysis of their strategies across different levels presents a more rounded picture.

The second focus of this special issue is to identify at least a few of the most pressing challenges of sustainable development across Eurasia and to attempt to understand their triggers, outcomes, and potential solutions. Table 1 outlines the structure, logic, and summary of the main ideas advanced in this special issue.

Strategies: nation-states as global, regional, and national actors

The first article after this foreword, by Tosun and Shyrokykh (2021), presents a detailed analysis of the strategies and activities of China and Russia in high-level forums on energy governance. The authors investigate China and Russia's involvement in the Clean Energy Ministerial (CEM). In line with literature on non-democracies, they contribute further to single out the different motivations of these actors for joining such high-level forums. The formal goals of involvement with high-level global forums is to cooperate in the reduction of greenhouse gas emissions (GHGs) through an exchange of information and practices. Informal goals, however, also include international image boosting and building a reputation as global benevolent actors (see, Tosun & Rinscheid, 2021). Another goal of both states is actual learning, networking, and contact building (see footnote 4). That is, membership in CEM not only facilitates access to technology and information, but also acts as an informal format for negotiation. Within this high-level forum, the article focuses on the strategies of the two state actors through unveiling their choice of policy initiatives undertaken at CEM. The study discovers an active and dynamic strategy on the part of China in attempting to take the lead in a number of initiatives at CEM. In contrast, Russia lags behind China in leadership strategies at CEM. The findings indicate that China has made more strategic use of the CEM compared to Russia.

The following two articles scale down from the global to the national arena, looking into how China, Russia, and Kazakhstan deal with environmental issues within their own borders. The article by Arthur L. Demchuk, Mile Mišić, Anastassia Obydenkova, and Jale Tosun (Demchuk et al., 2021) continues the comparison between China and Russia regarding environmental conflict management at the national level. It resumes a comparative approach towards the strategies employed by both states in dealing with multiple environmental conflicts at the domestic level. The study investigates strategies of environmental conflict management in China and Russia from a cross-cultural perspective. The authors argue that China and Russia share a number of characteristics, such as the role of Communism and its priorities for economic development at any cost, with its associated industrialisation and environmental degradation, but notes that both states also share a collectivist culture. The analysis of the two states also sheds light on the role played by sub-national and local governmental actors on the one hand, and on the role of public opinion and the people on the other. In the case of China, the article argues that *local governments often ally with the people*, supporting their viewpoint and helping local people negotiate the issues of environmental conflicts with central government. In contrast, in Russia, sub-national regional and local governments support 'the vertical of power',[6] thus being accountable only to the ruling elite. On the other hand, evidence also demonstrates that regional and local government may occasionally support business actors and their related projects, which initiate the environmental conflict in the first place. The latest strategy is explained through multiple studies of corruption at sub-national level in Russia. The later strategy of support of regional and local power to business is associated with financial benefits for local government and corruption. Despite existing legal channels to settle the environmental conflicts and protect public interests, the governmental actors at local and sub-national regional levels rarely support their people in Russia. Among secondary findings, the authors argue that the environmentalist movements in Russia enjoy some international support and influence. In contrast, environmental movements in China are all detached from international influence.

The third article after this foreword, by Marianna Poberezhskaya and Alina Bychkova (Poberezhskaya & Bychkova, 2021), completes the geographical picture of China and Russia by looking at their biggest neighbour, Kazakhstan, located between the two states. The geopolitical position of Kazakhstan and its wealthy natural resources (in both oil and gas) make it an important actor in Eurasia and also at a global level. The authors highlight the role of fossil fuels in the economy of Kazakhstan and the ambiguity of the Kazakhstani position in fighting climate change. While Kazakhstan is heavily dependent on the production and export of oil to China and the EU, it also faces the devastating consequences of climate change, including decreasing amounts of fresh water, a deteriorating agricultural sector, and the spread of desertification. On the other hand, the economy of Kazakhstan relies on oil exports to China and Russia. Therefore, the promotion of at least some environmental programmes, such as the construction of renewable energy plants, is not in the interests of Kazakhstan, either in the short or long term.

To address the controversial Kazakhstani standing on sustainable development, the authors study the national discourse on climate change by focusing on the analysis of legal documents and interviews conducted with experts. After in-depth analysis of the official narratives, the authors argue that Kazakhstan's calls to advance sustainable development seem to have been triggered by a strategy of image-building. That is, Kazakhstan is attempting *to appear* as a strong, environmentally friendly actor in the eyes of the national and international public. This image should also help attract much-needed foreign investments and boost economic development. In this latter aspect, Kazakhstan is echoing China and Russia's strategies at global energy forums as described in the article by Tosun and Shyrokykh in this special issue. However, Poberezhskaya and Bychkova (2021) also insightfully notice that many rhetorical promises and commitments to sustainable development made by the Government of Kazakhstan and by the president are not realistic and will likely remain unfulfilled. The authors point to similarities between modern discourse and the multiple, ambitious promises of the Soviet Union period. Modern rhetoric on sustainable development in Kazakhstan thus seems to be one of the historical legacies of Communism.

Challenges: emissions and nuclear chain

The second part of the special issue (articles Four, Five, and Six after this foreword) focuses on the specific challenges of sustainable development in Eurasia. It switches attention from a *state*-centred analysis (the *strategies* of nation-states) to a *problem*-centred analysis (that is, *challenge*-centred). The problem-centred approach looks into a few challenges, such as a reduction of emissions and nuclear chain. Within the analysis of these issues, the following three articles approach post-Soviet Eurasia within a larger comparative focus.

The second section starts with an article by Ilya A. Stepanov and Igor A. Makarov. The authors study the challenge of the regulation and reduction of GHG. The study looks into incentive-based instruments of GHG emissions regulation, such as carbon pricing. It analyzes this issue across the fossil fuel exporting economies in the world. The main target of the article is to learn the best global strategies for reducing GHG emissions and to apply them to the case of Russia. The main challenge analysed in this study is how to advance the carbon pricing strategy within a state with an economy that is dependent on exports of fossil fuels. Stepanov and Makarov elaborate a strategy and principles to advance incentives to reduce and regulate emissions, while also taking into account the importance of support to society and the economy in Russia. The study presents a sophisticated analysis of emissions regulations and schemes that work across the world in other states that are rich in fossil fuels, such as Norway, Canada, and Australia, but also in post-Soviet states, such as Kazakhstan. The authors investigate different approaches of advancing carbon pricing in energy-exporting countries across the world and call for learning their lessons in Russia, thus contributing to the literature on the diffusion of practices of sustainable development. Overall, the authors suggest adopting a balanced approach supporting vulnerable social layers and weak industries, promoting fiscal neutrality, and arguing in favour of gradual implementation of reforms, as well as the use of carbon offsets.

The article by Raufhon Salahodjaev and Arletta Isaeva continues the analysis of the environmental challenges posed by CO_2 emissions. The authors build on controversial literature on the effects of trade, financial development, and foreign direct investments (FDI) for emissions. A few studies on the topic point to the ability of FDI and trade to decrease emissions through the diffusion of technology, innovation, and global values.[7] This echoes studies on foreign aid as one of the triggers of democratisation (e.g. Wright, 2009). On the other hand, FDI and trade are associated with economic growth, without necessarily accounting for the environment. The authors test their hypotheses through looking at the effects of FDI and trade across post-Communist states and their implications for CO_2. They take into account a number of other important factors, such as consumption of energy and economic development over a two-decade period (1995–2017). Using quantitative analysis, the authors reveal that, across the 20 post-Communist states, trade and FDI are positively associated with an increase in emissions. The article echoes the previous study in calling for reforms aimed at improving the regulation of fossil fuel economies and at systematic efforts to reduce emissions across post-Communist states.

The final article by Ksenija Hanaček and Joan Martinez-Alier (Hanaček & Martinez-Alier, 2021) addresses the challenge of nuclear chain in post-Soviet Eurasia. Nuclear chain is not only a historical legacy started in the midst of the Cold War; it remains to this day and has been developed further across some post-Soviet states (e.g. in Belarus). The article focuses on socio-environmental conflicts and, thus, echoes the study by Demchuk et al. (2021) in this special issue. Hanaček and Martinez-Alier look into the public behaviour (protests) across former Soviet states. Public protests have grown into an anti-nuclear movement that is at the centre of the article. Hanaček and Martinez-Alier demonstrate that this movement is one of the few available tools capable of stopping and reverting nuclear chain and its devastating consequences for public health and for the environment.[8] The study is based on a sophisticated and meticulous analysis of 14 environmental conflicts associated with nuclear chain across the post-Soviet space, including current EU member Lithuania, the EU's closest neighbours (Belarus and Ukraine), the Caucasus (Armenia), and Central Asia (Kazakhstan, Kyrgyzstan, and Tadjikistan). The analysis also focuses on aspects such as protests against building nuclear reactors, protests against testing nuclear bombs, and protests against uranium mining. The article makes a few important discoveries. For example, one of the crucial factors that might make a difference in combating environmental conflicts is public protest – a movement that dates back to the 1970s in terms of the environment. Even within totalitarian Communist regimes, public movements survived and augmented in the 21st century. Out of the 14 examined environmental conflicts triggered by nuclear chain, seven were suspended due to public protests. Half of the identified conflicts remained. Overall, this highly impactful study not only addresses one of the biggest global environmental challenges of our time (nuclear chain); it also demonstrates the importance of civil society, transparency, and the nature of political regimes.

Conclusion

This volume contributes to multiple sets of literature and has raised a number of issues that are likely to stay on the research agenda. The collection of articles advances studies on the diffusion of values and practices, on the role of history, and importance of external influences for sustainable development (e.g. historical legacies of nuclear chain and emissions; external impact on environmental movements; environmental rhetoric). These concluding remarks outline some of these findings presented in this volume and place them within broader cross-disciplinary literature.

First, the special issue contributes to diffusion literature and studies of regionalism. It focuses on the international and national strategies of state actors and on environmental challenges. An important question is whether and how membership of states in different IOs (e.g. global climate clubs or the EU) matters in the fight against climate change (dealing with nuclear chain or emissions). As the study by Tosun and Shyrokykh (2021) argues, membership in climate clubs is associated with learning across states at the global level and allows direct access to the latest information, practices, and innovations. These activities, contacts, and formal and informal meetings within climate clubs (as well as within other IOs) are strongly associated with the diffusion of values and principles. Diffusion takes place at both cross-national and cross sub-national levels (Lankina et al., 2016a). On the other hand, the environmental commitments of China, Russia, and Kazakhstan can be analysed within the literature in terms of formal goals versus real motivations (see also, Libman & Obydenkova, 2018a, 2018b; Poberezhskaya & Bychkova, 2021). While formally proclaiming support for sustainable development, these non-democracies also seek to augment their international image as global, environmentally friendly actors (Kochtcheeva, 2021; Tosun & Rinscheid, 2021). This is in line with existing literature on the strategy of Russia in global environmental politics. In the words of Henry and McIntosh Sundstrom (Henry & McIntosh Sundstrom, 2007, p. 47), 'Russia's strategy will emphasise maximising profits through treaty mechanisms over maximising emissions reductions.' Henry and McIntosh Sundstrom also argue that such actions at international level (for example, the ratification of the Kyoto Protocol by Russia in 2004) aim to augment the status of Russia in other international negotiations and to 'contribute to an image of itself as a good member of the club of advanced industrialized states' (Henry & McIntosh Sundstrom, 2007, p. 47).[9] The collection of articles in this special issue makes the next step in considering the international and national strategies of both China and Russia.

Strategies are associated with diffusion. Previous literature has mainly focused on the diffusion of liberal values and associated it with democratisation (see Footnotes 2–3). However, values and practices can be diffused in very different ways: learning can spill over from democracies to autocracies (e.g. Ambrosio et al., 2021), but diffusion can also take place across autocracies, facilitating their learning from each other. In a way, the case study of Kazakhstan reflects these two different worlds and suggests two directions in development (Poberezhskaya & Bychkova, 2021). On the one hand, Kazakhstan seems to imitate the environmental activism of China at the global level (in line with the study of Tosun and Shyrokykh). On the other, it clearly exhibits the under-fulfilment of existing environmental commitments: its support to sustainable development seems to be more rhetorical, and its promises are not realistic (Poberezhskaya & Bychkova, 2021). Articles by Demchuk et al. (2021) and by Hanaček and Martinez-Alier (2021) also point to external influences coming from Europe and from the EU on the environmental movements in Russia (but not in China). Though this topic is not the focus of these two articles, it is still important for better understanding the triggers of environmental movements in a non-democratic context.

In line with diffusion literature, the article by Stepanov and Makarov (2021) directly engages with learning about the most efficient environmental practices used in fossil fuel democracies (e.g. Norway or Canada). The authors argue that climate change policies employed in resource-rich democracies could be imported to Russia without damaging either society or business. The topic of diffusion continues in the study by Salahodjaev and Isaeva (2021) in this issue. They discuss the potentially positive impact of FDI and foreign trade on the improvement of the environment, which could be associated with the diffusion of values through contacts, meetings, and collaboration with foreign investors.[10] This expectation, however, has been refuted by empirical findings, suggesting that FDI and trade increase emissions. It is crucial to keep in mind that the study does not distinguish between FDI and trade *with democracies* (e.g. in Europe) versus investments and trade *with autocracies* (e.g. with China).[11] Through investment and foreign trade, it is likely that states were more subject of diffusion from such donors as China and Russia rather than from European democracies. This mystery will certainly remain for further analysis and investigation.

Finally, another two sets of literature that have inspired this special issue focused on the role of historical legacies and political regimes. Existing literature on the legacies of Communism has analysed a wide range of issues, such as public behaviour, social and political trust, public health, economic equality, and even firm innovation, tolerance, and migration, among many others (Beissinger and Kotkin 2014; Pop-Eleches and Tucker 2017; Arpino & Obydenkova, 2020; Libman & Obydenkova, 2019, 2020; Nazarov & Obydenkova, 2020; Nazarov & Obydenkova, 2021a). Yet, the implications of Communism for sustainable development seem somewhat outside the focus of these studies. Building on this literature, and as some contributions to this special issue have demonstrated, historical legacies remain highly important in existing multiple environmental challenges and their management on the part of society and governmental actors (e.g. nuclear chain; environmental conflicts).

As to political regimes, it is hard to overestimate the implications of democracy for a number of the issues discussed in this volume. Previous studies have argued that democracy is an essential component of environmental politics, environmental movements and public awareness, as well as of effectiveness of policy implementation (e.g. Fredriksson & Wollscheid, 2007; Neumayer, 2002; Obydenkova & Salahodjaev, 2016; Fredriksson & Mohanty, 2021; Obydenkova & Salahodjaev, 2017; Venable, 2011). Obviously, democracies are far more sensitive to public concerns, permitting freedom of mass media and transparency, freedom of movements and protests. While protests may take place within a non-democratic context, democracies are still more responsive and sensitive to public opinion, demands, and choices (e.g. the anti-nuclear movement). On the other hand, non-democratic states withhold information, encourage manipulation via the official mass media to mislead the public, and may suppress protests and movements (be they political or environmental). Hence, expectations would be that environmental movements are less efficient and less developed in such a context.

Bringing together economists and political scientists specialising in sustainable development and political regimes, this collection of articles offers more insights into the nexus of environmental challenges and strategies employed by the largest actors, not only in Eurasia, but in the world – China and Russia. Building on interdisciplinary literature on political regimes and sustainable development, the special issue unites perspectives on economics, international relations, and social and political science. The issues raised within this volume, inter-disciplinary findings of articles and their further implications and considerations, should stay on the research agenda of sustainable development in Eurasia and beyond.

Notes

1. I would like thank all the contributors to this special issue for their inspiration and support: Joan Martinez-Alier and Ksenija Hanaček, Jale Tosun and Karina Shyrokykh, A. L. Demchuk and Mile Mišić, Marianna Poberezhskaya and Alina Bychkova, Ilya A. Stepanov and Igor A. Makarov, Raufhon Salahodjaev and Arletta Isaeva. I take this opportunity to thank the Basic Research Programme of the National Research University Higher School of Economics (HSE University) for funding the research presented in this article.
2. On the legacies of Communism, see (Beissinger and Kotkin 2014; Pop-Eleches and Tucker 2017; Libman & Obydenkova, 2020; Obydenkova & Libman, 2012; Lankina et al., 2016b).
3. On the EU and diffusion of democracy, see, (Ambrosio, 2010; Börzel & Solingen, 2014; Kopstein & Reilly, 2000; Lankina et al., 2016a; Levitsky & Way, 2010; Obydenkova, 2008; Pevehouse, 2005; Whitehead, 1996). On democratisation in Eurasia, see for example, Teorell (2010).
4. Izotov & Obydenkova, (2021); Kneuer & Demmelhuber, (2016); Libman & Obydenkova, (2018a, 2018b).
5. On Russia and China, see, (Sun & Alex, 2016; Tosun & Rinscheid, 2021; Venable, 2011; Yu, 2015; Zhang et al., 2019; Zhang & Xue-Feng, 2019). On IOs as actors of sustainable development, see, Biermann and Bauer (2004). On the EU's impact, see, Andonova and Tuta (2014).
6. On the vertical of power and territorial (de-)centralisation in Russia, see for example, Obydenkova and Swenden (2013). On sub-national actors in environmental politics (deforestation) see, Libman and Obydenkova (2014); and on subnational corruption in Russia, see for example, Dinino and Orttung (2005), Obydenkova and Libman (2015).
7. Previous studies have pointed out that loans, trade, and investment might include environmental conditionality (e.g. on banks, see, Ambrosio et al., 2021; Anastassia et al., 2021; Djalilov & Hartwell, 2021; Gutner, 2002; Hall et al., 2021). Other studies demonstrate that, in some cases, financial development *reduces* CO_2 emissions, while economic growth may increase CO_2 emissions (e.g. Shahbaz et al., 2013).
8. The importance of public opinion, transparency, and the power of independent mass media in environmental conflict management was outlined in a number of studies (e.g. Mišić & Obydenkova, 2021).
9. A similar argument can also be found in Kochtcheeva (2021).

10. To some extent, this argument echoes studies on the diffusion of (democratic) values and practices developed within international dimension of democratisation (e.g. Kopstein & Reilly, 2000; Lankina et al., 2016a; Obydenkova, 2008).
11. Very recent studies have demonstrated that even loans and investment coming from the EBRD and associated with strong environmental conditionality can be subverted by China (see for example, Anastassia et al., 2021).

Disclosure statement

No potential conflict of interest was reported by the author(s).

ORCID

Anastassia Obydenkova http://orcid.org/0000-0001-5099-5294

References

Whitehead, L. (ed.). (1996). *International dimension of democratization: Europe and the Americas*. Oxford University Press.

Beissinger, M., and Kotkin, S. (eds.). (2014). *Historical legacies of communism in Russia and Eastern Europe*. Cambridge University Press: Cambridge.

Ambrosio, T., Hall, A., & Obydenkova, A. (2021). Sustainable development agendas of regional international organizations: The European Bank of reconstruction and development and the Eurasian development bank. *Problems of Post-Communism*, 1–13. Accessed on 3 December, 2021. https://doi.org/10.1080/10758216.2021.1979412

Ambrosio, T. (2010). Constructing a framework of authoritarian diffusion: Concepts, dynamics, and future research. *International Studies Perspective*, *11*(4), 375–392. https://doi.org/10.1111/j.1528-3585.2010.00411.x

Andonova, L. B., & Tuta, I. A. (2014). Transnational networks and paths to EU environmental compliance: Evidence from new member states. *JCMS: Journal of Common Market Studies*, *52*(4), 775–793. https://doi.org/10.1111/jcms.12126

Arpino, B., & Obydenkova, A. V. (2020). Democracy and political trust before and after the great recession 2008: The European Union and the United Nations. *Social Indicators Research*, *148*(2), 395–415. https://doi.org/10.1007/s11205-019-02204-x

Biermann, F., & Bauer, S. (2004). Assessing the effectiveness of intergovernmental organizations in international environmental politics. *Global Environmental Change*, *14*(2), 189–193. https://doi.org/10.1016/S0959-3780(03)00025-6

Demchuk, A. L., Mišić, M., Obydenkova, A., & Tosun, J. (2021). Environmental conflict management: A comparative cross-cultural perspective of China and Russia. *Post-Communist Economies*, 1–23. Accessed on 3 December, 2021. https://doi.org/10.1080/14631377.2021.1943915

Dininio, P., & Orttung, R. (2005). Explaining patterns of corruption in the Russian regions. *World Politics*, *57*(4), 500–529. https://doi.org/10.1353/wp.2006.0008

Djalilov, K., & Hartwell, C. (2021). Do social and environmental capabilities improve bank stability? Evidence from transition countries. *Post-Communist Economies*, 1–23. Accessed on 3 December, 2021. https://doi.org/10.1080/14631377.2021.1965359

Fredriksson, P. G., & Mohanty, A. (2021). COVID-19 regulations, political institutions, and the environment. *Environmental and Resource Economics*. Accessed on 3 December, 2021. https://doi.org/10.1007/s10640-021-00628-z

Fredriksson, P. G., & Neumayer, E. (2013). Democracy and climate change policies: Is history important? *Ecological Economics*, *95*, 11–19. https://doi.org/10.1016/j.ecolecon.2013.08.002

Fredriksson, P. G., & Wollscheid, J. R. (2007). Democratic institutions versus autocratic regimes: The case of environmental policy. *Public Choice, 130*(3–4), 381–393. https://doi.org/10.1007/s11127-006-9093-1

Gutner, T. (2002). *Banking on the environment: Multilateral development banks and their environmental performance in central and Eastern Europe*. MIT Press.

Hall, S. G. F., Lenz, T., & Obydenkova, A. (2021). Environmental commitments and rhetoric over the Pandemic crisis: Social media and legitimation of the AIIB, the EAEU, and the EU. *Post-Communist Economies*, 1–26. Accessed on 3 December, 2021. https://doi.org/10.1080/14631377.2021.1954824

Hanaček, K., & Martinez-Alier, J. (2021). Nuclear supply chain and environmental justice struggles in Soviet and Post-Soviet countries. *Post-Communist Economies*, 1–29. Accessed on 3 December, 2021. https://doi.org/10.1080/14631377.2021.1943917

Henry, L. A., & McIntosh Sundstrom, L. (2007). Russia and the Kyoto protocol: Seeking an alignment of interests and image. *Global Environmental Politics, 7*(4), 47–69. https://doi.org/10.1162/glep.2007.7.4.47

Izotov, V. S., & Obydenkova, A. V. (2021). Geopolitical games in Eurasian regionalism: Ideational interactions and regional international organisations. *Post-Communist Economies, 33*(2–3), 150–174. https://doi.org/10.1080/14631377.2020.1793584

Kneuer, M., & Demmelhuber, T. (2016). Gravity centers of authoritarian rule: A conceptual approach. *Democratization, 23*(5), 775–796. https://doi.org/10.1080/13510347.2015.1018898

Kochtcheeva, L. V. (2021). Foreign policy, national interests, and environmental positioning: Russia's post Paris climate change actions, discourse, and engagement. *Problems of Post-Communism*, 1–13. Accessed on 3 December, 2021. https://doi.org/10.1080/10758216.2021.1968912

Kopstein, J., & Reilly, D. (2000). Geographic diffusion and the transformation of the postcommunist world. *World Politics, 53*(1), 1–37. https://doi.org/10.1017/S0043887100009369

Lankina, T. V., Libman, A., & Obydenkova, A. (2016b). Appropriation and subversion. *World Politics, 68* (2), 229–274. https://doi.org/10.1017/S0043887115000428

Lankina, T., Libman, A., & Obydenkova, A. (2016a). Authoritarian and democratic diffusion in post-communist regions. *Comparative Political Studies, 49*(12), 1599–1629. https://doi.org/10.1177/0010414016628270

Levitsky, S., & Way, L. (2010). *Competitive authoritarianism: Hybrid regimes after the Cold War*. Cambridge University Press.

Libman, A., & Obydenkova, A. V. (2018a). Understanding authoritarian regionalism. *Journal of Democracy, 29*(4), 151–165. https://doi.org/10.1353/jod.2018.0070

Libman, A., & Obydenkova, A. V. (2018b). Regional international organizations as a strategy of autocracy: The Eurasian economic union and Russian foreign policy. *International Affairs, 94*(5), 1037–1058. https://doi.org/10.1093/ia/iiy147

Libman, A., & Obydenkova, A. (2014). Governance of commons in a large nondemocratic country: The case of forestry in the Russian federation. *Publius: The Journal of Federalism, 44*(2), 298–323. https://doi.org/10.1093/publius/pjt065

Libman, A., & Obydenkova, A. (2019). Inequality and historical legacies: Evidence from post-communist regions. *Post-Communist Economies, 31*(6), 699–724. https://doi.org/10.1080/14631377.2019.1607440

Libman, A., & Obydenkova, A. (2020). Proletarian internationalism in action? Communist legacies and attitudes towards migrants in Russia. *Problems of Post-Communism, 67*(4–5), 402–416. https://doi.org/10.1080/10758216.2019.1640068

Mišić, M., & Obydenkova, A. (2021). Environmental conflict, renewable energy, or both? Public opinion on small hydropower plants in Serbia. *Post-Communist Economies*, 1–30. Accessed on 3 December, 2021. https://doi.org/10.1080/14631377.2021.1943928

Nazarov, Z., & Obydenkova, A. (2020). Democratization and firm innovation: Evidence from the European and Central Asian post-communist states. *Post-Communist Economies, 32*(7), 833–859. https://doi.org/10.1080/14631377.2020.1745565

Nazarov, Z., & Obydenkova, A. (2021a). Public health, democracy, and transition: Global evidence and post-communism. *Social Indicators Research*. Accessed on 3 December, 2021. https://doi.org/10.1007/s11205-021-02770-z

Nazarov, Z., & Obydenkova, A. (2021b). Environmental challenges and political regime transition: The role of historical legacies and the European Union in Eurasia. *Problems of Post-Communism*, 1–14. Accessed on 3 December, 2021. https://doi.org/10.1080/10758216.2021.1995437

Neumayer, E. (2002). Do democracies exhibit stronger international environmental commitment? A cross-country analysis. *Journal of Peace Research*, *39*(2), 139–164. https://doi.org/10.1177/0022343302039002001

Obydenkova, A. V., & Salahodjaev, R. (2017). Climate change policies: The role of democracy and social cognitive capital. *Environmental Research*, *157*, 182–189. https://doi.org/10.1016/j.envres.2017.05.009

Obydenkova, A., & Libman, A. (2012). The impact of external factors on regime transition: Lessons from the Russian regions. *Post-Soviet Affairs*, *28*(3), 346–401. https://doi.org/10.2747/1060-586X.28.3.346

Obydenkova, A., & Libman, A. (2015). The survival of post-communist corruption in contemporary Russia: The influence of historical legacies. *Post-Soviet Affairs*, *31*(4), 304–338. https://doi.org/10.1080/1060586X.2014.931683

Obydenkova, A., Rodrigues Vieira, V. G., & Tosun, J. (2021). The impact of new actors in global environmental politics: The European bank for reconstruction and development meets China. *Post-Communist Economies*. Accessed on 3 December, 2021. https://doi.org/10.1080/14631377.2021.1954825

Obydenkova, A., & Salahodjaev, R. (2016). Intelligence, democracy, and international environmental commitment. *Environmental Research*, *147*(1), 82–88. https://doi.org/10.1016/j.envres.2016.01.042

Obydenkova, A., & Swenden, W. (2013). Autocracy-sustaining versus democratic federalism: Explaining the divergent trajectories of territorial politics in Russia and Western Europe. *Territory, Politics, Governance*, *1*(1), 86–112. https://doi.org/10.1080/21622671.2013.763733

Obydenkova, A. (2008). Regime transition in the regions of Russia: The freedom of mass media: Transnational impact on sub-national democratization? *European Journal of Political Research*, *47*(2), 221–246. https://doi.org/10.1111/j.1475-6765.2007.00727.x

Pevehouse, J. (2005). *Democracy from above? Regional organizations and democratization*. Cambridge University Press.

Poberezhskaya, M., & Bychkova, A. (2021). Kazakhstan's climate change policy: Reflecting national strength, green economy aspirations and international agenda. *Post-Communist Economies*, 1–22. Accessed on 3 December, 2021. https://doi.org/10.1080/14631377.2021.1943916

Pop-Eleches, G., & Tucker, J. A. (2017). *Communism's shadow: Historical legacies and contemporary political attitudes*. Princeton University Press: Princeton.

Salahodjaev, R., & Isaeva, A. (2021). Post-Soviet states and CO2 emissions: The role of foreign direct investment. *Post-Communist Economies*, 1–22. Accessed on 3 December, 2021. https://doi.org/10.1080/14631377.2021.1965360

Shahbaz, M., Solarin, S. A., Mahmood, H., & Arouri, M. (2013). Does financial development reduce CO2 emissions in Malaysian economy? A time series analysis. *Economic Modelling*, *35*, 145–152. https://doi.org/10.1016/j.econmod.2013.06.037

Solingen, E. , Börzel, T. A. (2014). Introduction to Presidential Issue: The Politics of International Diffusion—A Symposium. *International Studies Review*, *16*(2), 173–187. http://www.jstor.org/stable/24032870

Stepanov, I. A., & Makarov, I. A. (2021). Greenhouse gas emissions regulation in fossil fuels exporting countries: Opportunities and challenges for Russia. *Post-Communist Economies*, 1–28. Accessed on 3 December, 2021. https://doi.org/10.1080/14631377.2021.1943918

Sun, Y., & Alex, L. (2016). Carbon trading in China: Environmental discourse and politics. Houndmills, UK: Palgrave Macmillan. *Global Environmental Politics*, *16*(3), 159–161. https://doi.org/10.1162/GLEP_r_00372

Teorell, J. (2010). *Determinants of democratization: Explaining regime change in the World, 1972–2006.* Cambridge University Press.

Tosun, J., & Rinscheid, A. (2021). The clean energy ministerial: Motivation for and policy consequences of membership. *International Political Science Review*, *42*(1), 114–129. https://doi.org/10.1177/0192512120942303

Tosun, J., & Shyrokykh, K. (2021). Leadership in high-level forums on energy governance: China and Russia compared. *Post-Communist Economies*, 1–24. Accessed on 3 December, 2021. https://doi.org/10.1080/14631377.2021.1964742

Venable, S. (2011). Red to green: Environmental activism in post-soviet Russia. *Global Environmental Politics*, *11*(3), 154–156. https://doi.org/10.1162/GLEP_r_00076

Wright, J. (2009). How foreign aid can foster democratization in authoritarian regimes. *American Journal of Political Science*, *53*(3), 552–571. https://doi.org/10.1111/j.1540-5907.2009.00386.x

Yu, J. (2015). *Entering the mainstream: An evolution in China's climate diplomacy.* China Dialogue. https://chinadialogue.net/en/climate/8369-entering-the-mainstream-an-evolution-in-china-s-climate-diplomacy/

Zhang, D., Fan, F., & Pak, S. D. (2019). Network analysis of actors and policy keywords for sustainable environmental governance: Focusing on Chinese environmental policy. *Sustainability*, *11*(15), 4068. https://doi.org/10.3390/su11154068

Zhang, N., & Xue-Feng, J. (2019). The effect of environmental policy on Chinese firm's green productivity and shadow price: A metafrontier input distance function approach. *Technological Forecasting and Social Change*, *144*, 129–136. https://doi.org/10.1016/j.techfore.2019.04.015

Leadership in high-level forums on energy governance: China and Russia compared

Jale Tosun and Karina Shyrokykh

ABSTRACT
This study investigates the participation of China and Russia in the Clean Energy Ministerial (CEM). In which policy initiatives have these two countries participated? In which initiatives have they taken the lead? Building on the club theory and international relations literature, we approach the research questions by offering an in-depth analysis of the policy dynamics inside the CEM. From a theoretical viewpoint, we posit that China has been more active in the CEM than Russia, which our empirical analysis confirms. However, Russia has also been involved in several CEM initiatives. Concerning leadership, China has demonstrated a greater interest in playing that role than Russia. We conclude that, overall, China makes a better strategic use of the CEM in terms of gathering information and developing networks with other member states as well as private actors in order to implement measures for overcoming the challenges of clean energy transition.

Introduction

Effective climate change mitigation requires state and non-state actors at different scales of governance to engage in the swift and sustained reduction of greenhouse gas (GHG) emissions. The negotiations of the 1992 United Nations Framework Convention on Climate Change (UNFCCC) and the 1997 Kyoto Protocol were hailed by policymakers, civil society organisations and scientists as a breakthrough in international climate action (Victor, 2015). However, in 2009, the international community witnessed how difficult it is to negotiate an international agreement on climate change in which the governments around the world would commit to curbing GHG emissions (see Bäckstrand et al., 2017). The disappointment over the negotiation outcomes of the 15th Conference of the Parties to the UNFCCC accelerated a process that had already started in the early 2000s, that is, the launch of international cooperation formats involving 'more than two and less than the full multilateral set of countries party to the UNFCCC and that [have] not reached the degree of institutionalization of an international organization' (Weischer et al., 2012, p. 177). Such 'climate clubs' play an important role in global climate governance, enabling parties to cooperate when a broader coalition of international actors is unachievable (Hovi et al., 2019; Nordhaus, 2015; Victor, 2015; Widerberg & Stenson, 2013).

In more abstract terms, a club is a 'voluntary group deriving mutual benefits from sharing the costs of producing an activity that has public-good characteristics' (Nordhaus, 2015, p. 1340). Climate clubs share some features of international organisations (IOs), but also differ from the latter in two important ways. First, climate clubs are smaller formats of cooperation where participation is not restricted to states. Second, climate clubs are flexible and do not have the institutionalised and rigid structures that IOs often have. The benefits of club participation can come in the form of reputation, as well as access to information and technology (Potoski & Prakash, 2005). In climate clubs, participating parties agree to undertake harmonised emissions reduction actions and non-participating states are 'penalised' to the degree that they do not have access to information and technology available for the club members (Nordhaus, 2015). Essentially, cooperation in climate clubs can be seen as a bottom-up strategy for an international climate regime, and as an alternative approach to climate cooperation that does not require an agreement between multiple parties.

Evidently, climate clubs are just one type of organisation that have started to populate and alter the character of global climate and energy governance (Biermann et al., 2009; Goldthau & Sitter, 2020), which, according to Abbott (2012, p. 571), has become 'complex, fragmented, and decentralized, operating without central coordination.' In existing publications, scholars have paid considerable attention to hybrid formats of climate governance that involve state actors at different scales (e.g. the Covenant of Mayors; see also Domorenok et al., 2020) and non-state actors (pertaining to transnational private actors, non-governmental organisations and social movements; see Bäckstrand et al., 2017).

Although various actors spanning numerous levels of governance participate in global climate governance, states retain their dominant role. In fact, Ostrom's (2010, 2012) concept of 'polycentric' climate change governance provides a compelling argument as to why scholars should pay attention to the role of states in climate governance: there are multiple scales at which states must take climate action for climate change mitigation (Jordan et al., 2015; Jordan & Huitema, 2014; Tobin, 2017). As states remain the key actors in climate change governance, we consider it important to understand how states choose in which climate clubs to participate and what goals they pursue within such clubs.

In this study, we investigate how China and Russia participate in climate clubs. China and Russia are not only 'great powers' (Allison, 2020), but also major GHG emitters (jointly producing about one-third of global carbon dioxide emissions; see BP, 2020). Both states are defined as authoritarian regimes with their own, often imitative initiatives for launching IOs (Libman & Obydenkova, 2013, 2018a, 2018b). A number of studies have discussed the importance of the political regimes of states in their choice of environmental policies (Demchuk et al., 2021; Fredriksson & Neumayer, 2013; Fredriksson et al., 2005; Fredriksson & Wollscheid, 2007; Obydenkova, 2012; Obydenkova & Salahodjaev, 2016; Wu & Martus, 2020). They found that democracies and authoritarian regimes behave differently not only with regard to national environmental policy choices but also in respect of world politics, including global environmental governance (Libman & Obydenkova, 2014; Obydenkova et al., 2016; Payne, 1995; Shandra, 2007). These studies conclude that authoritarian regimes, in general, are less concerned with the environmental agenda than are democracies, be that at a national level (e.g. in the management of national forest governance) or at a global level (e.g. the ratification of international environmental agreements). By comparing the behaviour of two large non-democratic states, such as post-Communist Russia and China, in high-level forums on energy governance, we aspire to provide new insights into the nexus of autocracies and their global environmental standing.

In the last two decades, we have been able to witness continuity and change regarding the climate policy positions of both Russia and China. Thus, under President Dmitry Medvedev (2008–2012), Russia supported international climate cooperation and indicated its willingness to mitigate GHG emissions, whereas in the years before, the country surprised observers by how long it took it to ratify the Kyoto Protocol (Andonova & Alexieva, 2012). And effectively, the ratification was driven by the European Union (EU), which made it conditional for accepting Russia's accession to the World Trade Organisation (Henry & Sundstrom, 2007). After holding the view for many years that climate action should be taken by the developed world (Brenton, 2013), China changed its position on climate policy in 2009/2010 and assumed a more proactive role in global climate governance (Dong, 2017; Hilton & Kerr, 2017).

While there exist several climate clubs (for an overview, see Weischer et al., 2012), here we focus on how China and Russia have participated in the Clean Energy Ministerial (CEM). In contrast to other climate clubs, the CEM has been regarded as one of the most 'successful' (see Yu, 2019). It has increased its membership size from 23 (in 2010) to 29 (in 2021) . Moreover the CEM has produced numerous initiatives, which we will discuss in detail in the remainder of this study, indicating that the organisation is well capable of facilitating collaboration between its members (Tosun & Rinscheid, 2021). Lastly, the success of the CEM is also reflected in the fact that other high-level forums on energy governance have replicated its organisational design, such as the Mission Innovation founded in 2015.

Since the CEM covers areas of strategic importance for both China and Russia, this case is likely to reveal broader insights into the factors that may drive autocracies' participation in climate cooperation in clubs. Lastly, we focus on Russia's and China's participation in the CEM because it allows us to tackle the questions of when and why countries display leadership in such organisations. Over time, the CEM has moved from an organisation dominated by the United States to a more multilateral one, allowing other member states to launch initiatives and exercise leadership. And because both China and Russia are two geopolitically powerful actors, which are, however, dependent on energy markets (Belyi & Goldthau, 2015 Belyi & Talus, 2015), albeit for different reasons, they are two likely candidates for attempting to act as leaders, setting up initiatives that would benefit them.

Taken together, in this article we aim to understand how authoritarian regimes participate in climate clubs. We are particularly interested in understanding when autocratic states engage in climate governance and in what format – are they leaders or followers in such organisations? How have China and Russia participated in the CEM? And have their attempts to exercise leadership in the CEM changed over time? To address these questions, we focus on the period between 2010 and 2021, as this allows us to examine whether changes in global leadership patterns can stimulate autocracies to take a more active part in climate governance.

The remainder of this study unfolds as follows. First, we present background information on the energy and GHG emission profiles of China and Russia. Then, we develop our theoretical argument. We subsequently provide some clarifications on our methodological approach before assessing our hypotheses. In a last step, we discuss our findings and provide some concluding remarks.

Energy and emission profiles of China and Russia

China was one of the poorest countries in the world four decades ago, but this started to change drastically when the country opened up its economy and adopted a series of (experimental) economic reforms in 1978 (Haini, 2020, p. 1). Its accession to the World Trade Organisation in 2001 gave the economic modernisation agenda a major boost (Hopewell, 2015). The outcome of these reforms is that today China is the second largest economy in the world after the United States. At the time of opening up its economy, agriculture was the dominant sector, but this has since been replaced by industry. The size of China's industry sector is one of the reasons why China has seen a significant increase in GHG emissions since 1990 (see Figure 1). Additional reasons are population density, urbanisation, and a sharp increase in the number of passenger vehicles (Meidan, 2020).

Rapid industrialisation and urbanisation processes also increased energy consumption. While the share of coal in the energy mix has decreased since the 1970s, China continues to rely heavily on coal, as indicated by Figure 2. The second largest component of China's energy consumption profile is oil, due to increased demand for passenger vehicles. While the Communist Party has reacted to the sharp rise in passenger cars by promoting electric cars instead of conventional fuel cars (e.g. Yang et al., 2017), the country's oil needs are still considerable and can only be met through imports. China imports crude oil from countries in the Middle East, which make its economy vulnerable to supply disruptions (Meidan, 2020). China's energy policy has focused on ensuring that there is sufficient energy supply to facilitate the smooth running of economic activities, a goal it has attempted to realise by diversifying the domestic energy mix. In the quest for energy

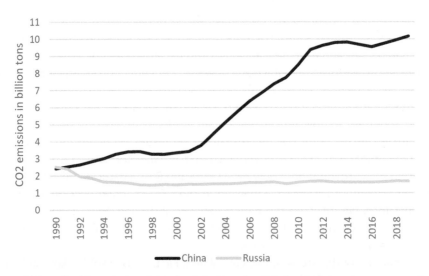

Figure 1. Carbon dioxide emissions from fossil fuel combustion for energy and cement production, 1990–2019. Remarks: Own elaboration based on https://ourworldindata.org/co2-emissions.

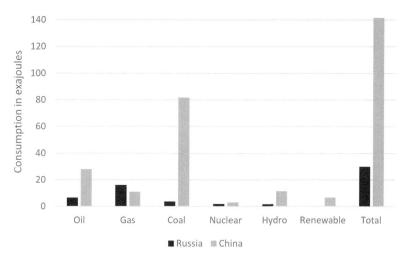

Figure 2. Primary energy consumption by fuel type, 2010. Remarks: Own elaboration based on www.bp.com.

diversification, the production of hydroelectricity and renewable energy have increased (see Figure 2).

The need to promote alternative energy sources and energy efficiency, together with a significant degree of environmental degradation, induced China's Central Committee and the State Council to adopt a series of climate mitigation policies, as shown by Figure 3 (Dong, 2017, pp. 34–35). Likewise, the level of problem pressure in terms of GHG emissions and environmental degradation can be seen as the main reason why China started to become active in international climate politics after 2009 (Hilton & Kerr, 2017) and has even attempted to claim a leadership role in global climate governance (Dong, 2017, p. 34). Because China's contributions to global GHG emissions are so significant, the country possesses a 'structural power' – without its involvement in mitigation efforts the goal of limiting global warming will not be met (Liefferink & Wurzel, 2018).

In its Nationally Determined Contribution to the Paris Agreement, the Chinese government indicated that its carbon dioxide emissions would peak by 2030, with best efforts to peak earlier. It also pledged to generate 20% of its energy from low-carbon sources by 2030 and to cut emissions per unit of the Gross Domestic Product by 60–65% of 2005 levels by 2030, potentially facilitating a peak by 2027.[1] Furthermore, in 2020, President Xi Jinping pledged to become carbon neutral by 2060. Overall, China has embarked upon an ambitious mission to stimulate economic growth, reduce its dependence on energy imports, and decarbonise its economy (Meidan, 2020).

Russia, on the other hand, is the third largest producer and consumer of energy resources in the world (after China and the United States). It is a major exporter of natural gas, crude oil, and coal (BP, 2020), which makes it a key player in international energy markets and climate change and energy governance (Henderson & Mitrova, 2020). The state-owned energy company Gazprom enjoys a privileged position in the Russian energy sector as well as in the economy as a whole (Belyi & Locatelli, 2015; Henderson & Moe, 2016). Economic growth in Russia relies greatly on fossil fuels, and the subsidisation of

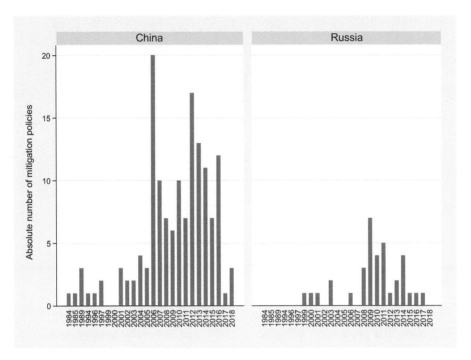

Figure 3. Climate change mitigation policies, 1984–2018. Remarks: Own elaboration based on data on climate mitigation policies from New Climate Policy Database (http://climatepolicydatabase.org/index.php/Climate_Policy_Database).

energy prizes has resulted in significant GHG emissions (Li et al., 2020). As Figure 2 shows, the share of renewable energy in energy consumption is negligible although it is slowly expanding (Lanshina et al., 2018), and officially is not projected to rise above 1% by 2035. Optimising the energy structure and improving energy efficiency as well as changing the structure of the country's industry would have a positive effect on GHG emissions reduction.

However, instead of this, the Russian government continues investing in energy-intensive industries (Li et al., 2020) and the expansion of the coal sector (Martus, 2019). Arguably, the entire socio-economic development of the former Soviet states (e.g. preservation of former Soviet trade ties well beyond the oil and gas industries) and also of some post-Communist EU member-states can be explained by the literature on the historical legacies of Communism (Arpino & Obydenkova, 2020; Beissinger & Kotkin, 2014; Lankina et al., 2016; Nazarov & Obydenkova, 2020; Pop-Eleches & Tucker, 2017; Lankina et al., 2016a, 2016b). These studies argue that decades under Communism left a profound mark not only on the countries' choices regarding economic development, but also on their societies, public behaviour and opinion, and people's trust in political institutions, among many other issues. This considered, it is easier to understand the historically traditional choices of Russia, be that in economic or climate and energy policy choices.

By continuing its energy policy as it was under Communism, Henderson and Mitrova (2020, p. 95) argue that Russia is explicitly acknowledging that its energy exports should promote its external policy, indicating the government's awareness of its geopolitical power, especially over the Central-Asian states as well as states in Central and Eastern Europe (Izotov & Obydenkova, 2020). Likewise, Western European states, such as Germany, Finland and Austria, are largely dependent on Russian energy imports. In total, about 40% of EU imports of natural gas come from Russia (BP, 2020). Energy exports are often used by Russia as a geopolitical tool. For example, the Russian government suspended oil exports to Latvia when the Russian pipeline operator wanted to buy the oil port of Ventspils but had its offer rejected (Tosun, 2011). In a complementary fashion, ever since the EU has embarked on diversifying its energy imports (Tosun et al., 2015), Russia has also tried to diversify its export markets by venturing into Asia (Belyi, 2015).

In line with the findings of the literature on non-democracies and environmentalism, climate policy has not been a priority issue on the political agenda of the Russian government, which also becomes apparent when inspecting the adoption of climate mitigation policies presented in Figure 3. In its Nationally Determined Contribution to the Paris Agreement, the Russian government indicated that it would aim for a 5–30% domestic reduction in GHGs by 2030 compared to 1990 levels.[2] Furthermore, it committed the government to the voluntary obligation of limiting GHG emissions to 70–77% of the 1990 levels by 2030, provided that forest schemes were counted as efforts to offset carbon emissions. As Figure 1 shows, the country's GHG emissions have been on the same level over the last three decades, which suggest that to meet even this low-ambition pledge the government needs to take mitigation-related actions.

Generally, environmental and climate-related issues do not find much response among Russian policymakers. Russia's climate mitigation activities lag behind the pace and the level of ambition displayed by global efforts due to the lack of political will to address this issue and its denial of the anthropogenic origins of climate change (Korppoo & Kokorin, 2017). Thus, President Vladimir Putin has expressed his distrust of climate activists on multiple occasions, assuming that climate campaigns are orchestrated by some 'international forces' rather than being bottom-up movements led by citizens.[3] From a bottom-up perspective, public opinion and behaviour, both in general and towards environmental issues especially, are heavily influenced by official state-controlled mass media and in particular by the national television broadcasters, whose distorted presentations of reality arguably constitute one of the historical legacies of Communism (Tynkkynen, 2010; Tynkkynen & Tynkkynen, 2018; Obydenkova & Arpino, 2018). Therefore, the presidential distrust of environmental activists occupies the central place in the official mass media, forming public opinion on the green agenda and related aspects.

Despite wildfires in Siberia, more frequent floods, biodiversity loss, the melting permafrost, deforestation, and poor forest governance, the state does not respond to climate change (e.g. Libman & Obydenkova, 2014). Being greatly dependent on the exportation of natural resources, progressive climate policies would go against the status quo and require significant economic as well as political reforms that the Kremlin and its cronies are not ready to put in place. Because of the vested interests of powerful veto players, endemic corruption in Russia, and the state control of mass media, adequate climate change policies are unlikely to be adopted as long as climate change mitigation entails costs (e.g. in a form of reduced exports or substantial investments in low-emission development) (Korppoo & Kokorin, 2017).

Russia's participation in international environmental cooperation has always been determined by its foreign policy objectives (Henderson & Mitrova, 2020), foremost those related to economic growth, and it has been characterised by unpredictability in international climate negotiations (Andonova & Alexieva, 2012). While the country's political and business elites are slowly becoming aware of the need to reform its economic and energy policy, this issue has received relatively little political attention. As Figure 3 shows, there was a visible surge in climate mitigation policies in 2008–2012. This was a time when the political climate towards climate action was relatively favourable. At that time, climate policy was framed in the public discourse in three ways: first, as a means to improve Russia's international image; second, as an undertaking that entails economic and political costs; third, climate change as a problem that Russia must help to solve (Tynkkynen, 2010). When Vladimir Putin took over the presidency from Dmitry Medvedev, becoming President for the third time, the public discourse on climate change began to be dominated by climate denial (Tynkkynen & Tynkkynen, 2018).

Theoretical argument

Our theoretical argument departs from the rationalist assumption that states partake in international cooperation to minimise transaction costs and receive information otherwise not available, and that this decision is based on cost-benefit calculations. However, joining a climate club or any other IO is one thing, but acting as an active member let alone as a leader is another. Following Sprinz et al. (2018), we expect member states to take on one of the following three conceivable roles. First, a state can act as a *leader*, launching new initiatives and promoting climate policies for the common good. Second, a state can act as a *follower*, joining existing initiatives started by others. Lastly, states can choose the role of a *symbolic member*, staying largely outside of climate actions.

The question of leadership in clubs is crucial. First, in smaller organisations, leadership is more likely to occur naturally. There is a general tendency of countries to maintain the status quo, but if a leader changes behaviour, in a small group, this may compel others to follow (Heal & Kunreuther, 2017). Changing the behaviour of some, therefore, may change the behaviour of all the members in a club.

Second, climate clubs emerge when a few actors that agree to cooperate incur the upfront costs of a new technology for reducing GHG emissions. Other countries will then be willing to follow suit because they only have to incur the much smaller marginal costs (Heal & Kunreuther, 2017). However, states might decide to serve as leaders only on some rather than all initiatives. The challenge is to explain when states are more likely to decide to serve as leaders. Following the functionalist International Relations (IR) tradition, international cooperation is more likely to be established when it facilitates addressing an issue at hand, minimising transaction costs for the participating parties as well as providing information on partners' intentions (van de Graaf, 2013). And the decision of states to partake in international cooperation depends on their respective domestic preferences, carefully weighting costs and benefits (Moravcsik, 1997).

Building on the climate club literature and the functionalist reasoning, we hypothesise that the participation of China and Russia in the policy initiatives of the CEM is determined by the cost-benefit calculations nested in state preferences. More precisely, we argue that it is functional considerations that determine these two countries' participation. Serving as a leader in the CEM means that the members can place issues on the organisation's agenda that are important for being able to solve domestic climate and energy-related challenges. In this regard, it is important to note that China is under pressure to address its rapidly increasing emissions (see Figure 1), as well as its need for energy diversification (see Figure 2. In contrast, Russia's carbon dioxide emissions have been relatively constant over time (see Figure 1), and energy exports constitute the main source of revenue for the country (Mitrova & Melnikov, 2019), and so the country is expected to have less incentive to change the status quo. The situation in China is quite the opposite – adjustments being made in the energy sector to deploy clean energy technologies are very likely to contribute to the country's energy resilience. Thus, given the varying degree of urgency for climate action and the differences in the role of energy production, we hypothesise that *China (as an energy consumer) is more active in leading and participating in CEM initiatives than Russia (as an energy producer)* (Hypothesis 1).

While the first hypothesis builds on cross-country differences, to develop the second hypothesis, we draw on the sectoral differences that may shape Chinese and Russian climate cooperation interests. The climate club theory highlights that cooperation in clubs centres on the exact issues requiring joint problem solving (Green, 2017). Therefore, we expect China and Russia to participate in those CEM climate incentives that explicitly target the sectors most relevant to the respective country's economy and its economic and political interests.

While China's contribution to global GHG emissions is significantly higher than Russia's, both countries were signatories of the Kyoto Protocol when they entered the CEM in 2010 and both made pledges to reduce their carbon dioxide emissions when signing and ratifying the Paris Agreement. At the same time, there is a significant difference between the two countries and the ways in which they depend on energy – Russia is a major exporter of oil and natural gas, while China is one of the largest importers since its industrial production depends on reliable energy supply. Moreover, as shown in Figure 2, China relies heavily on coal power, but the Communist Party has also committed itself to increasing the production capacity of energy from renewable sources. In Russia, on the other hand, there is very little incentive to diversify energy sources or transit to renewables. Given these sector-level differences, we anticipate these countries to follow different paths in reducing emissions and therefore to participate differently in the CEM.

Thus, we expect China to participate in initiatives that cover aspects related to the development of renewable energy and decarbonisation. Meanwhile, since Russia is heavily engaged in energy exports and has little incentive to diversify its energy supply, we expect Russia to be less interested in participating or leading initiatives on issues such as renewable energy. Our reasoning is supported by Mitrova and Melnikov (2019, p. 75), who state that Russia's 'incentives to set ambitious national decarbonisation targets are very low, especially assuming that these additional efforts would require significant investments, which are not available in light of the economic stagnation and financial sanctions, and would also require higher prices for energy, which is socially unacceptable.' Therefore, we hypothesise that *China is more active in CEM incentives on renewable energy in comparison to Russia* (Hypothesis 2).

The next line of reasoning draws on the role of power constellations in IOs and is inspired by the realist tradition in IR. According to this perspective, international cooperation incentives such as those driven by climate clubs may simply be instruments of powerful states to achieve their objectives at the international level (Keohane & Nye, 1974). In situations when the dominant member of an IO loses its leadership status (like in the case of the United States in the CEM after 2016; see Tosun & Rinscheid, 2021), this may create an opportunity for other members to replace the former leader.

By replacing the formerly dominant member, a powerful country can re-direct climate cooperation to fit its needs and change the distribution of the benefits and costs among the members of a club – an outcome to which Stone (2011) refers as 'capture'. While we consider the term 'capture' too strong given the purpose of the CEM as a knowledge and communication platform, we agree with this view to the extent that the retreat of a dominant actor can induce other actors to take its place and to launch initiatives that may promote their respective interests.

Both China and Russia are important players in global energy governance – China's rapidly growing economy is hugely dependent on energy imports, while Russia's entire economy largely depends on energy export. Since both China and Russia are powerful states that have strong interests in how global climate change and energy governance are shaped, our third hypothesis postulates that *China and Russia are inclined to fill in a leadership gap in the CEM* (Hypothesis 3).

Methodological approach

In this study, we are interested in how China and Russia as two 'great powers' have participated in the CEM. Given our research interest, we carry out a comparative case study, in which we expect the differences in the energy and GHG emission profiles of the two countries to bring about differences in how they have participated in the CEM. To empirically assess the hypotheses, we rely on the energy and emission statistics presented in the above section, as they capture the values of our explanatory variables.

We draw on the methodology of comparative case study to reveal how country-level differences shape the strategy of a country's participation in CEM incentives. To that end, we utilise a cross-case method to test how differences between countries bring about a similar the outcome, which in this case is participation in the CEM (Mahoney, 2007).

Concerning the dependent variable, we work with two specifications: first, the number and type of initiatives in which China and Russia have acted as leaders; and second, the number and type of initiatives in which China and Russia have participated but not led. The initiatives are the main tool of the CEM to attain its organisational goals and are based on working plans with tangible expected outcomes. One or several members take the lead in proposing and designing initiatives, which are subsequently reviewed by independent experts. Member states do not have to be the leaders of initiatives and participate in them to help realise the goals of the CEM. The data for operationalising the dependent variables come from the CEM's website. On the occasion of the annual ministerial meetings, the CEM Secretariat publishes an overview of the members' participation in initiatives, which we used to code the dependent variables.

Both China and Russia represent the most likely cases to have a strong interest in steering international cooperation in the CEM. What is more, cross-country and cross-sectoral differences between the two countries provide us with an opportunity to investigate scope conditions under which participants of climate clubs are more likely to actively engage in climate governance. Lastly, a comparative analysis of these two cases allows us to shed some light on autocratic members of climate clubs, as most of the existing research focuses on the leadership and participation of democratic states in climate clubs (Hovi et al., 2016; Sprinz et al., 2018).

Overview of the clean energy initiatives

The CEM is an institutional platform for exchanging information on clean energy technologies and implementing projects cooperatively. It was initiated by the United States as one component of a broader policy strategy of the administration of Barack Obama to promote clean energy (Obama, 2017). The CEM is committed to improving energy efficiency, enhancing clean energy supply, and expanding access to clean energy. To attain these goals, the organisation advocates so-called initiatives that expand the deployment of the corresponding technologies (Tosun & Rinscheid, 2021). It supports the involvement of private-sector partners both in the annual ministerial meetings and in the technical work.

The CEM is one of several climate clubs, which Weischer et al. (2012) divide into four groups: i) political dialogue forums, ii) technical dialogue forums, iii) country strategy implementation groups, and iv) project implementation groups. The CEM is situated on the borderline between a country strategy implementation group and a project implementation group. It is important to note in this context that the CEM is not a renewable energy club in the narrow sense. While it naturally promotes renewable energy technologies, it has also always been open to negative emissions technologies that can remove carbon dioxide from the atmosphere (Fuss et al., 2014). One energy type excluded from the CEM activities are fossil fuels. When inspecting the organisation's initiatives, it becomes clear that the organisation works on a wide range of topics.

By 2021, the CEM had launched a total of 21 initiatives, of which some were modified and relaunched and others terminated. Among the initiatives started upon launch of the CEM is the *Super-Efficient Equipment and Appliance Deployment* initiative, which aims to develop a common technical foundation to facilitate governments to adopt cost-effective appliance efficiency policies and programmes. The *International Smart Grid Action Network* is an award for outstanding leadership and innovation in smart grid projects. The *Electric Vehicles Initiative* provides a forum for accelerating the introduction and adoption of electric vehicles worldwide. The *Clean Energy Solutions Centre* supports governments in designing policies and programmes for deploying low-carbon technologies. The *Clean Energy Education and Empowerment* initiative aims to increase gender diversity in clean energy professions.

Over the course of time, a few initiatives were terminated and started again but with a modified focus or scope. For example, the *Energy Management Working Group* (launched in 2015) succeeded the *Global Superior Energy Performance* (2010–2015). The aim of the *Energy Management Working Group* is to foster the diffusion of the ISO 50,001 standard around the globe.[4] Likewise, the initiative *Carbon Capture, Use, and Storage* was transformed into the *Carbon Capture, Utilisation and Storage Initiative* in 2018. The *Sustainable Cities* initiative, launched in 2012, was replaced in 2019 by the *Sustainable Cities and Eco-*

Energy Towns initiative. Originally, *the 21st Century Power Partnership* aimed to incubate immature clean energy sources, but now it focuses on planning for system-level transformation. The *Global Lighting and Energy Access Partnership* followed the *Solar and LED Energy Access Programme* in 2012; both addressed the development of commercial markets for energy access solutions before being transitioned out of the CEM in 2019. Further initiatives that were terminated include the *Multilateral Solar and Wind Working Group*, the *Multilateral Bioenergy Working Group*, and *Sustainable Development of Hydropower Initiative*.

Then, in 2018 and 2019, a new generation of initiatives was launched that reflects the preferences of the Trump Administration (2017–2021). Before agreeing on these initiatives, the United States expressed its intention to put its engagement with the CEM on halt. Consequently, the overview document prepared by the CEM Secretariat in 2017 contained a note that the United States' participation in and leadership of all initiatives were 'under review'. Taking a secondary role in global climate governance was not a particularity of cooperation within the CEM – the United States generally pursued a less active role in global climate governance under President Trump in comparison to his predecessor, President Obama (Aldy, 2017; Jotzo et al., 2018). The United States pulled out of the Paris Climate Agreement and cut federal funding for scientific, climate-related incentives.[5] The Trump Administration also removed some safety regulations related to offshore drilling and rolled back Obama-era mining regulations.[6]

It was only when the other members made concessions to the United States concerning the issues that were due to become subjects of collaboration within the CEM that the US government stopped questioning its membership and launched four new initiatives. The *Investment and Finance* initiative aims to support energy production in developing policies and to establish frameworks conducive to mobilising investment and financing. The *Regional and Global Energy Interconnection* initiative facilitates the transition of energy systems to electricity-centred and interconnected energy systems. The *Nuclear Innovation: Clean Energy Future Initiative* concentrates on collaboration on nuclear power, and the *Hydrogen Initiative* adopted most recently concentrates on hydrogen and fuel cell technologies.

Empirical analysis

Figure 4 gives an overview of the CEM member states and their willingness to lead initiatives in 2013 (the year with all first- and second-generation initiatives in place) and 2021 (the most recent year and with all 'third-generation' initiatives in place). It should be noted that this figure displays the original members of the organisation only in order to be able to carry out a comparison over time. Countries that joined the CEM after 2010 (i.e. Chile, the Netherlands, New Zealand, Poland, Portugal, and Saudi Arabia) and the European Commission are left out.

The most important observation when inspecting the figure is that the United States were by far the most active member of the CEM in terms of (co-)leading initiatives by 2013. With Donald Trump taking office as president, the United States scaled down its leadership in the organisation, as stated in the previous section. Nonetheless, in 2021, the United States was still the CEM member with the most pronounced leadership profile, and with President Joe Biden taking office in 2021, the country is likely to return playing a

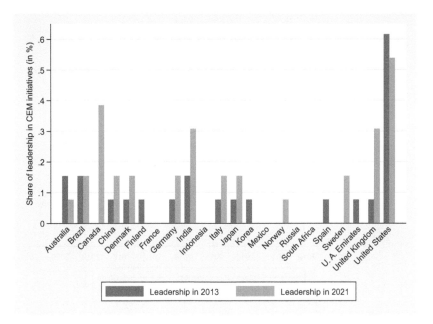

Figure 4. Leadership in CEM Initiatives, 2013 and 2021. Remarks: Own elaboration based on data gathered by Tosun and Rinscheid (2021).

more active role in the CEM. Interestingly, it was neither China nor Russia that attempted to fill the power vacuum in the CEM that indeed existed in 2017 and 2018, but Canada, as indicated by the number of initiatives for which it took the lead.

However, China's leadership profile outperforms that of Russia. China leads the *Regional and Global Energy Interconnection* initiative, in which Chile, Finland, Korea, South Africa, and the United Arab Emirates participate. This initiative pursues three goals: first, mutual learning on policies and regulation in relation to regional and global energy interconnection; second, building consensus on increasing the proportion of renewable energy in energy consumption and enhanced grid interconnection; third, encouraging the members of the organisation to join this initiative and to seize its potential for collaboration. As flagged above, not all CEM initiatives aim at promoting renewable energy, but this is one of them. Furthermore, together with Canada, China co-leads the *Electric Vehicles Initiative*, in which 12 other member states participate, among them Chile, several European states, India, Japan, and the United States.

Russia, too, has acted as a co-leader of an initiative. Together with Korea, Russia exercised leadership in the *Sustainable Cities and Eco-Energy Towns* initiative until it was completed in 2020. That initiative targeted the overall improvement of energy efficiency and sustainability in cities and towns as well as rural areas and concentrated on developing benchmarks and an international database, engaging with key stakeholders, and increasing awareness of sustainable cities development. Participants of this initiative were China, Mexico, Saudi Arabia, and the United Arab Emirates.

Figure 5 presents the leadership in initiatives of China and Russia over time, starting in 2013 (before that year the CEM did not provide information on leadership). The data presented in the figure are calculated as the absolute number of leaderships in

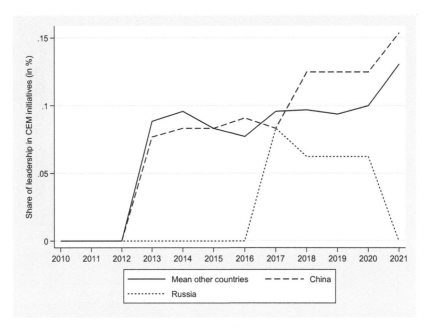

Figure 5. Leadership of CEM Initiatives over Time, 2013–2021. Remarks: Own elaboration based on data gathered by Tosun and Rinscheid (2021).

initiatives relative to the absolute number of all initiatives in place at a given point in time – therefore we refer to it as the share of leadership in CEM initiatives. This measurement approach is necessary for capturing the temporal variation in the initiatives and for providing a more meaningful insight. In addition, the figure presents the mean share of leadership in initiatives exercised by countries other than China and Russia.

When we compare the country profiles, we can see that China's share in leadership has been above the average since 2017, whereas Russia's has continuously been below. In fact, Russia stopped leading any CEM initiatives after the *Sustainable Cities and Eco-Energy Towns* initiative was completed in 2020. Consequently, the corresponding line for Russia declines sharply in 2021. Another observation worth noting is the time trend of the mean share of leadership in initiatives, which has been positive and with a steep slope since 2016. This indicates that leadership in CEM initiatives has become more distributed among the member states: there are more members co-leading an initiative. Against this background, the evolution of Russia's participation in the CEM is even more striking, since it suggests that it remains unaffected by the evident indications of 'multilateralisation' within the organisation.

In 2021, China participated in seven out of 13 initiatives led by other countries, covering topics that ranged from the promotion of renewable energy to the *Carbon Capture, Utilisation and Storage Initiative*. Interestingly, China does not participate in the initiative on nuclear innovation, which was launched in 2018 by the Trump Administration. The opposite holds true for Russia, which is one of the world's largest producers of nuclear energy and is steadily expanding the domestic role of nuclear energy (e.g. Tarasova, 2018). It also exports nuclear goods and services.[7]

Russia participated in four out of 13 initiatives, which in addition to nuclear power cover collaboration on negative emissions technologies, grid issues, energy management and energy efficiency, and hydrogen. A comparison of the participation profiles of the two countries reveals that China collaborates with the other CEM members on issues related to renewable energy, energy efficiency, and negative emissions technologies. Russia's profile is heavier on energy efficiency, negative emissions technologies, and technologies for clean energy beyond renewable energy.

Comparing China's and Russia's participation with the profiles of the other CEM members (see Figure 6) shows that they qualify for being assigned to a 'medium-active' group. Neither China nor Russia is excessively active in initiatives led by other CEM members. Finland, India, Mexico, South Africa, and the United Kingdom stood out in 2021, as those were the CEM members with the broadest participation in CEM initiatives that they did not (co-)lead.

Figure 7 compares the participation levels of China and Russia with the participation level averaged across all of the CEM members. This figure is useful since it shows that China's engagement level rose sharply after 2015, and in 2021 it was much higher than the mean participation level. This picture aligns with the research literature, which has found that China has adopted a more ambitious approach to climate and energy policy in the last few years (e.g. Dong, 2017; Hilton & Kerr, 2017). We expect this to be reflected in its level of participation in international climate action. In the case of Russia, we can also witness an increase in the participation level but only after 2017. Interestingly, Russia's elevated participation level coincides with the launch of initiatives by the Trump Administration that shifted the focus away from renewable energy and onto other energy topics. From the perspective of two-level games (Putnam, 1988), this indicates that Russia

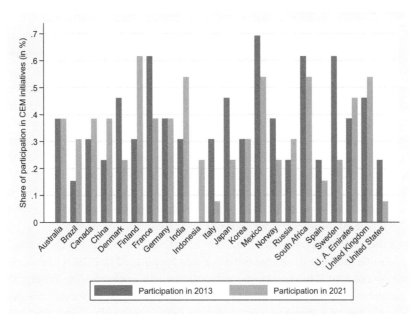

Figure 6. Participation in CEM Initiatives, 2013 and 2021. Remarks: Own elaboration based on gathered by from Tosun and Rinscheid (2021).

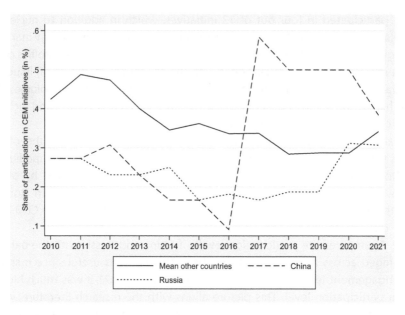

Figure 7. Participation in CEM Initiatives over Time, 2013–2021. Remarks: Own elaboration based on data gathered by Tosun and Rinscheid (2021).

began to regard the CEM a more attractive organisation to engage with when it offered a set of policy initiatives that align more closely with the interests of the Russian government.

Discussion of the findings

In the theory section, we formulated three hypotheses, which we can now evaluate based on the insights provided in the previous section. In the first hypothesis, we claimed that China would be more active in leading and participating in CEM initiatives than Russia. With regard to this hypothesis, it is first important to state that the level of leadership with states other than the United States – and to some extent Canada – is rather low, although there is a positive trend which suggests that more CEM members are willing to (co-)lead initiatives. Leadership of initiatives provides states with the opportunity to put specific energy-related themes on the agenda and to benefit from collaboration with the other member states and private organisations (most importantly business actors) on that theme. In theory, this provides a relatively cost-efficient way of developing solutions that contribute to meeting the GHG emission reduction goals the states committed to in their Nationally Determined Contributions to the Paris Agreement.

Despite the potential benefits of leading initiatives, Russia has exercised leadership only in one initiative, and since that initiative was terminated in 2020 it has not launched a new one. In contrast, China co-leads one initiative and leads another initiative by itself. The *Electric Vehicles Initiative* is particularly noteworthy because it concerns the promotion of electric vehicles and therefore represents an area of particular (economic) interest to China (e.g. Yang et al., 2017). Another feature worth noting about this initiative is that many member states participate in it, including influential members such as the United

States. Thus, in our view, China's leadership in the CEM is more manifest than Russia's. We consider this finding to support the rationale underlying the first hypothesis.

The second hypothesis postulated that China is leading and participating in initiatives that place a greater emphasis on renewable energy and decarbonisation in comparison to Russia. We found it striking that both countries participate in a rather diverse set of initiatives. Even in the case of Russia, we could observe that the country used to work on the issue of renewable energy, foremost in the context of the *Sustainable Cities and Eco-Energy Towns* initiative, which it co-led. However, when inspecting the participation profile of Russia more closely, it is dominated by initiatives that concentrate on energy efficiency as well as on technologies for producing 'clean' rather than renewable energy (on this, see Obama, 2017). In this regard, Russia – like China – has been active in the initiative on carbon capture, utilisation, and storage, which is an end-of-pipe technology for removing carbon dioxide emissions rather than preventing them. What is particularly interesting, however, is that Russia joined the initiative on nuclear power technologies, which was launched by the Trump Administration.

Altogether, the Russian participation profile is not less diverse than the Chinese one, but it places greater emphasis on clean energy technologies. As expected, the Chinese participation profile reveals a stronger interest in renewable energy technologies and in innovative low-carbon technologies, as most importantly indicated by the *Electric Vehicle Initiative*. Consequently, the empirical findings support the second hypothesis.

Turning to the third hypothesis, which pertains to the temporary power gap in the CEM, we must state that neither China nor Russia attempted to replace the United States. Interestingly, the lack of political support for the CEM during the Trump Administration was used by Canada to exercise leadership. While Russia has not changed its leadership or participation profile in the last four years, China has to some extent by pursuing its own interests and by not joining initiatives that shifted the CEM's focus onto technologies that it originally did not support, such as nuclear power. In this context, it is also worth noting that China was an observer of the hydrogen initiative also launched by the Trump Administration, but it decided not to join it. In sum there is no indication that China strived to replace the United States as the leading state in the CEM. The same holds true for Russia, and therefore we must reject hypothesis 3.

Interestingly, Russia is a participant of both initiatives launched by the Trump Administration. It became a more explicit follower of the initiatives led by the United States in the period 2017–2020 than it was before. We would argue that recent changes to Russia's participation in CEM initiatives is a response to two stimuli. First, the Russian government has to some extent become aware that it must somehow respond to the global diffusion of low-carbon energy technologies and the growing risk of lower demand for its exports of energy-intensive goods (Makarov et al., 2020). Second, the persistence of the Russian energy system results not only from a limited political will to adopt corresponding policies and regulations, but also from an insufficient capacity to put the policies adopted into practice (Lanshina et al., 2018). The combination of wishing not to fall behind in the development of low-carbon energy technologies and the low capacity for transforming the energy system result in the fact that Russia participates in CEM initiatives, but only in a manner that aligns with the status quo and can bring about incremental changes.

Overall, this study offers new insights into how authoritarian regimes participate in international cooperation (e.g. Mattes & Rodríguez, 2014) and further contributes to the study of participation and leadership in climate clubs (e.g. Tosun & Rinscheid, 2021). As we have shown, the amount of attention paid to clean energy cooperation depends on country-level factors – if participation in the CEM directly serves autocracies' interests and addresses their needs, such cooperation can be achieved. This also implies that the opposite is true: international cooperation is less likely to be achieved on issues that do not relate to autocracies' immediate interests, or international cooperation will be pursued by regional IOs set up by authoritarian governments (Libman & Obydenkova, 2018b).

Conclusion

Climate change poses a major challenge for modern societies all around the world. For climate change governance to be effective, it does not suffice to take action within the cooperation framework provided by the UNFCCC; instead, a more polycentric approach is needed, where different entities at different scales can invent a variety of solutions (Aldy, 2017; Jordan et al., 2015; Jordan et al., 2018; Ostrom, 2010, 2012). The emergence of climate clubs corresponds to this polycentric perspective on climate change governance. Polycentric governance and the emergence of climate clubs provide incentive structures for states to intensify their efforts in relation to fighting climate change. How do China and Russia as two powerful autocracies participate in this new landscape of climate change governance?

Our analysis focused on the internal policy dynamics of the CEM, one of several climate clubs founded since the early 2000s (Weischer et al., 2012), and revealed that China and Russia are willing to engage in such organisations, yet differently. While the leadership and participation profile of China qualifies it as a more 'emerging' leader within the CEM than Russia, we could not find evidence that China has attempted to dominate the organisation. There are signs that the country aspires to play a more prominent role in the CEM, but it has not yet openly displayed leadership within it. During the observation period, Russia's leadership and participation profile corresponded to that of a 'follower' (Sprinz et al., 2018), although from our viewpoint it is more accurate to refer to it as a 'selective' follower, as the empirical analysis revealed that the Russian government was selective in the initiatives in which it chose to engage. The participation profile clearly reflects the country's cost-benefit calculus as postulated more generally by Tosun and Rinscheid (2021) and the differing openness of stakeholders in the energy sector to proactive climate policy (Martus, 2019). Our analysis of Russia's participation in the CEM adds more nuance to the country's participation in global climate governance and suggests that it is worthwhile to systematically assess its participation in other climate clubs, especially since the major importers of Russian fossil fuels have turned towards decarbonisation, thereby posing risks to the country's economy (Makarov et al., 2020).

Overall, we consider the analysis of how authoritarian regimes participate in climate clubs and other (small) IOs that form part of the new landscape of global climate governance as a valuable complement to understanding international climate politics. Climate clubs in particular provide an institutional setting for continued collaboration and they are less politicised than international climate negotiations. From this perspective – and as stated, for example, by Victor (2015) – such organisations could indeed provide a favourable context for more effective collaboration on climate change.

Consequently, we invite future research to replicate this analysis and to apply it to other climate clubs. Furthermore, it appears promising to compare the participation of China and Russia in climate clubs and IOs that work on climate-related issues, such as the International Renewable Energy Agenda (van de Graaf, 2013). It would be intriguing to observe different participation patterns depending on whether the organisation comprises of many or only a few members. These issues should remain on the agenda for further studies.

Notes

1. Information was gathered from the following website: https://climateactiontracker.org/countries/china/pledges-and-targets/.
2. Information was gathered from the following website: https://climateactiontracker.org/countries/russian-federation/.
3. For example, President Putin expressed scepticism regarding the Fridays For Future movement and doubted that it is independent: https://www.bbc.com/news/world-europe-49918912.
4. ISO 50,001 is an international standard that defines the criteria for establishing, implementing, maintaining, and improving an energy management system, enabling organisations to follow a systematic approach in their endeavours to realise the continual improvement of energy performance.
5. For budget, see https://budget.house.gov/publications/report/president-trump-s-2020-budget-dangerous-exercise-ignoring-reality-and-threat.
6. For safety regulations, see https://www.npr.org/2019/05/03/720008093/trump-administration-moves-to-roll-back-offshore-drilling-safety-regulations?t=1615135288548. For mining regulations, see https://www.reuters.com/article/usa-mining-resolution-trump/trump-moves-to-loosen-mining-regulations-approve-projects-as-he-exits-idINKBN29D1G7.
7. For more, see https://www.world-nuclear.org/information-library/country-profiles/countries-o-s/russia-nuclear-power.aspx.

Acknowledgments

We thank Rui Luo, Anastassia Obydenkova and three anonymous reviewers for valuable comments on earlier drafts of this article. Laurence Crumbie deserves credit for language editing.

Disclosure statement

No potential conflict of interest was reported by the author(s).

ORCID

Jale Tosun http://orcid.org/0000-0001-9367-5039
Karina Shyrokykh http://orcid.org/0000-0002-1326-6129

References

Abbott, K. W. (2012). The transnational regime complex for climate change. *Environment and Planning C: Government & Policy*, *30*(4), 571–590. https://doi.org/10.1068/c11127

Aldy, J. E. (2017). Real world headwinds for Trump climate change policy. *Bulletin of the Atomic Scientists*, *73*(6), 376–381. https://doi.org/10.1080/00963402.2017.1388673

Allison, G. (2020). The new spheres of influence: Sharing the globe with other great powers. *Foreign Affairs*, *99*(2), 30–40. https://www.foreignaffairs.com/articles/united-states/2020-02-10/new-spheres-influence

Andonova, L. B., & Alexieva, A. (2012). Continuity and change in Russia's climate negotiations position and strategy. *Climate Policy*, *12*(5), 614–629. https://doi.org/10.1080/14693062.2012.691227

Arpino, B., & Obydenkova, A. V. (2020). Democracy and political trust before and after the great recession 2008: The European Union and the United Nations. *Social Indicators Research*, *148*(2), 395–415. https://doi.org/10.1007/s11205-019-02204-x

Bäckstrand, K., Kuyper, J. W., Linnér, B.-O., & Lövbrand, E. (2017). Non-state actors in global climate governance: From Copenhagen to Paris and beyond. *Environmental Politics*, *26*(4), 561–579. https://doi.org/10.1080/09644016.2017.1327485

Beissinger, M., & Kotkin, S. (2014). *Historical legacies of communism in Russia and Eastern Europe*. Cambridge University Press.

Belyi, A. V. (2015). Russia's gas export reorientation from West to East: Economic and political considerations. *The Journal of World Energy Law & Business*, *8*(1), 76–86. https://doi.org/10.1093/jwelb/jwu037

Belyi, A. V., & Goldthau, A. (2015). *Between a rock and a hard place: International market dynamics, domestic politics and Gazprom's strategy* (European University Institute 2015/22). European University Institute. https://econpapers.repec.org/paper/rscrsceui/2015_2f22.htm

Belyi, A. V., & Locatelli, C. (2015). State and markets in Russia's hydrocarbon sectors: Domestic specificities and interrelations with the West. In Belyi, A.V. and Talus, K. (Eds.), *States and markets in hydrocarbon sectors* (pp. 103–121). Springer.

Belyi, A. V., & Talus, K. (2015). *States and Markets in Hydrocarbon Sectors*. Springer.

Biermann, F., Pattberg, P., van Asselt, H., & Zelli, F. (2009). The fragmentation of global governance architectures: A framework for analysis. *Global Environmental Politics*, *9*(4), 14–40. https://doi.org/10.1162/glep.2009.9.4.14

BP. (2020). *Statistical review of world energy* (69th ed.).

Brenton, A. (2013). 'Great powers' in climate politics. *Climate Policy*, *13*(5), 541–546. https://doi.org/10.1080/14693062.2013.774632

Demchuk, A. L., Mišić, M., Obydenkova, A., & Tosun, J. (2021). Environmental conflict management: A comparative cross-cultural perspective of China and Russia. *Post-Communist Economies*, 1–23. forthcoming. https://doi.org/10.1080/14631377.2021.1943915

Domorenok, E., Acconcia, G., Bendlin, L., & Campillo, X. R. (2020). Experiments in EU climate governance: The unfulfilled potential of the Covenant of Mayors. *Global Environmental Politics*, *20*(4), 1–22. https://doi.org/10.1162/glep_a_00563

Dong, L. (2017). Bound to lead? Rethinking China's role after Paris in UNFCCC negotiations. *Chinese Journal of Population Resources and Environment*, *15*(1), 32–38. https://doi.org/10.1080/10042857.2017.1286144

Fredriksson, P. G., & Neumayer, E. (2013). Democracy and climate change policies: Is history important? *Ecological Economics*, *95*(1), 11–19. https://doi.org/10.1016/j.ecolecon.2013.08.002

Fredriksson, P. G., Neumayer, E., Damania, R., & Gates, S. (2005). Environmentalism, democracy, and pollution control. *Journal of Environmental Economics and Management*, *49*(2), 343–365. https://doi.org/10.1016/j.jeem.2004.04.004

Fredriksson, P. G., & Wollscheid, J. R. (2007). Democratic institutions versus autocratic regimes: The case of environmental policy. *Public Choice*, *130*(34), 381–393. https://doi.org/10.1007/s11127-006-9093-1

Fuss, S., Canadell, J. G., Peters, G. P., Tavoni, M., Andrew, R. M., Ciais, P., Jackson, R. B., Jones, C. D., Kraxner, F., & Nakicenovic, N. (2014). Betting on negative emissions. *Nature Climate Change*, *4*(10), 850–853. https://doi.org/10.1038/nclimate2392

Goldthau, A., & Sitter, N. (2020). Horses for courses. The roles of IPE and global public policy in global energy research. *Policy and Society*, 1–17. forthcoming. https://doi.org/10.1080/14494035.2020.1864100

Green, J. F. (2017). The strength of weakness: Pseudo-clubs in the climate regime. *Climatic Change*, *144*(1), 41–52. https://doi.org/10.1007/s10584-015-1481-4

Haini, H. (2020). The evolution of China's modern economy and its implications on future growth. *Post-Communist Economies*, 1–25. forthcoming. https://doi.org/10.1080/14631377.2020.1793610

Heal, G., & Kunreuther, H. (2017). An alternative framework for negotiating climate policies. *Climatic Change*, *144*(1), 29–39. https://doi.org/10.1007/s10584-017-2043-8

Henderson, J., & Mitrova, T. (2020). Implications of the global energy transition on Russia. In S. Tagliapietra & M. Hafner (Eds.), *Lecture notes in energy. The geopolitics of the global energy transition* (Vol. 73, pp. 93–114). Springer Nature. https://doi.org/10.1007/978-3-030-39066-2_5

Henderson, J., & Moe, A. (2016). Gazprom's LNG offensive: A demonstration of monopoly strength or impetus for Russian gas sector reform? *Post-Communist Economies*, *28*(3), 281–299. https://doi.org/10.1080/14631377.2016.1203206

Henry, L. A., & Sundstrom, L. M. (2007). Russia and the Kyoto Protocol: Seeking an alignment of interests and image. *Global Environmental Politics*, *7*(4), 47–69. https://doi.org/10.1162/glep.2007.7.4.47

Hilton, I., & Kerr, O. (2017). The Paris agreement: China's 'New Normal' role in international climate negotiations. *Climate Policy*, *17*(1), 48–58. https://doi.org/10.1080/14693062.2016.1228521

Hopewell, K. (2015). Different paths to power: The rise of Brazil, India and China at the World Trade Organization. *Review of International Political Economy*, *22*(2), 311–338. https://doi.org/10.1080/09692290.2014.927387

Hovi, J., Sprinz, D. F., Sælen, H., & Underdal, A. (2016). Climate change mitigation: A role for climate clubs? *Palgrave Communications*, *2*(1), 1-9. https://doi.org/10.1057/palcomms.2016.20

Hovi, J., Sprinz, D. F., Sælen, H., & Underdal, A. (2019). The club approach: A gateway to effective climate co-operation? *British Journal of Political Science*, *49*(3), 1071–1096. https://doi.org/10.1017/S0007123416000788

Izotov, V. S., & Obydenkova, A. V. (2020). Geopolitical games in Eurasian regionalism: Ideational interactions and regional international organisations. *Post-Communist Economies*, *2*(2), 1–25. https://doi.org/10.1080/14631377.2020.1793584

Jordan, A., Huitema, D., Schoenefeld, J., van Asselt, H., & Forster, J. (2018). Governing climate change polycentrically. In A. Jordan, D. Huitema, H. van Asselt, & J. Forster (Eds.), *Governing climate change: Polycentricity in action?* (pp. 3–26). Cambridge University Press. https://doi.org/10.1017/9781108284646.002

Jordan, A., & Huitema, D. (2014). Innovations in climate policy: The politics of invention, diffusion, and evaluation. *Environmental Politics*, *23*(5), 715–734. https://doi.org/10.1080/09644016.2014.923614

Jordan, A., Huitema, D., Hildén, M., van Asselt, H., Rayner, T. J., Schoenefeld, J. J., Tosun, J., Forster, J., & Boasson, E. L. (2015). Emergence of polycentric climate governance and its future prospects. *Nature Climate Change*, *5*(11), 977–982. https://doi.org/10.1038/nclimate2725

Jotzo, F., Depledge, J., & Winkler, H. (2018). US and international climate policy under President Trump. *Climate Policy*, *18*(7), 813–817. https://doi.org/10.1080/14693062.2018.1490051

Keohane, R. O., & Nye, J. S. (1974). Transgovernmental relations and international organizations. *World Politics*, *27*(1), 39–62. https://doi.org/10.2307/2009925

Korppoo, A., & Kokorin, A. (2017). Russia's 2020 GHG emissions target: Emission trends and implementation. *Climate Policy*, *17*(2), 113–130. https://doi.org/10.1080/14693062.2015.1075373

Lankina, T., Libman, A., & Obydenkova, A. (2016b). Authoritarian and democratic diffusion in post-communist regions. *Comparative Political Studies*, *49*(12), 1599–1629. https://doi.org/10.1177/0010414016628270

Lankina, T., Libman, A., & Obydenkova, A. (2016a). Appropriation and subversion. *World Politics*, *68*(2), 229–274. https://doi.org/10.1017/S0043887115000428

Lanshina, T. A., Laitner, J. A., Potashnikov, V. Y., & Barinova, V. A. (2018). The slow expansion of renewable energy in Russia: Competitiveness and regulation issues. *Energy Policy*, *120*(1), 600–609. https://doi.org/10.1016/j.enpol.2018.05.052 10.1016/j.enpol.2018.05.052

Li, R., Jiang, H., Sotnyk, I., Kubatko, O., & Almashaqbeh, Y. A., I. (2020). The CO2 emissions drivers of post-communist economies in Eastern Europe and Central Asia. *Atmosphere*, *11*(9), 1019. https://doi.org/10.3390/atmos11091019

Libman, A., & Obydenkova, A. (2013). Communism or communists? Soviet legacies and corruption in transition economies. *Economics Letters*, *119*(1), 101–103. https://doi.org/10.1016/j.econlet.2013.02.003

Libman, A., & Obydenkova, A. (2014). Governance of commons in a large nondemocratic country: The case of forestry in the Russian Federation. *Publius: The Journal of Federalism*, *44*(2), 298–323. https://doi.org/10.1093/publius/pjt065

Libman, A., & Obydenkova, A. V. (2018a). Regional international organizations as a strategy of autocracy: The Eurasian Economic Union and Russian foreign policy. *International Affairs*, *94*(5), 1037–1058. https://doi.org/10.1093/ia/iiy147

Libman, A., & Obydenkova, A. V. (2018b). Regional international organizations as a strategy of autocracy: The Eurasian economic Union and Russian foreign policy. *International Affairs*, *94*(5), 1037–1058. https://doi.org/10.1093/ia/iiy147

Liefferink, D., & Wurzel, R. K. W. (2018). Leadership and Pioneership. In A. Jordan, D. Huitema, H. van Asselt, & J. Forster (Eds.), *Governing climate change: Polycentricity in action?* (pp. 135–151). Cambridge University Press. https://doi.org/10.1017/9781108284646.009

Mahoney, J. (2007). Qualitative methodology and comparative politics. *Comparative Political Studies*, *40*(2), 122–144. https://doi.org/10.1177/0010414006296345

Makarov, I., Chen, H., & Paltsev, S. (2020). Impacts of climate change policies worldwide on the Russian economy. *Climate Policy*, *20*(10), 1242–1256. https://doi.org/10.1080/14693062.2020.1781047

Martus, E. (2019). Russian industry responses to climate change: The case of the metals and mining sector. *Climate Policy*, *19*(1), 17–29. https://doi.org/10.1080/14693062.2018.1448254

Mattes, M., & Rodríguez, M. (2014). Autocracies and international cooperation. *International Studies Quarterly*, *58*(3), 527–538. https://doi.org/10.1111/isqu.12107

Meidan, M. (2020). China: Climate leader and villain. In S. Tagliapietra & M. Hafner (Eds.), *Lecture notes in energy. The geopolitics of the global energy transition* (Vol. 73, pp. 75–91). Springer Nature. https://doi.org/10.1007/978-3-030-39066-2_4

Mitrova, T., & Melnikov, Y. (2019). Energy transition in Russia. *Energy Transitions*, *3*(1), 73–80. https://doi.org/10.1007/s41825-019-00016-8

Moravcsik, A. (1997). Taking preferences seriously: A liberal theory of international politics. *International Organization*, *51*(4), 513–553. https://doi.org/10.1162/002081897550447

Nazarov, Z., & Obydenkova, A. V. (2020). Democratization and firm innovation: Evidence from European and Central Asian post-Communist States. *Post-Communist Economies*, *32*(7), 833–859. https://doi.org/10.1080/14631377.2020.1745565

Nordhaus, W. (2015). Climate clubs: Overcoming free-riding in international climate policy. *American Economic Review*, *105*(4), 1339–1370. https://doi.org/10.1257/aer.15000001

Obama, B. (2017). The irreversible momentum of clean energy. *Science (New York, N.Y.)*, *355*(6321), 126–129. https://doi.org/10.1126/science.aam6284

Obydenkova, A., Nazarov, Z., & Salahodjaev, R. (2016). The process of deforestation in weak democracies and the role of Intelligence. *Environmental Research*, *148*(1), 484–490. https://doi.org/10.1016/j.envres.2016.03.039

Obydenkova, A., & Salahodjaev, R. (2016). Intelligence, democracy, and international environmental commitment. *Environmental Research*, *147*(1), 82–88. https://doi.org/10.1016/j.envres.2016.01.042

Obydenkova, A. V. (2012). Democratization at the grassroots: The European Union's external impact. *Democratization*, *19*(2), 230–257. https://doi.org/10.1080/13510347.2011.576851

Obydenkova, A. V., & Arpino, B. (2018). Corruption and trust in the European Union and National Institutions: Changes over the great recession across European States. *JCMS: Journal of Common Market Studies*, *56*(3), 594–611. https://doi.org/10.1111/jcms.12646

Ostrom, E. (2010). Polycentric systems for coping with collective action and global environmental change. *Global Environmental Change*, *20*(4), 550–557. https://doi.org/10.1016/j.gloenvcha.2010.07.004

Ostrom, E. (2012). Nested externalities and polycentric institutions: Must we wait for global solutions to climate change before taking actions at other scales? *Economic Theory*, *49*(2), 353–369. https://doi.org/10.1007/s00199-010-0558-6

Payne, R. A. (1995). Freedom and the environment. *Journal of Democracy*, *6*(3), 41–55. https://doi.org/10.1353/jod.1995.0053

Pop-Eleches, G., & Tucker, J. A. (2017). *Communism's shadow: Historical legacies and contemporary political attitudes*. Princeton University Press.

Potoski, M., & Prakash, A. (2005). Green clubs and voluntary governance: ISO 14001 and firms' regulatory compliance. *American Journal of Political Science*, *49*(2), 235–248. https://doi.org/10.1111/j.0092-5853.2005.00120.x

Putnam, R. D. (1988). Diplomacy and domestic politics: The logic of two-level games. *International Organization*, *42*(3), 427–460. https://doi.org/10.1017/S0020818300027697

Shandra, J. M. (2007). The world polity and deforestation. *International Journal of Comparative Sociology*, *48*(1), 5–27. https://doi.org/10.1177/0020715207072157

Sprinz, D. F., Sælen, H., Underdal, A., & Hovi, J. (2018). The effectiveness of climate clubs under Donald Trump. *Climate Policy*, *18*(7), 828–838. https://doi.org/10.1080/14693062.2017.1410090

Stone, R. W. (2011). *Controlling institutions: International organizations and the global economy* (1. publ). Cambridge University Press. http://site.ebrary.com/lib/alltitles/docDetail.action?docID=10469103 https://doi.org/10.1017/CBO9780511793943

Tarasova, E. (2018). (Non-) alternative energy transitions: Examining neoliberal rationality in official nuclear energy discourses of Russia and Poland. *Energy Research & Social Science*, *41*(1), 128–135. https://doi.org/10.1016/j.erss.2018.04.008

Tobin, P. (2017). Leaders and laggards: Climate policy ambition in developed states. *Global Environmental Politics*, *17*(4), 28–47. https://doi.org/10.1162/GLEP_a_00433

Tosun, J. (2011). When the grace period is over: Assessing the new Member States' compliance with EU requirements for oil stockholding. *Energy Policy*, *39*(11), 7156–7164. https://doi.org/10.1016/j.enpol.2011.08.035

Tosun, J., Biesenbender, S., & Schulze, K. (2015). Building the EU's energy policy Agenda: An introduction. In J. Tosun, S. Biesenbender, & K. Schulze (Eds.), *Lecture notes in energy: Vol. 28. Energy policy making in the EU: Building the agenda* (Vol. 28, pp. 1–17). Springer. https://doi.org/10.1007/978-1-4471-6645-0_1

Tosun, J., & Rinscheid, A. (2021). The clean energy ministerial: Motivation for and policy consequences of membership. *International Political Science Review*, *42*(1), 114–129. https://doi.org/10.1177/0192512120942303

Tynkkynen, N. (2010). A great ecological power in global climate policy? Framing climate change as a policy problem in Russian public discussion. *Environmental Politics*, *19*(2), 179–195. https://doi.org/10.1080/09644010903574459

Tynkkynen, V.-P., & Tynkkynen, N. (2018). Climate denial revisited: (Re)contextualising Russian public discourse on climate change during putin 2.0. *Europe-Asia Studies*, *70*(7), 1103–1120. https://doi.org/10.1080/09668136.2018.1472218

van de Graaf, T. (2013). Fragmentation in global energy governance: Explaining the creation of IRENA. *Global Environmental Politics*, *13*(3), 14–33. https://doi.org/10.1162/GLEP_a_00181

Victor, D. G. (2015). *The case for climate clubs*. International Centre for Trade and Sustainable Development/World Economic Forum.

Weischer, L., Morgan, J., & Patel, M. (2012). Climate clubs: Can small groups of countries make a big difference in addressing climate change? *Review of European Community & International Environmental Law*, *21*(3), 177–192. https://doi.org/10.1111/reel.12007

Widerberg, O., & Stenson, D. E. (2013). Climate clubs and the UNFCCC. Stockholm: *FORES*.

Wu, F., & Martus, E. (2020). Contested environmentalism: The politics of waste in China and Russia. *Environmental Politics*, *12*(4), 1–20. https://doi.org/10.1080/09644016.2020.1816367

Yang, X., Jin, W., Jiang, H., Xie, Q., Shen, W., & Han, W. (2017). Car ownership policies in China: Preferences of residents and influence on the choice of electric cars. *Transport Policy*, *58*(1), 62–71. https://doi.org/10.1016/j.tranpol.2017.04.010

Yu, B. (2019). *Climate clubs and global decarbonization: A comparison of the APP and the CEM*. EGL Working Paper 20191. Toronto. Munk School of Global Affairs & Public Policy, University of Toronto.

Environmental conflict management: a comparative cross-cultural perspective of China and Russia

Arthur L. Demchuk, Mile Mišić, Anastassia Obydenkova and Jale Tosun

ABSTRACT
How are environmental conflicts managed in China and Russia? Both states are territorially large non-democracies affected by environmental degradation due to industrialisation and economic growth, and both are characterised by collectivist culture resulting from pronounced historical legacies and Communism. Our analysis of China indicates the important role played by local governments often supporting local people; and role of the negotiation between the central and the local governments. In contrast, in Russia local governments ally with businesses involved in environmental conflicts; or tend to support central government view on the conflict. However, the environmentalists' movements in Russia are better connected to external (international) support. In contrast, China exhibits more isolation of environmental movements that are less influenced by Western environmentalism, if at all. The paper aspires to bring further insights in understanding of the public environmentalism and management of environmental conflicts in Eurasia.

Introduction

In recent decades, almost all world regions have experienced environmental conflicts.[1] These conflicts are caused mainly by the incompatibility of the goals of various political actors in relation to the preservation of the environment or the use of natural resources with those of fast economic development and pragmatic benefits at any cost (Martínez-Alier, 2002; Martínez-Alier & Schlüpmann, 1990 [1993]). The peculiarities of the formation of the modern world market economy have led to an inequality in the development of world production and consumption. The positive and negative social and environmental consequences of globalisation are uneven in time and space, and they are felt differently by different peoples and regions (Christoff & Eckersley, 2013). Industrialised democracies and urban agglomerations are in a favourable position, while non-democracies, developing and rural economies are in a disadvantaged position (Obydenkova & Salahodjaev,

2016, 2017) Research on climate change in particular has revealed the exposure and vulnerability of poverty-stricken people to adverse consequences such as droughts, floods, heat waves, and the impacts on agriculture and food production as well as on ecosystem services (Hallegatte et al., 2018). As a result, the Sustainable Development Goals adopted by the United Nations in 2015 strive to link the issues of economic development, poverty reduction and urbanisation to environmental and climate action (Tosun & Leininger, 2017).

Existing research has indeed shown that the different incentive structures can be shaped to make long-term goals of sustainable development compatible with economic benefits. For example, drawing on the influential study by Vogel (1997), empirical investigations have shown that economic development can also prompt policymakers to strengthen their environmental policies. In this context, the post-Communist countries and Communist China are particularly intriguing cases. Until the late 1980s, post-Communist countries had closed trade regimes, highly centralised and inter-dependent economies (ties that survived until the twenty-first century) that prioritised short-term economic benefits over environmental policies (Andonova et al., 2007; Lankina, T. et al., 2016a; Lankina, T. V. et al., 2016b). In the early 1990s, under the influence of the European Union (EU) and other external actors, most of the post-Communist states in Central and Eastern Europe and even some regions in Russia experienced diffusion of democracy, freedom of mass media and salience of environmental issues (Obydenkova, 2008; Obydenkova, 2012). As for the EU accession states from the Central Europe, the regime transition was coupled with the adoption of significant pro-environmental policies. But while some countries put strict environmental regulations in place, others opted for lax ones (Tosun, 2013). Previous research has highlighted the importance of international trade and accession to the European Union to both democratisation and the promotion of environmental politics and policies in this part of the world (Andonova et al., 2007; Nazarov & Obydenkova, 2020; Tosun, 2013; Tosun & Schulze, 2015). Many studies have also shown how the Central and Eastern European Member States have cut ties to their Communist legacies.[2]

In contrast, this literature paid less attention to the environmental agendas of non-democracies, especially those located in Eurasia, such as Russia and China. This is not surprising, as these states are known for their lack of transparency, controlling mass media to manipulate public opinion, and propaganda (Libman & Obydenkova, 2018). Within the studies on sustainable development, environmental justice, environmental movements, and conflicts occupy a special place (Martínez-Alier, 2002). Environmental conflicts are defined here as the interaction of two or more parties which believe that their goals in relation to changing (or preserving) the state of the natural environment (life support systems-ecosystems) are incompatible (Demchuk, 2020). The goals of the conflict parties and the strategies they use are based on their *perception* and assessment of the situation. To a large extent, behaviour in an environmental conflict is determined by political culture – *cultural attitudes* (see, e.g. Gupta & McIver, 2016; Mi et al., 2020). Thus, socio-cultural perception is a key variable in the formation of attitudes towards environmental conflicts, which in turn affect the long-term management of these conflicts.

This article gives an overview of environmental conflicts and how they are managed in two countries that have a similar collectivist culture – Russia (exhibiting a legacy of

Communism) and China, currently a Communist state. The specificity of the collective culture in both cases presumably increases an individuals' willingness to engage in environmental movements, as argued by Hofstede et al. (2010) On the other hand, authoritarian regimes are associated with a lack of transparency, corruption, pragmatism, and the prioritisation of the economy (Libman & Obydenkova, 2014; Obydenkova & Libman, 2016). These factors are likely to discourage an individual from engaging in environmental movements, in both China and Russia. Recent research on environmental governance in general (e.g. Tosun & Shyrokykh, 2021; Wu & Martus, 2020) and on environmental protests (e.g. Plantan, 2018) in particular has shown that this comparison yields intriguing insights.

The remainder of this article unfolds as follows. First, we provide a definition of environmental conflicts and environmental conflict management. Then, we provide additional clarifications on the cases of China and Russia. Subsequently, we give an overview of the pertinent literatures and discuss their main findings. In a last step, we summarise our findings and conclude.

Environmental conflicts and environmental conflict management

The focal point of all environmental conflicts are environmental issues that arise from environmentally damaging economic and social activities, such as urban planning and construction (Glasbergen, 1995). Environmental issues can take many forms and relate to land use, natural resource management, waste management, and different kinds of air, water, and soil pollution (Bingham & Conservation Foundation, 1986; Jackson & Pradubraj, 2004). They culminate in environmental conflicts when there are clashes over how resources should be used or what preventive or corrective actions should be taken (see Scheidel et al., 2020). Geographically, environmental conflicts can be localised within a single country or they can have a transboundary (see, e.g. Mianabadi et al., 2020) or global scope, such as climate change (see, e.g. Trombetta, 2012).

Another important feature is the intensity of environmental conflicts. As the literature does not provide a uniform definition of this phenomenon, anything from differences in values, political discussions, and policy debates, to violent conflicts within a single state or between countries can be considered as environmental conflict (Fisher, 2014). This makes the empirical analysis of this phenomenon challenging. Most scholars regard environmentally-motivated mass mobilisation as an indicator of environmental conflict (see, e.g. Plantan, 2018), but this is only one of several ways in which conflicts can unfold. From this perspective, the Environmental Justice Atlas (Temper et al., 2018) represents a valuable new analytical tool, as it offers data on environmental conflicts worldwide (Hanaček & Martinez-Alier, 2021; Martinez-Alier, 2021)

While there is not a single theoretical model for explaining how environmental conflicts emerge, much of the literature has focused on the concept of resource scarcity, contending that the occurrence and intensity of conflicts increase as resources become scarcer (see Scheidel et al., 2020). In line with this, there are three potential pathways to environmental conflicts (Hauge & Ellingsen, 1998). First is the *supply-induced scarcity*, which is when resources diminish faster that they can be renewed. An example of this would be overfishing, overdrafting, or pollution that renders a certain resource unfit for consumption. The second is *demand-induced* scarcity, which is triggered by higher resource consumption per capita, or simply by population growth, and leads to insufficient quantities of resources. Finally, *structural scarcity* refers to the uneven allocation of resources.[3] The notion of structural scarcity can be also applied to pollution when certain geographical areas and populations would be asymmetrically affected by environmental pollution. These three paths should not be taken separately, but rather as a continuum where supply- or demand-induced scarcities would lead to structural scarcities or uneven results for different groups.

Considering this, it is reasonable to expect that various social actors would have different values, interests, needs, positions, motivations, and objectives when it comes to environmental issues and associated conflicts (Castro & Nielsen, 2003; Redpath et al., 2013). In essence, conflicts could emerge between competing users of a certain resource (e.g. fishers), between groups that seek to protect and conserve a certain resource and those who want to use it, and between any of these groups and decision-makers (Fisher, 2014). Moreover, environmental conflicts can be fuelled by effects that environmental changes (resource availability, quality, or access) can have on societal actors (Fisher, 2014).

In this article, we are predominantly interested in intra-state environmental conflicts between local environmental movements and communities, and various levels of the national government in two large authoritarian countries. The political contexts of these states determine to some extent how the environmental conflicts are managed, and whether environmental movements are successful. The literature on comparative environmental movements lists the nature of a regime, political institutions and access to the policy process, the opportunity to find allies and opponents, as well as a state's capacity for repression as crucial explanatory variables (O'Neill, 2012). Some political systems, even authoritarian ones, will respond to the demands of environmental activists under certain conditions, whereas others will not (Y. Li et al., 2016; O'Brien & Li, 2006; Plantan, 2018). Our goal is to offer insights into how Chinese and Russian local authorities have dealt with environmental conflicts.

Motivation for the case selection

A comparison of China and Russia concerning the resolution of environmental conflicts appears promising for a few reasons. First, both countries have highly polluting industrial sectors. In the case of China, it is mostly manufacturing, the production of electricity from coal, and the increase in registered passenger vehicles that contribute to environmental degradation, whereas in Russia energy production and extractive industries are the main sources of environmental pollution and stress (Y. Li et al., 2016; Martus, 2017; Mol, 2009; O'Brien & Li, 2006; Plantan, 2018; Tosun & Shyrokykh, 2021; Wu & Martus, 2020; X.Yang et al., 2017; Yanitsky, 2012). As a result, the governments of the two countries should have an incentive to mitigate and remedy environmental degradation by means of environmental policy.

Second, both countries are non-democracies, yet of different types (e.g. Libman & Obydenkova, 2021). China's main regime-related feature is that it is a one-party system, whereas Russia is considered an electoral autocracy (see, e.g. Kailitz & Stockemer, 2017). Although they differ in many details, both regimes can be characterised as 'participatory authoritarianism', which stresses the resulting "practices of local governance that, on the one hand, enable citizens to engage directly with local officials in the policy process, but limit, direct, and control civic participation on the other" (Owen, 2020, p. 415). In light of our interest in environmental conflicts and their governance, this common feature makes the comparison particularly valuable.

Third, following Hofstede et al. (2010) and compared to other countries, China and Russia stand out as countries that have a collectivist culture in place (see Figure 1). According to Hofstede et al. (2010), in 'individualist' cultures the individual is the main unit of society, and the concern for the individual is the concern for all. In 'collectivist' cultures the main unit of society is a small group, most often the family. People in such cultures have an inherent orientation towards others, and a person identifies herself as a member of a particular group. They are focused not so much on the result of their activities but on maintaining good relationships. We expect individuals in both China and Russia to be generally aware of environmental grievances and, in principle, willing to engage in collective action to prevent or correct these (Mi et al., 2020). However, given the countries' unfavourable political contexts, poor respect for human rights (if any), and the lack of complete information and transparency, we also expect these aspirations to be suppressed by risk-avoiding behaviour. Therefore, developing a sense of what the environmental movements in these countries look like and how willing they are to engage in environmental conflicts appears promising.

This figure shows the similarity of the individualism scores for China and Russia: Both states have the lowest individualism scores of all the countries, followed by Japan, Germany, the UK, and the USA (the latter two demonstrate significant similarity). The data presented in the figure allow us to identify China and Russia as highly collectivist countries, making a comparative analysis especially meaningful.

Environmental conflicts and environmental authoritarianism in China

Over the past 40 years, the People's Republic of China has shown unprecedented stable economic growth and become a world power, launching different regional initiatives in Eurasia and establishing new international organisations as hubs for the diffusion of values and ideas (R. Li et al., 2020).[4] As a 'side' effect of its rapid development of industrial and agricultural production, however, environmental conflicts have emerged. Environmental protests have taken place as a consequence of this, despite the country's non-democratic context, and even resulted in some high-profile, large campaigns (Plantan, 2018). The conflicts have mostly arisen over the planning, construction and operation of industrial facilities in cities (Y. Li et al., 2016), over nuclear plants (Wu, 2017), over infrastructure, coal mining, and waste management (Lang & Xu, 2013), over the extraction of mineral ores and building materials, and big dams (Xie & van der Heijden, 2010).[5] It is important to highlight that the environmental conflicts in China are driven by concerns over how environmental pollution affects human health rather than considerations in relation to environmental degradation more generally. These health-related concerns seem to be substantiated when considering that both Chinese and Western media have identified the existence of 'cancer villages' (Lora-Wainwright et al., 2012).

Distinctive features of environmental conflicts in China have been the development of various forms of activism (Lora-Wainwright et al., 2012), including the mobilisation of demonstrations against projects, public protests, and sometimes even the use of violence. In the great majority of cases, environmental activism and conflicts occur in urban areas. For example, Jian and Chan (2016) provide a detailed assessment of environmental action against a proposed industrial wastewater disposal project in the city of Qidong in 2012. In this regard, the authors show how the collective identity of the protestors was constructed and reconstructed through their interaction with political actors during the mobilisation process.

According to Plantan (2018), Chinese environmental activists have reduced their formal involvement in high-profile campaigns and have also limited the visible horizontal linkages between each other. Environmental activism is less common in rural areas. In the opinion of Lora-Wainwright et al. (2012), one explanation for this is that rural populations tend to perceive environmental problems as 'inevitable', which stems from their sense of subordination to political leaders, their dependence on local industries, and the framing of the exploitation of local resources as part of a broader national project of development.

The general literature on environmental conflicts and their management has alluded to the effectiveness of resolving such conflicts through negotiation, reaching consensus, and finding a consensus (Rauschmayer & Wittmer, 2006). However, in modern China, the regulation of urban environmental conflicts works somewhat differently (Y. Li et al., 2016; Liu et al., 2017). That is, the country's environmental policy is defined mainly by the central government in Beijing and the local authorities implement it (Y. Li et al., 2016). Local authorities enjoy a notable level of discretion and power to resolve local issues of importance to their respective populations, including those related to environmental conflicts. In fact, China grants local authorities 'conditional autonomy' (Charron & Lapuente, 2011). This means that local authorities are free to choose the means of regulating social conflicts, but the central government of the People's Republic of China reserves the right to intervene in the situation if the local government does not cope well (O'Brien & Li, 2006). In addition, local officials are appointed 'from above', which makes them feel accountable (considering themselves subordinates) primarily to those who appointed them. In the past, this institutional arrangement, referred to as 'environmental authoritarianism', has favoured 'selective' implementation efforts in which the local governments aligned their approaches with the preferences of the central government (X. Li et al., 2019).

The higher/national authorities in China wield considerable power over the local ones and can influence their decisions (Cai, 2010). This central government's regulatory oversight of policy implementation has further increased the incentive for local governments to take action according to the preferences of the central government (X. Li et al., 2019).

However, there are signs that the Chinese authorities are gradually moving away from the previous authoritarian 'all-controlling' model to a more thoughtful and comprehensive one. In this emerging, 'responsive' environmental authoritarianism, states respond to the requests and demands of citizens, while maintaining political control over society (Van Rooij et al., 2016). Responsive environmental authoritarianism does not adopt any single approach but has shown to be adaptive to differing conflict situations. As demonstrated by Cai (2010), local governments in China can respond to social conflicts in four ways:

- ignore the protest (refusal of direct interaction with citizens);
- suppress the protest (forceful repression);
- find a compromise (fulfilling part of the citizens' demands to reduce social tension while punishing individual citizens for 'violating the law');

- giving in to all the citizens' demands (refusing to implement the project or transferring it to another place).

With the first two strategies, the authorities do not deviate from the original decisions, and in the last two cases, they change the original decision partially or completely. In the situation of environmental conflicts, local authorities in China find themselves 'between two fires' and must choose between the interests of economic development (construction and operation of new industrial facilities) and environmental interests (reducing the negative impact on ecosystems, maintaining public order and stability) (Deng & Yang, 2013; Mertha, 2009).

The factors that determine the local governments' choice of a particular method for approaching and resolving environmental conflicts in China are listed in Table 1.

We will now discuss some of these factors in greater depth. The scale of a protest (i.e. the number of participants) and the presence or absence of violence influence how the local authorities govern environmental conflicts (Y. Li et al., 2016). The construct underpinning this argument is the scope of public discontent that environmental activism can produce. Similar to the central government, local authorities in China are sensitive to public discontent and potential unrest (O'Brien & Li, 2006). Along these lines, Y. Li et al. (2016) contend that if environmental protests include the use of violence, there is a higher chance that local authorities will change their initial decisions on an environmental issue in an attempt to prevent escalation.

The costs of meeting the demands of the environmental activists is another important factor for explaining the role that local governments play in resolving environmental conflicts (Y. Li et al., 2016; O'Brien & Li, 2006). If the costs and losses of meeting the demands of the protesters are too great, then the authorities stick to the original decision (Cai, 2010). The frequency of environmental conflicts is also significant, because multiple conflicts in one place can attract the attention of the whole of China (Shi & Cai, 2006). Local authorities, therefore, should aim to apply the chosen strategies carefully so as not to make the protests swell or spark new social upheavals (Cai, 2008).

How do the abovementioned factors influence the results of environmental conflict management in China? Scholars generally argue that the smaller the scale of protest actions, the less likely they are to succeed. Large-scale protests become a 'political risk' for local authorities, and can put pressure on them to change their initial decisions regarding the project that caused the protest (Cai, 2008; McAdam & Boudet, 2012). But there are exceptions. As the analysis of environmental protests in Beijing, Guangzhou, and Wujiang by Lang and Xu (2013) shows, even small-scale protests can be successful if their participants use network resources, which include contacts to journalists, media editors, non-governmental environmental organisations, and experts.

Environmental conflicts concerning the planning, construction, and operation of urban industrial facilities at different stages of implementation are assessed differently by local authorities in terms of costs. Accordingly, the local authorities chose a strategy for regulating a particular conflict and responding to citizens' protests. In this regard, Kemberling and Roberts (2009), for example, found in their analysis of the United States that it is much easier to fight against plans to build a new object than against the continuation of one whose construction has already commenced, and it is even harder to campaign for the closure of an object that has already been built or commissioned. This

Table 1. Overview of factors determining environmental conflict governance in China.

Factor	Underlying mechanism(s)	Reference
Media and social networks	Pressure of the media and social networks increases the conflicts' visibility.	Y. Li et al., 2016; Yang & Calhoun, 2007
Accountability of office holders	Giving citizens a voice so that they can raise their concerns positively affects problem solving.	He & Thøgersen, 2010
Scale and form of protests	Large scale protests are associated with higher chances of success.	Y. Li et al., 2016
Conflict nature	Whether the protests are violent or peaceful dictates, among other things, how the government will respond. Violent protests might have higher chances of success.	Y. Li et al., 2016
Stakeholders	Stakeholder structure affects how the issue will be managed.	Liu et al., 2017; Wang et al., 2015
Central government's position	Central government can remain silent, support, contradict, or oppose the conflict. The absence of support from the national government is usually a *conditio sine qua non* for local governments to change their position.	Y. Li et al., 2016
Costs and benefits	If high costs are associated with meeting the citizens' demands, this might lead to either ignoring the demands or repression. Similarly, high costs associated with ongoing protests might lead the local government to bend.	Cai, 2008; Y. Li et al., 2016; Y. Li, 2019
Project stage	Late-stage projects are usually treated differently to early-stage ones, as the former tend to be more expensive to cancel.	Y. Li et al., 2016
Information and knowledge	Scholars can affect what form the conflict might take in various ways.	L. Yang et al., 2015
External forces	External forces (e.g. large-scale industrial pollution in China) might raise overall concern regarding the environment and motivate new stakeholders to participate.	van Rooij et al., 2016

Own elaboration.

is quite understandable: at the planning stage, the costs of changing the project (relocation, for example) are small, so the local authorities are more likely to renege on their decision. An example of this is the relocation of a waste incineration power plant in Beijing, when the government faced stiff opposition from the local population (Y. Li, 2019). On the other hand, the local authorities will persistently 'protect' the project if it is in the final stages of construction, because the price of making changes to it will be unacceptably high, as was the case of the paraxylene plant in Pengzhou (Y. Li et al., 2016).

How the local governments will react to environmental conflicts and resistance depends on many factors (see Table 1). However, there are some patterns in environmental conflict management on the local level that are common across the country (Y. Li, 2019; Y. Li et al., 2016). The necessary condition for a local government to change its decision is lack of support from the central government (Y. Li, 2019; Y. Li et al., 2016). If a local government receives support from the central government, the change is unlikely. If the national government does not offer support, however, a local government is likely to compromise if faced with large-scale violent protests, even if a project is in a late stage of development (Y. Li et al., 2016). Large-scale violent confrontations, as in the case of the Wuxi waste incineration power plant, are highly undesirable and perceived by the national government as something that can spill over from the local level and damage the state legitimacy (Y. Li et al., 2016). Conversely, peaceful demonstrations, whether large- or small-scale, at the early stages of a project can also lead to compromise. This, arguably, is due to the low costs of relocating or abandoning a project (Y. Li et al., 2016).

Environmental conflicts and vertical of power in Russia

After the fall of the Soviet Union, Russia experienced an upswing of civic activism and demands for citizens' participation in decision-making at all levels of government, which was quite a natural manifestation of the processes of democratisation and decentralisation in the 1990s (Henry, 2011; Henry & Douhovnikoff, 2008; Newell & Henry, 2016; Obydenkova and Swenden 2013). However, from 2001 onwards, Russia has witnessed a critical turn in its development entailing radical re-centralisation (known as vertical of power), the suppression of (mass) media freedom, disinformation, and democratic backsliding.

These political changes, have led to a rise in the number and intensity of environmental conflicts since the 2000s (Pickvance, 2019). However, similar to the patterns observed in China, environmental issues are no permanent feature of the public agenda in Russia. Attention to the environmental experiences its' 'ups' and 'downs', as Downs (1972) put it famously. One likely reason for the disrupted public interest in environmental issues is the media landscape in Russia and fluctuation in the state's control over the media and in the available information. Most newspapers, for example, rely on Russian officials as information sources. Furthermore, most of the Russian newspapers do not criticise the state of the environment or the corresponding policies (Poberezhskaya, 2015). The Russian political and cultural tradition is characterised by the dominant role of the state (government) in decision-making (Tsygankov, 2014). Despite growth in the values of individualism over recent decades, the majority of Russians are characterised by the values of collectivism and communitarianism (Tower et al., 1997). Indeed, Figure 1 above demonstrated that Russia falls closest to China, as compared to other states with large economies. On the one hand, collectivism is associated with engagement in pro-environmental activities, potentially benefitting not only one-self but society more broadly (see, e.g. Baldwin et al., 2019; Cho et al., 2013). On the other hand, the legacy of Communism has left its mark on social perceptions, patterns of public behaviour, and distrust of political institutions and officials (Libman & Obydenkova, 2019, 2020, 2021) Therefore, when considering the socio-cultural perspective of environmental movements and environmental conflict management, it is essential to account for the impact of history as well as realities of modern politics.

From the cultural perspective of collectivism, one may expect Russians to have a higher likelihood of becoming involved in environmental movements. But from the perspective of legacies of Communism and existing political constraints (e.g. suppression of public freedoms, passivity of civil society, and above all, *misinformation* disseminated by official mass media), we should expect a weaker response to the official policies affecting the environment. In fact, it is not surprising that the environmental movement in Russia has been described as relatively weak, often relying on volunteers or on the support of foreign environmental organisations and foundations (Crotty, 2006).

Another important factor is that the environmental movement in Russia is fragmented and the organisational strength of the individual groups varies considerably across the country (Yanitsky, 2012). This is not counter-intuitive, as multiple studies have shown that the regions of Russia vary significantly in their economic development, level of democracy, civil society, independence of mass media and even in access to the internet and social media, among other issues (Lankina et al. 2016a; Obydenkova, 2008; Obydenkova, 2012). Because of the uneven distribution of wealth across regions, business actors in Russia have a much greater influence over the formation and implementation of environmental policy than civil society does in Western countries (Feldman & Blokov, 2012). This economic, social, and political heterogeneity across Russia is partially responsible for the

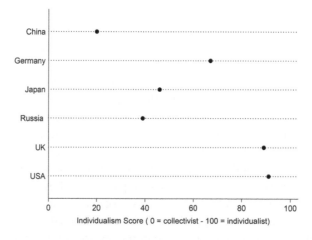

Figure 1. Individualism in China and Russia versus Democracies with Major Economies. Own elaboration based on data collected from the following website: https://www.hofstede-insights.com/country-comparison/.

difference in regional public responses to environmental conflicts and for the actors involved in conflict management.

Recently, environmental issues have become one of the most popular and resonant on the agenda of many regions of the Russian Federation, giving rise to conflict situations. The Environmental Justice Atlas mentions 58 major cases of environmental conflicts across Russia.[6] Those located in the European part of Russia are mainly related to industrial and infrastructural development, urban waste management, the construction of nuclear power plants, and radioactive waste management (Klyuev, 2019; Wu & Martus, 2020), whereas environmental conflicts in the Urals, Siberia, and the Far East are mainly over water management, mineral ores, fossil fuels, the extraction of building materials, and forest (mis-)management (Libman & Obydenkova, 2014; Pierk & Tysiachniouk, 2016). Due to the geographical variation across Russian regions, various demographic groups are involved in these environmental conflicts, including urban residents (mainly those employed in the non-industrial sphere), residents of rural areas, and representatives of the indigenous peoples of Siberia and the Far East, etc.

The goals of the protestors and the responses of the state differ on a case-by-case basis. Sometimes (e.g. in Khimki Forest), environmental issues become a serious weapon in political campaigns aimed at discrediting local authorities (Evans, 2012; Petrov et al., 2014; Plantan, 2018; Vinogradov, 2013). In others, pollution concerns become a tool in inter-corporate conflicts (Shvarts et al., 2016). There are also cases of 'alliances' being formed between local administrations and environmentalists in order to put pressure on economic interests (Henry, 2011). This latter aspect is somewhat similar to the case of China, as described above, when local authorities may ally with the local population on environmental issues.

What is critically important about non-democracies is that due to the lack of independent mass media, misinformation, and low levels of transparency, people do not know if certain governmental policies and decisions triggered an environmental conflict unless the consequences of this conflict become visible and obvious. Therefore, there is no direct link between the environmental situation in the locality and the level of public activity on environmental issues (Vinogradov, 2013) As Vinogradov (2013) states, it is only possible to mobilise citizens once environmental degradation becomes obvious and visible (e.g. during the implementation of projects that will alter the landscape for the sake of new industrial construction, roads, or pipelines). The idea of the 'self-worth' of the current order of things,[7] regardless of the actual state of the environment (unknown to public), is likely to be the most efficient trigger of an ecological movement. In some cases, an additional factor may be regional patriotism, which reinforces the idea of the importance of local historical sites.

The most common environmental conflicts in Russia are those caused by the pollution or destruction of natural resources (e.g. forest, the ocean). A typical pathway for such a conflict is as follows: after an incident occurs, activists organise a rally to collect signatures for petitions and write complaints to local authorities or enterprises, requesting that they intervene and resolve the issue (Bogdanova et al., 2018). The studies demonstrate that even after public protests have taken place, the conflict is often most often ignored by authorities or, in a few case, becomes the basis for a prosecutor's check (Ibid). Either way, the management of environmental conflicts can barely be described as efficient or satisfactory in any way. More importantly, it takes place 'post-factum' – *after* so much environmental damage has been caused that it is visible to the public. (Vinogradov, 2013) Like all other forms of public (mis-)management, environmental conflict management suffers from inefficient bureaucracy, corruption at all levels, and a lack of clarity regarding the rules and the procedure (e.g. Bogdanova et al., 2018; Libman & Obydenkova, 2014; Vinogradov, 2013). Territorial centralisation accounts for a significant portion of this mismanagement, as studies cited above indicate. The result of this type of conflict is environmental litigation, which has been the battlefield of Russian environmentalism since the late 1990s (Yanitsky, 2012, p. 938).

However, it should be noted that the incentive structures vary noticeably across regions in Russia. In a number of oil-producing regions, the authorities *and involved business* adopt a 'solidarity' approach (in contrast to China, where solidarity between local government *and people* take place). For example, in the Komi Republic environmental conflicts are 'resolved' on the basis of denial, manipulation, and ignoring (Buryj, 2014) According to a study by Buryj (2014), big businesses, *with the support of the regional authorities*, deny the fact that environmental rules have been violated and they restrict public access to the site. When it becomes impossible to hide (e.g. an oil spill), the manipulation of public opinion begins. During the implementation of conciliation procedures, the strongest environmental activists of civil society are pushed out of the negotiations by businesses and the authorities, and often replaced by more flexible actors. The process of finding a solution is highly bureaucratic and informal in nature. Finally, if the conflict cannot be resolved, the authorities try to silence it, suppressing the official media.

The above-cited studies single out at least two trends in environmental movements unfolding across Russia as the triggers of different types of public behaviour. The first trend is when an environmental movement does not take place due to the solidarity between business and government, which triggers opportunistic behaviour on the part of bureaucracy and the development of the shadow economy. In this case, the public is kept misinformed to fit the interest of business and, by default, corrupted local bureaucracy. The second trend is when environmental protests take place in response to 'visible' changes: e.g. the preservation of cultural and natural objects (Bogdanova et al., 2018). Such conflicts emerge when businesses or the authorities wish to alter a park, pond, square, or other such amenity, but society wishes to preserve it. Even when a government wishes to improve a park, for example, conflict can be the result as the plans may entail construction work. Hence, the most important factor in the prevention of environmental conflicts of this type is a public relations campaign to promote initiatives, whatever those may be. In most cases, society reacts negatively to changes because of lack of information. The solution in democracies, therefore, is to hold public hearings or place information posters at the construction site, explaining in detail the developers' goals (Drazkiewicz et al., 2015; Harrison & Sundstrom, 2010; Manowong & Ogunlana, 2008; Sun et al., 2016). Due to the low accountability of the Russian government (at all levels) to its people, the public often witnesses the actions of Government and the outcomes of informal deals between businesses and administrations without having been given any prior information.

Other examples of this second trend relate to waste disposal, namely the fight against illegal landfills and the fight against building incinerators close to residential areas. In the first case, landfills cause dissatisfaction among local residents, as they pollute the environment (Wu & Martus, 2020). This type of conflict is particularly important in the Moscow

Region, where significant volumes of waste are produced by the numerous households as well as by industry. The second type of conflict is the movement of society against building incinerators near residential areas (Mingaleva et al., 2020; Wu & Martus, 2020). Whenever a similar dispute takes place in Moscow and St. Petersburg (the two cities with the most developed civil society and access to social media), they receive substantial attention from the mass media. In contrast, remote regions with more limited access to the internet and controlled official mass media have less information on waste disposal in their respective regions and situation is silenced by local governments.

In accordance with the country's collectivist culture, a notable feature of environmental movements in Russia is that the initiators are *ordinary residents* (Bogdanova et al., 2018). State bodies and municipalities may become involved in a conflict, but they are never the initiators of environmental concerns. The authorities, just like the public, pay attention to conflicts once they have escalated. Likewise, policymakers only reach out to civil society actors – if at all – following the escalation of a conflict (Plantan, 2018), or after it has gained international attention and resulted in external pressure on the government (Henry, 2010).

The need to create either internal or external pressure is probably the reason why the Russian environmental activists have often chosen the strategy of mass mobilisation and coordinated protests across the country (Plantan, 2018). In addition, environmental activists also seek to create coalitions with environmental organisations outside of Russia. A good example is the Baikal movement against the Eastern Siberia-Pacific Ocean oil pipeline, which included a coalition of local non-governmental organisations (NGOs), Greenpeace, the World Wide Fund for Nature (WWF), as well as other Russian environmental NGOs. Besides organising a series of protests across large cities in Russia, the coalition reached out to the UNESCO World Heritage Committee, and eventually managed to get the project cancelled (Plantan, 2018).

The basis of environmental conflicts is usually costs related to the distribution of environmental externalities, such as air, water, or soil pollution (Khovavko, 2016). Specific tools that ensure the internalisation of environmental externalities are direct regulatory methods (standards), market-based methods (Pigouvian tax, user fees, and permits trade system), and institutional approaches (disclosure strategy and voluntary business initiatives) (e.g. Sterner, 2003). One of the most important, widespread policy instruments for identifying and managing externalities is the *Environmental Impact Assessment* (EIA) (see, e.g. Busch & Jörgens, 2005; Knill & Tosun, 2009; Tosun et al., 2019). In Russia, EIAs are a obligatory assessment process where companies planning a project must evaluate its potential negative impacts on the environment (Schuhmann & Kropp, 2018). The Regulation of the year 2000 defines EIA as 'a process encouraging an ecologically informed administrative decision on implementation of economic and other activities through identification of possible adverse impacts, assessment of ecological impacts, taking into account public opinions, and developing measures to mitigate and prevent negative impacts' (Solodyankina & Koeppel, 2009, pp. 77–78).

Consequently, an integral part of the EIA procedure is the discussion of the project with the public, which is intended to give local populations an opportunity to express their opinion on the project under consideration (Cherp & Golubeva, 2004). The results of these public hearings are subsequently presented to the 'state ecological assessment.' The final decision is made by the collective decision-making body of the commission of experts; it is decided by majority vote and includes the participation of non-state experts (Schuhmann & Kropp, 2018). Despite the legal obligation to consult the public, Schuhmann and Kropp (2018) have identified cases in which the competent subnational authorities approved the EIAs due to pressure from companies or higher political levels and prevented public hearings. More broadly, the authors show that the EIAs are implemented very differently throughout Russia, sometimes resulting in the proper participation of civil society and sometimes sidelining them (see also Khovavko, 2016). Similar observations are reported by Yanitsky (2012) for the role played by regional and local chambers involved in environmental conflict resolution: in the end, the interests of the local administration tend to prevail.

Another way to effectively influence the government's environmental policy is provided by the tools of direct democracy and most importantly referendums. In the second half of the 1990s, the Russian Federation adopted numerous legislative acts regulating the holding of referenda at the different levels of its political system (Hill & White, 2018). The issues that can be submitted for a referendum are limited, and the procedure for initiating a referendum is complicated. As a result, the very demand for a referendum has become a form of protest movement aimed at forcing the authorities to sit down at the negotiating table. However, with democratic backsliding in the last two decades, the rights to protests and referendums have become rhetorical lip-service. Other institutions that are suitable for reaching a compromise in order to resolve environmental conflicts, such as formal meetings, public examinations, conciliation commissions, and instruments of representative democracy, are either absent or do not function properly.[8]

The most important factor in preventing and resolving environmental conflicts is considering the views of local communities and populations. This is important for a number of reasons. First, there are always winners and losers in the implementation of economic activity projects. The beneficiaries can be the initiators of the project, the authorities of various levels, or even the people, if the project is of national significance. The losers are almost always local communities due to environmental degradation, but as already indicated above, these are often in a situation where all they can do is socially licence the operation of such activities, as in the case of oil and gas projects in the Komi Republic (Wilson, 2016).

Secondly, the local populations, especially indigenous ones, are guided by the long-term goals of sustainable development (their ancestors lived on this land and their children will live on it). Therefore, there are also cultural reasons for local populations to oppose projects that are potentially harmful to the environment (Novikova, 2016).

Third, communities with strong intra-community ties are able to make decisions about the use of resources that ensure collective interests are met, as stated by pertinent theories such as the Institutional Analysis and Development Framework as put forth by Ostrom (2011). By following a set of common rules, these communities can escape the tragedy of the commons (Hardin, 1968) and achieve long term resource explanation sustainability. These rules should set clear boundaries regarding use of the common resource, as well as clear access rules. Moreover, provision and resource exploitation should be adapted to local natural conditions, with an established system for sanctions as well as rules of renegotiation (Ostrom, 2015).

Conclusion

Across Eurasia, environmental conflicts are spreading fast and affecting people from different social groups. Resolving such disputes and conflicts in non-democracies requires more effort and resources. In this article, we gave an overview of environmental conflicts and how they are managed in two non-democracies with collectivist cultures – China and Russia. Our findings revealed that in China the relationship between the local and the central government (environmental authoritarianism) are key for understanding how environmental conflicts are resolved. In Russia, environmental conflict resolution seems to depend more on the capacity of civil society (environmental groups), which varies regionally and locally (Yanitsky, 2012), rather than on the support of local administrations and governments due to vertical of power. Moreover, the procedural rules are open to interpretation by local and regional authorities, making it easy to fit them to the interests of central government, business and opportunistic bureaucracy.[9]

The democracies with developing economies are under pressure to bring national environmental standards in line with those adopted in more economically developed countries – something that became visible in the case of the EIA procedure (Cherp & Golubeva, 2004; Khovavko, 2016; Solodyankina & Koeppel, 2009). In contrast, autocracies with strong economies (China and Russia) prioritise their economic and security benefits over the agenda of sustainable development (Hall et al., 2021). That is why the role of people and society cannot be under-evaluated in these states. The cultural perspective sheds light on the importance of the collectivist cultures shared by Russia and China and their impact on sustaining environmental movements in these states.

In contrast to the cultural approach, the 'exporting' of environmental mediation from the West to other countries can be only partially useful if they do not relate to local political, cultural, or institutional contexts. The importance of cultural attitudes in solving the problems of a particular country was demonstrated in the studies on policy transfer (Dolowitz & Marsh, 2000).

When using various technologies of environmental conflict management in China and Russia, a number of difficulties have to be overcome: the weakness of legal mechanisms, the limited powers of environmental agencies, the competition of various government bodies with each other, the reluctance of various actors to abandon direct 'power' actions, corruption at all levels of government, political lobbying, lack of financial resources, qualified personnel, and professional knowledge (Evans, 2012; Feldman & Blokov, 2012).

Despite some cultural similarities, China and Russia have a number of differences when it comes to protest mobilisation and governmental response. Environmental activists in Russia seem to prefer the strategy of mass mobilisation across the country, with the involvement of large internationals environmental organisations whenever possible. Their tactic is to create a network of NGOs and put the pressure on the regime, both internally and externally, through coordinated action (Plantan, 2018). In China, conversely, environmental non-governmental organisations usually avoid working together, and especially coordinating with international organisations. International and global environmental actors and organisations do no reach out to key societal or national actors, as the political regime is fairly closed in China to any external influences of this kind (e.g. Ambrosio, 2008). Therefore, the relationship between the local and the national governments seems to be crucial for the success of protest movements in China (Y. Li, 2019; Y. Li et al., 2016; O'Brien & Li, 2006).

In a world of increasing globalisation, it is important to consider the interests and positions of local communities, as these have their own views on the optimal use of natural resources and have formed them over centuries. This is even more crucial for non-democratic states, where people lack information on a number of topics, including environmental challenges. Traditional knowledge on the functioning of local ecosystems can be a significant and often the only tool available for the public to put pressure on governments. It also helps experts who evaluate various alternatives to environmental policy and the management of environmental conflicts (Berkes et al., 1994;Muradian et al., 2003). The approach of taking culture into account is, in fact, in line with the ideals of democracy and universal participation in decision-making as valued in modern Western society. Yet, we argue that traditional and alternative methods of environmental conflict resolution should become complementary, not mutually exclusive. This study aimed to use new cultural perspectives to enhance our understanding of environmental movements, conflicts, and their management. The issue is of the highest importance for Eurasia and should stay on the agenda for further studies.

Notes

1. Co-authors are listed alphabetically and they contributed equally to this paper.
2. However, even after the Enlargement of the EU in the 2000s, the new EU Member States still display different patterns of public opinion and behaviour which could be explained by historical legacies of Communism that survived the Global Financial Crisis 2008 (e.g. Armingeon & Guthmann, 2014; Arpino & Obydenkova, 2020; Obydenkova and Arpino2018; Beissinger & Kotkin, 2014)
3. This goes well beyond environmental conflicts and has been applied to political and economic development by Libman and Obydenkova (2014) who call it the 'limiting factor'. Limiting factors emerge when there is a scarce and unique source that keeps an entire economy developing.
4. An analysis of 'environmental authoritarianism' by X. Li et al. (2019) is presented later in this section.
5. Information collected from the Environmental Justice Atlas (https://ejatlas.org/country/china).
6. Environmental Justice Atlas – https://ejatlas.org/country/russia
7. The public in Russia can be described as 'traditionalist' as it often resists changes, including those taking place in the countryside (Libman and Obydenkova2021).
8. This observation aligns with the findings of Mol (2009) on Russia's environmental deinstitutionalisation.
9. However, it is fair to assume that a similar trend can be found in the case of China and its regions, and that this is due to the generally high level of corruption reported for China at a national level (however, the Corruption Perception Index still presents China as in a better situation than Russia).

Acknowledgments

The authors are very grateful to two anonymous reviewers of this paper for their excellent comments and insights.

Disclosure conflicts of interest statement

No potential conflict of interest was reported by the author(s).

Funding

This research has been supported by the Interdisciplinary Scientific and Educational School of Moscow University 'Preservation of the World Cultural and Historical Heritage', by the Basic Research Program of the National Research University Higher School of Economics, and by the Konrad Adenauer Foundation (KAS).

ORCID

Arthur L. Demchuk http://orcid.org/0000-0002-9285-7823
Mile Mišić http://orcid.org/0000-0002-6554-1962
Anastassia Obydenkova http://orcid.org/0000-0001-5099-5294
Jale Tosun http://orcid.org/0000-0001-9367-5039

References

Ambrosio, T. (2008). Catching the 'Shanghai Spirit': How the Shanghai cooperation organization promotes authoritarian norms in Central Asia. *Europe-Asia Studies*, *60*(8), 1321–1344. https://doi.org/10.1080/09668130802292143

Andonova, L., Mansfield, E. D., & Milner, H. V. (2007). International trade and environmental policy in the postcommunist world. *Comparative Political Studies*, *40*(7), 782–807. https://doi.org/10.1177/0010414006293215

Armingeon, K., & Guthmann, K. (2014). Democracy in crisis? The declining support for national democracy in European countries, 2007-2011. *European Journal of Political Research*, *53*(3), 423–442. https://doi.org/10.1111/1475-6765.12046

Arpino, B., & Obydenkova, A. V. (2020). Democracy and political trust before and after the great recession 2008: The European Union and the United Nations. *Social Indicators Research*, *148*(2), 395–415. https://doi.org/10.1007/s11205-019-02204-x

Baldwin, E., Carley, S., & Nicholson-Crotty, S. (2019). Why do countries emulate each others' policies? A global study of renewable energy policy diffusion. *World Development*, *120*, 29–45. https://www.sciencedirect.com/science/article/abs/pii/S0305750X19300701

Beissinger, M., & Kotkin, S. (2014). *Historical legacies of communism in Russia and Eastern Europe*. Cambridge University Press. https://doi.org/10.1017/CBO9781107286191

Berkes, F., Folke, C., & Gadgil, M. (1994). Traditional ecological knowledge, biodiversity, resilience and sustainability. In C. A. Perrings, K.-G. Mäler, C. Folke, C. S. Holling, & B.-O. Jansson (Eds.), *Biodiversity conservation: Problems and policies. Papers from the biodiversity programme Beijer International Institute of Ecological Economics Royal Swedish Academy of Sciences* (pp. 269–287). Springer Netherlands. https://doi.org/10.1007/978-94-011-1006-8_15

Bingham, G., & Conservation Foundation. (1986). *Resolving environmental disputes: A decade of experience*. Conservation Foundation. https://books.google.de/books?id=aOssAQAAMAAJ

Bogdanova, E., Cook, L. J., & Kulmala, M. (2018). The carrot or the stick? Constraints and opportunities of Russia's CSO Policy. *Europe-Asia Studies*, *70*(4), 501–513. https://doi.org/10.1080/09668136.2018.1471803

Buryj, O. V. (2014). Institucional'nyj rakurs ekologicheskih konfliktov v nedropol'zovanii (primer Respubliki Komi) [Institutional perspective of Environmental Conflicts in subsurface use (example of the Komi Republic)]: Actual problems, directions and mechanisms of development of the productive forces of the North-2014. Materials of the Fourth All-Russian Scientific Seminar: in 2 parts, 51–57. https://www.elibrary.ru/download/elibrary_23352312_68214852.pdf

Busch, P.-O., & Jörgens, H. (2005). International patterns of environmental policy change and convergence. *European Environment, 15*(2), 80–101. https://doi.org/10.1002/eet.374

Cai, Y. (2008). Local governments and the suppression of popular resistance in China. *The China Quarterly, 193*, 24–42. https://www.cambridge.org/core/journals/china-quarterly/article/abs/local-governments-and-the-suppression-of-popular-resistance-in-china/C1339AA94E85581CC9AE29F5D926AB07

Cai, Y. (2010). *Collective resistance in China: Why popular protests succeed or fail.* Stanford University Press.

Castro, A., & Nielsen, E. (2003). *Natural resource conflict management case studies: An analysis of power, participation and protected areas.* Food and Agriculture Organization of the United Nations.

Charron, N., & Lapuente, V. (2011). Which dictators produce quality of government? *Studies in Comparative International Development, 46*(4), 397–423. https://doi.org/10.1007/s12116-011-9093-0

Cherp, A., & Golubeva, S. (2004). Environmental assessment in the Russian Federation: Evolution through capacity building. *Impact Assessment and Project Appraisal, 22*(2), 121–130. https://doi.org/10.3152/147154604781766030

Cho, Y.-N., Thyroff, A., Rapert, M. I., Park, S.-Y., & Lee, H. J. (2013). To be or not to be green: Exploring individualism and collectivism as antecedents of environmental behavior. *Journal of Business Research, 66*(8), 1052–1059. https://doi.org/10.1016/j.jbusres.2012.08.020

Christoff, P., & Eckersley, R. (2013). *Globalization and the environment.* Rowman & Littlefield Publishers.

Crotty, J. (2006). Reshaping the hourglass? The environmental movement and civil society development in the Russian Federation. *Organization Studies, 27*(9), 1319–1338. https://doi.org/10.1177/0170840606064107

Demchuk, A. L. (2020). *Ekologicheskie konflikty v sovremennoj politike: Teoreticheskie osnovy i nacional'nye modeli [Environmental conflicts in modern politics: Theoretical foundations and national models].* Moscow University Publishers. http://ruspolitology.ru/biblioteka/10224

Deng, Y., & Yang, G. (2013). Pollution and protest in China: Environmental mobilization in context. *The China Quarterly, 214*, 321–336. https://www.cambridge.org/core/journals/china-quarterly/article/abs/pollution-and-protest-in-china-environmental-mobilization-in-context/8E0B1C7D81B5C57AA93DB4971EABC28D

Dolowitz, D. P., & Marsh, D. (2000). Learning from abroad: The role of policy transfer in contemporary policy-making. *Governance, 13*(1), 5–23. https://doi.org/10.1111/0952-1895.00121

Downs, A. (1972). Up and down with ecology - the Issue-Attention cycle. *The Public Interest, 28*, 51–64. https://www.nationalaffairs.com/public_interest/detail/up-and-down-with-ecologythe-issue-attention-cycle

Drazkiewicz, A., Challies, E., & Newig, J. (2015). Public participation and local environmental planning: Testing factors influencing decision quality and implementation in four case studies from Germany. *Land Use Policy, 46*, 211–222. https://www.sciencedirect.com/science/article/abs/pii/S0264837715000496

Evans, A. B. (2012). Protests and civil society in Russia: The struggle for the Khimki Forest. *Communist and Post-Communist Studies, 45*(3–4), 233–242. https://doi.org/10.1016/j.postcomstud.2012.06.002

Feldman, D. L., & Blokov, I. (2012). *The politics of environmental policy in Russia. Managing Environmental Conflict.* Edward Elgar Publishing.

Fisher, J. (2014). Managing environmental conflict. In Peter T. Coleman, Morton Deutsch, Marcus, Eric C. (Eds.). *Handbook of conflict resolution. Theory and practice.* San Francisco, CA: Jossey-Bass

Glasbergen, P. (1995). Environmental dispute resolution as a management issue. In P. Glasbergen (Ed.), *Environment & management: Vol. 5. Managing environmental disputes: Network management as an alternative* (Vol. 5, pp. 1–17). Kluwer. https://doi.org/10.1007/978-94-011-0766-2_1

Gupta, K., & McIver, R. (2016). Does national culture affect attitudes toward environment friendly practices? In G. N. Gregoriou & V. Ramiah (Eds.), *Handbook of environmental and sustainable* finance (pp. 241–263). Academic Press an imprint of Elsevier. https://doi.org/10.1016/B978-0-12-803615-0.00012-1

Hall, S., Lenz, T., & Obydenkova, A. (2021). Green rhetoric over the pandemic crisis: social media and legitimation in the AIIB, the EAEU, and the EU. *Post-Communist Economies*. forthcoming.

Hallegatte, S., Fay, M., & Barbier, E. B. (2018). Poverty and climate change: Introduction. *Environment and Development Economics*, *23*(3), 217–233. https://doi.org/10.1017/S1355770X18000141

Hanaček, K., & Martinez-Alier, J. (2021). *Nuclear chain environmental conflicts: Peripheralization and critical environmental justice in post-Soviet countries*. Post-Communist Economies (forthcoming).

Hardin, G. (1968). The tragedy of the commons. *Science (New York, N.Y, 162*(3859), 1243. https://doi.org/10.1126/science.162.3859.1243

Harrison, K., & Sundstrom, L. M. (Eds). (2010). Global commons, domestic decisions. The comparative politics of climate change. MIT Press: Cambridge, Mass.

Hauge, W., & Ellingsen, T. (1998). Beyond environmental scarcity: Causal pathways to conflict. *Journal of Peace Research*, *35*(3), 299–317. https://doi.org/10.1177/0022343398035003003

He, B., & Thøgersen, S. (2010). Giving the people a voice? Experiments with consultative authoritarian institutions in China. *Journal of Contemporary China*, *19*(66), 675–692. https://doi.org/10.1080/10670564.2010.485404

Henry, L. A. (2010). Between transnationalism and state power: The development of Russia's post-Soviet environmental movement. *Environmental Politics*, *19*(5), 756–781. https://doi.org/10.1080/09644016.2010.508308

Henry, L. A. (2011). *Red to green: Environmental activism in post-Soviet Russia*. Cornell University Press.

Henry, L. A., & Douhovnikoff, V. (2008). Environmental issues in Russia. *Annual Review of Environment and Resources*, *33*(1), 437–460. https://doi.org/10.1146/annurev.environ.33.051007.082437

Hill, R. J., & White, S. (2018). Russia, the Former Soviet Union and Eastern Europe. In M. Qvortrup (Ed.), *Referendums Around the World: With a foreword by Sir David Butler* (pp. 113–145). Springer International Publishing. https://doi.org/10.1007/978-3-319-57798-2_4

Hofstede, G., Hofstede, G. J., & Minkov, M. (2010). *Cultures and organizations: Software of the mind: Intercultural cooperation and its importance for survival (Revised and expanded third edition)*. McGraw-Hill.

Jackson, L., & Pradubraj, P. (2004). Introduction: Environmental conflict in the Asia-Pacific. *Asia Pacific Viewpoint*, *45*(1), 1–11. https://doi.org/10.1111/j.1467-8376.2004.00224.x

Jian, L., & Chan, -C. K.-C. (2016). Collective identity, framing and mobilisation of environmental protests in Urban China: A case study of Qidong's protest. *China: An International Journal*, *14*(2), 102–122. https://muse.jhu.edu/article/618402

Kailitz, S., & Stockemer, D. (2017). Regime legitimation, elite cohesion and the durability of autocratic regime types. *International Political Science Review*, *38*(3), 332–348. https://doi.org/10.1177/0192512115616830

Kemberling, M., & Roberts, J. T. (2009). When time is on their side: Determinants of outcomes in new siting and existing contamination cases in Louisiana. *Environmental Politics*, *18*(6), 851–868. https://doi.org/10.1080/09644010903345637

Khovavko, I. I. (2016). Returning Environmental Impact Assessment to Its Former Role. *Problems of Economic Transition*, *58*(10), 864–875. https://doi.org/10.1080/10611991.2016.1290440

Klyuev, N. N. (2019). Air Quality in Russian Cities for 1991–2016. *Regional Research of Russia*, *9*(2), 204–212. https://doi.org/10.1134/S2079970519020072

Knill, C., & Tosun, J. (2009). Hierarchy, networks, or markets: How does the EU shape environmental policy adoptions within and beyond its borders? *Journal of European Public Policy*, *16*(6), 873–894. https://doi.org/10.1080/13501760903088090

Lang, G., & Xu, Y. (2013). Anti-incinerator campaigns and the evolution of protest politics in China. *Environmental Politics*, *22*(5), 832–848. https://doi.org/10.1080/09644016.2013.765684

Lankina, T., Libman, A., & Obydenkova, A. (2016a). Authoritarian and democratic diffusion in post-communist regions. *Comparative Political Studies*, *49*(12), 1599–1629. https://doi.org/10.1177/0010414016628270

Lankina, T. V., Libman, A., & Obydenkova, A. (2016b). Appropriation and subversion. *World Politics, 68*(2), 229–274. https://doi.org/10.1017/S0043887115000428

Li, R., Jiang, H., Sotnyk, I., Kubatko, O., & Almashaqbeh, Y. A., . I. (2020). The CO2 emissions drivers of post-communist economies in Eastern Europe and Central Asia. *Atmosphere, 11*(9), 1019. https://doi.org/10.3390/atmos11091019

Li, X., Yang, X., Wei, Q., & Zhang, B. (2019). Authoritarian environmentalism and environmental policy implementation in China. *Resources, Conservation and Recycling, 145*(1), 86–93. https://doi.org/10.1016/j.resconrec.2019.02.011

Li, Y. (2019). Governing environmental conflicts in China: Lessons learned from the case of the Liulitun waste incineration power plant in Beijing. *Public Policy and Administration, 34*(2), 189–209. https://doi.org/10.1177/0952076717709521

Li, Y., Koppenjan, J., & Verweij, S. (2016). Governing environmental conflicts in China: Under what conditions do local governments compromise? *Public Admininistration, 94*(3), 806–822. https://doi.org/10.1111/padm.12263

Libman, A., & Obydenkova, A. (2014). Governance of commons in a large nondemocratic country: The case of forestry in the Russian federation. *Publius: The Journal of Federalism, 44*(2), 298–323. https://doi.org/10.1093/publius/pjt065

Libman, A., & Obydenkova, A. (2019). Inequality and historical legacies: Evidence from post-communist regions. *Post-Communist Economies, 31*(6), 699–724. https://doi.org/10.1080/14631377.2019.1607440

Libman, A., & Obydenkova, A. (2021). *Historical legacies of the communism: Modern politics, society, and economic development*. Cambridge University Press.

Libman, A., & Obydenkova, A. V. (2018). Understanding authoritarian regionalism. *Journal of Democracy, 29*(4), 151–165. https://doi.org/10.1353/jod.2018.0070

Libman, A., & Obydenkova, A. V. (2020). Proletarian Internationalism in Action? Communist legacies and attitudes towards migrants in Russia. *Problems of Post-Communism, 67*(4–5), 402–416. https://doi.org/10.1080/10758216.2019.1640068

Liu, X., Stoutenborough, J., & Vedlitz, A. (2017). Bureaucratic expertise, overconfidence, and policy choice. *Governance, 30*(4), 705–725. https://doi.org/10.1111/gove.12257

Lora-Wainwright, A., Zhang, Y., Wu, Y., & van Rooij, B. (2012). Learning to live with pollution: The making of environmental subjects in a Chinese industrialized village. *The China Journal, 68*, 106–124. https://www.journals.uchicago.edu/doi/10.1086/666582

Manowong, E., & Ogunlana, S. O. (2008). Critical factors for successful public hearing in infrastructure development projects: A case study of the on nuch waste disposal plant project. *International Journal of Construction Management, 8*(1), 37–51. https://doi.org/10.1080/15623599.2008.10773107

Martínez-Alier, J. (2002). *The environmentalism of the poor: A study of ecological conflicts and valuation*. Edward Elgar Publishing. http://site.ebrary.com/lib/alltitles/docDetail.action?docID=10471526

Martínez-Alier, J., & Schlüpmann, K. (1990 [1993]). *Ecological economics: Energy, environment and society (Repr)*. Blackwell.

Martinez-Alier, J. (2021). Mapping ecological distribution conflicts: The EJAtlas. *The Extractive Industries and Society*, Advance online publication. https://www.sciencedirect.com/science/article/abs/pii/S2214790X21000289?via%3Dihub

Martus, E. (2017). Contested policymaking in Russia: Industry, environment, and the "best available technology" debate. *Post-Soviet Affairs, 33*(4), 276–297. https://doi.org/10.1080/1060586X.2016.1209315

McAdam, D., & Boudet, H. (2012). *Putting social movements in their place: Explaining opposition to energy projects in the United States, 2000–2005*. Cambridge University Press.

Mertha, A. (2009). "Fragmented Authoritarianism 2.0": Political pluralization in the Chinese policy process. *The China Quarterly, 200*, 995–1012. https://www.cambridge.org/core/journals/china-quarterly/article/abs/fragmented-authoritarianism-20-political-pluralization-in-the-chinese-policy-process/EA5E4FE9316DA47EB53C777C879DCA29

Mi, L., Qiao, L., Xu, T., Gan, X., Yang, H., Zhao, J., Qiao, Y., & Hou, J. (2020). Promoting sustainable development: The impact of differences in cultural values on residents' pro-environmental behaviors. *Sustainable Development, 28*(6), 1539–1553. https://doi.org/10.1002/sd.2103

Mianabadi, A., Davary, K., Mianabadi, H., & Karimi, P. (2020). International environmental conflict management in transboundary river basins. *Water Resources Management, 34*(11), 3445–3464. https://doi.org/10.1007/s11269-020-02576-7

Mingaleva, Z., Vukovic, N., Volkova, I., & Salimova, T. (2020). Waste management in green and smart cities: A case study of Russia. *Sustainability, 12*(1), 94. https://doi.org/10.3390/su12010094

Mol, A. P. J. (2009). Environmental Deinstitutionalization in Russia. *Journal of Environmental Policy & Planning, 11*(3), 223–241. https://doi.org/10.1080/15239080903033812

Muradian, R., Martinez-Alier, J., & Correa, H. (2003). International capital versus local population: The environmental conflict of the Tambogrande mining project, Peru. *Society & Natural Resources, 16*(9), 775–792. https://doi.org/10.1080/08941920309166

Nazarov, Z., & Obydenkova, A. V. (2020). Democratization and Firm Innovation: Evidence from European and Central Asian post-Communist States. *Post-Communist Economies, 32*(7), 833–859. https://doi.org/10.1080/14631377.2020.1745565

Newell, J. P., & Henry, L. A. (2016). The state of environmental protection in the Russian Federation: A review of the post-Soviet era. *Eurasian Geography and Economics, 57*(6), 779–801. https://doi.org/10.1080/15387216.2017.1289851

Novikova, N. I. (2016). Who is responsible for the Russian Arctic? Co-operation between indigenous peoples and industrial companies in the context of legal pluralism. *Energy Research & Social Science, 16*, 98–110. https://www.sciencedirect.com/science/article/abs/pii/S2214629616300469

O'Brien, K. J., & Li, L. (2006). *Rightful resistance in rural China*. Cambridge University Press.

O'Neill K. (2012). The comparative study of environmental movements. In: Steinberg P.F. and VanDeveer, S. D. (Eds.), *Comparative environmental politics: Theory, practice, and prospects*. (pp. 115-142). Cambridge, Mass. https://www.jstor.org/stable/j.ctt5vjs7f

Obydenkova, A. (2008). Regime transition in the regions of Russia: The freedom of mass media: Transnational impact on sub-national democratization? *European Journal of Political Research, 47*(2), 221–246. https://doi.org/10.1111/j.1475-6765.2007.00727.x

Obydenkova, A., & Libman, A. (2016). *Autocratic and democratic external influences in post-Soviet Eurasia. Post-Soviet Politics*. Routledge. https://ebookcentral.proquest.com/lib/gbv/detail.action?docID=4442951

Obydenkova, A., & Salahodjaev, R. (2016). Intelligence, democracy, and international environmental commitment. *Environmental Research, 147*, 82–88. https://www.sciencedirect.com/science/article/abs/pii/S001393511630041X?via%3Dihub

Obydenkova, A. & Swenden, W. (2013). Autocracy-sustaining versus democratic federalism: Explaining the divergent trajectories of territorial politics in Russia and Western Europe. *Territory, Politics, Governance,1*(1), 86–112. https://doi.org/10.1080/21622671.2013

Obydenkova, A. V. (2012). Democratization at the grassroots: The European Union's external impact. *Democratization, 19*(2), 230–257. https://doi.org/10.1080/13510347.2011.576851

Obydenkova, A. V., & Arpino, B. (2018). Corruption and trust in the European union and national institutions: Changes over the great recession across European states. *JCMS: Journal of Common Market Studies, 56*(3), 594–611. https://doi.org/10.1111/jcms.12646

Obydenkova, A. V., & Salahodjaev, R. (2017). Climate change policies: The role of democracy and social cognitive capital. *Environmental Research, 157*, 182–189. https://www.sciencedirect.com/science/article/abs/pii/S0013935117306382

Ostrom, E. (2011). Background on the institutional analysis and development framework. *Policy Studies Journal, 39*(1), 7–27. https://doi.org/10.1111/j.1541-0072.2010.00394.x

Ostrom, E. (2015). *Governing the commons: The evolution of institutions for collective action. Canto classics*. Cambridge University Press. https://doi.org/10.1017/CBO9780511807763

Owen, C. (2020). Participatory authoritarianism: From bureaucratic transformation to civic participation in Russia and China. *Review of International Studies, 46*(4), 415–434. https://doi.org/10.1017/S0260210520000248

Petrov, N., Lipman, M., & Hale, H. E. (2014). Three dilemmas of hybrid regime governance: Russia from Putin to Putin. *Post-Soviet Affairs*, *30*(1), 1–26. https://doi.org/10.1080/1060586X.2013.825140

Pickvance, K. (2019). *Democracy and Environmental Movements in Eastern Europe: A Comparative Study of Hungary and Russia*. Routledge.

Pierk, S., & Tysiachniouk, M. (2016). Structures of mobilization and resistance: Confronting the oil and gas industries in Russia. *The Extractive Industries and Society*, *3*(4), 997–1009. https://doi.org/10.1016/j.exis.2016.07.004

Plantan, E. (2018). Mass mobilization in China and Russia: From unexpected victories to unintended consequences. *Russian Politics*, *3*(4), 513–547. https://doi.org/10.1163/2451-8921-00304004

Poberezhskaya, M. (2015). Media coverage of climate change in Russia: Governmental bias and climate silence. *Public Understanding of Science (Bristol, England)*, *24*(1), 96–111. https://doi.org/10.1177/0963662513517848

Rauschmayer, F., & Wittmer, H. (2006). Evaluating deliberative and analytical methods for the resolution of environmental conflicts. *Land Use Policy*, *23*(1), 108–122. https://doi.org/10.1016/j.landusepol.2004.08.011

Redpath, S. M., Young, J., Evely, A., Adams, W. M., Sutherland, W. J., Whitehouse, A., Amar, A., Lambert, R. A., Linnell, J. D. C., Watt, A., & Gutiérrez, R. J. (2013). Understanding and managing conservation conflicts. *Trends in Ecology & Evolution*, *28*(2), 100–109. https://doi.org/10.1016/j.tree.2012.08.021

Scheidel, A., Del Bene, D., Liu, J., Navas, G., Mingorría, S., Demaria, F., Avila, S., Roy, B., Ertör, I., Temper, L., & Martínez-Alier, J. (2020). Environmental conflicts and defenders: A global overview. *Global Environmental Change*, *63*, 102104. https://www.sciencedirect.com/science/article/pii/S0959378020301424

Schuhmann, J., & Kropp, S. (2018). Environmental impact assessment: Between facilitating public contribution and arbitrary involvement of NGOs. In S. Kropp, A. Aasland, M. Berg-Nordlie, J. Holm-Hansen, & J. Schuhmann (Eds.), *Governance in Russian regions: A policy comparison* (pp. 73–104). Springer International Publishing. https://doi.org/10.1007/978-3-319-61702-2_4

Shi, F., & Cai, Y. (2006). Disaggregating the state: Networks and collective resistance in Shanghai. *The China Quarterly*, *186*, 314–332. https://www.cambridge.org/core/journals/china-quarterly/article/abs/disaggregating-the-state-networks-and-collective-resistance-in-shanghai/B053ECA1916921B23FEA11F92123C1D2

Shvarts, E. A., Pakhalov, A. M., & Knizhnikov, A. Y. (2016). Assessment of environmental responsibility of oil and gas companies in Russia: The rating method. *Journal of Cleaner Production*, *127*(3), 143–151. https://doi.org/10.1016/j.jclepro.2016.04.021

Solodyankina, S., & Koeppel, J. (2009). The environmental impact assessment process for oil and gas extraction projects in the Russian Federation: Possibilities for improvement. *Impact Assessment and Project Appraisal*, *27*(1), 77–83. https://doi.org/10.3152/146155109X430344

Sterner, T. (2003). *Policy instruments for environmental and natural resource management*. Routledge.

Sun, L., Zhu, D., & Chan, E. H. W. (2016). Public participation impact on environment NIMBY conflict and environmental conflict management: Comparative analysis in Shanghai and Hong Kong. *Land Use Policy*, *58*, 208–217. https://www.sciencedirect.com/science/article/abs/pii/S0264837716300436

Temper, L., Demaria, F., Scheidel, A., Del Bene, D., & Martinez-Alier, J. (2018). The global environmental justice atlas (EJAtlas): Ecological distribution conflicts as forces for sustainability. *Sustainability Science*, *13*(3), 573–584. https://doi.org/10.1007/s11625-018-0563-4

Tosun, J. (2013). *Environmental policy change in emerging market democracies: Eastern Europe and Latin America compared*. University of Toronto Press.

Tosun, J., Francesco, F., & Peters, B. G. (2019). From environmental policy concepts to practicable tools: Knowledge creation and delegation in multilevel systems. *Public Administration*, *97*(2), 399–412. https://doi.org/10.1111/padm.12544

Tosun, J., & Leininger, J. (2017). Governing the Interlinkages between the sustainable development goals: Approaches to attain policy integration. *Global Challenges (Hoboken, NJ)*, *1*(9), 1700036. https://doi.org/10.1002/gch2.201700036

Tosun, J., & Schulze, K. (2015). Compliance with EU biofuel targets in South-Eastern and Eastern Europe: Do interest groups matter? *Environment and Planning. C, Government & Policy, 33*(5), 950–968. https://doi.org/10.1177/0263774X15605923

Tosun, J., & Shyrokykh, K. (2021). *Leadership in high-level forums on energy governance: China and Russia compared*. Post-Communist Economies. forthcoming.

Tower, R. K., Kelly, C., & Richards, A. (1997). Individualism, collectivism and reward allocation: A cross-cultural study in Russia and Britain. *British Journal of Social Psychology, 36*(3), 331–345. https://doi.org/10.1111/j.2044-8309.1997.tb01135.x

Trombetta, M. J. (2012). Climate change and the environmental conflict discourse. In J. Scheffran, M. Brzoska, H. G. Brauch, P. M. Link, & J. Schilling (Eds.), *Climate change, human security and violent conflict: Challenges for societal stability* (pp. 151–164). Springer Berlin Heidelberg. https://doi.org/10.1007/978-3-642-28626-1_7

Tsygankov, A. P. (2014). *The strong state in Russia: Development and crisis*. Oxford University Press.

van Rooij, B., Stern, R. E., & Fürst, K. (2016). The authoritarian logic of regulatory pluralism: Understanding China's new environmental actors. *Regulation & Governance, 10*(1), 3–13. https://doi.org/10.1111/rego.12074

Vinogradov, M. (2013). *Environmental conflicts in the regions of Russia" [Ekologicheskie konfliti v regionah Rossii]*. Ekodelo. https://ecodelo.org/obshchestvo/ekologicheskoe_dvizhenie/20148-ekologicheskie_konflikty_v_rossiiskikh_regionakh-statia

Vogel, D. (1997). *Trading up: Consumer and environmental regulation in a global economy*. Harvard University Press.

Wang, X., Yang, H., Shi, M., Zhou, D., & Zhang, Z. (2015). Managing stakeholders' conflicts for water reallocation from agriculture to industry in the Heihe River Basin in Northwest China. *The Science of the Total Environment, 505*, 823–832. https://www.sciencedirect.com/science/article/abs/pii/S0048969714015083

Wilson, E. (2016). What is the social licence to operate? Local perceptions of oil and gas projects in Russia's Komi Republic and Sakhalin Island. *The Extractive Industries and Society, 3*(1), 73–81. https://doi.org/10.1016/j.exis.2015.09.001

Wu, F., & Martus, E. (2020). Contested environmentalism: The politics of waste in China and Russia. *Environmental Politics, 12*(4), 1–20. https://doi.org/10.1080/09644016.2020.1816367

Wu, Y. (2017). Public acceptance of constructing coastal/inland nuclear power plants in post-Fukushima China. *Energy Policy, 101*, 484–491. https://www.sciencedirect.com/science/article/abs/pii/S0301421516306024

Xie, L., & van der Heijden, H.-A. (2010). Environmental movements and political opportunities: The case of China. *Social Movement Studies, 9*(1), 51–68. https://doi.org/10.1080/14742830903442527

Yang, G., & Calhoun, C. (2007). Media, civil society, and the rise of a green public sphere in China. *China Information, 21*(2), 211–236. https://doi.org/10.1177/0920203X07079644

Yang, L., Lan, G. Z., & He, S. (2015). Roles of scholars in environmental community conflict resolution. *International Journal of Conflict Management, 26*(3), 316–341. https://doi.org/10.1108/IJCMA-05-2012-0019

Yang, X., Lou, F., Sun, M., Wang, R., & Wang, Y. (2017). Study of the relationship between greenhouse gas emissions and the economic growth of Russia based on the environmental Kuznets curve. *Applied Energy, 193*(2), 162–173. https://doi.org/10.1016/j.apenergy.2017.02.034

Yanitsky, O. N. (2012). From nature protection to politics: The Russian environmental movement 1960-2010. *Environmental Politics, 21*(6), 922–940. https://doi.org/10.1080/09644016.2012.724216

∂ OPEN ACCESS

Kazakhstan's climate change policy: reflecting national strength, green economy aspirations and international agenda

Marianna Poberezhskaya and Alina Bychkova

ABSTRACT
This article looks at how Kazakhstan's heavy dependence on fossil fuels and its political context shape national discourse on climate change. Based on extensive analysis of the country's strategic documents and expert interviews, we argue that although Kazakhstan's economy relies on fossil fuels, the government is keen to promote sustainable development to attract international investments and advance its image as a 'strong state' for the domestic audience, and as a progressive and reliable partner for the international audience. Whilst there is little evidence of 'post-colonial' rhetoric appearing in Kazakhstan's official climate change discourse, the state's past is evident in its instrumental approach to environmental issues which in turn translates into inconsistencies in its climate change policy.

Introduction

Kazakhstan positions itself as a regional leader in terms of implementing climate change mitigation measures while also being the largest recipient of global multilateral climate funds in Central Asia (CA) (OECD, 2016). The state made commitments under the Paris Agreement, and in 2013 declared its intention to transform to a green economy by 2050. However, the feasibility of these national strategies is doubtful. The Kazakh economy relies heavily on fossil fuels, which accounted for 21% of its GDP in 2020, and around 70% of the country's exports (World Bank, n.d.). Kazakhstan is the 9th largest crude oil and 14th largest natural gas exporter in the world, and it ranks in the top 14 states in terms of natural gas reserves (CIA.gov, 2021). Natural gas production increased twofold from 2013–2016, and oil production reached its peak in 2019 with policymakers planning to double output by 2025 (IEA, 2020). Kazakhstan lags behind other fossil fuel exporters in terms of energy efficiency and diversity[1] (IRENA, n.d.) as its energy mix is dominated by coal which makes up 47% of the country's total primary energy supply (TPES) followed by oil and gas which account for around 25% each (IEA, 2020). Whilst Kazakhstan has managed to reduce greenhouse gas (GHG) emissions' by 3–5% by 2020[2] (from 1990 levels), an increase of 6–9% is likely by 2030[3] if the state pursues a 'business as usual' approach (IEA, 2020). Thus, current state

---

This is an Open Access article distributed under the terms of the Creative Commons Attribution-NonCommercial-NoDerivatives License (http://creativecommons.org/licenses/by-nc-nd/4.0/), which permits non-commercial re-use, distribution, and reproduction in any medium, provided the original work is properly cited, and is not altered, transformed, or built upon in any way.

policies are insufficient to help meet the United Nations Framework Convention on Climate Change (UNFCCC) goal to keep warming below 1.5–2 C (Climate Analytics, 2019).

Over the last decade, we have seen an increase in studies on climate change politics in developing countries with semi-authoritarian/authoritarian forms of governance (e.g. Kopra, 2018; Korppoo, 2016; Poberezhskaya, 2016; Schreurs, 2011); however, CA in general and Kazakhstan in particular, remain largely ignored (Poberezhskaya & Danilova, 2021). This article contributes to the existing literature gap in the following ways. Firstly, it offers a comprehensive analysis of the decision-making process on climate change-related issues in Kazakhstan and how it fits with national and international policy agendas. Secondly, it analyses how the fossil fuel economy coexists with climate change politics and how their mutually exclusive goals are presented within official rhetoric. Thirdly, it looks at the reasons for policymakers to advance a 'green economy' discourse in resource dependent developing countries with authoritarian forms of governance. Lastly, the article contributes to the theoretical debate by exploring whether the country's post-colonial self-image plays a role in national climate change rhetoric. By the application of discourse analysis we argue that although Kazakhstan's economy is based on fossil fuels, the government promotes the idea of green development to attract international investments as well as to advance its image as a 'strong state' (for the domestic audience), and as a progressive and reliable partner (for international audiences).

To achieve these aims, we first look at Kazakhstan's vulnerabilities to climate change. We then offer theoretical and methodological considerations, followed by the analysis which is set in three sections looking at the domestic, international and green economy discourses. We conclude with a comprehensive discussion of the main narratives identified in Kazakhstan's climate policy.

Climate change in Kazakhstan: geography, threats and vulnerabilities

Kazakhstan is the 9th largest country in the world by territory, but its population is relatively small at around 18 million and is unevenly distributed throughout the country (mostly located in the south). The majority of the country is covered by desert, semi-desert, and steppes. It is these geographic characteristics that shed light on the country's climate change vulnerabilities. For instance, as in the rest of CA, climate change is negatively affecting Kazakhstan's already fragile water security situation (World Bank, 2014), this includes rapidly melting glaciers (the main source of drinking water) and a change in the 'peak flow of key rivers' impacting the growing season as well as further contributing to rapid land degradation and desertification, a reduction in agricultural yields, and transboundary conflicts in the region (Bernauer & Siegfried, 2012; Xenarios et al., 2019). As climate change worsens, according to the Asian Development Bank, by 2050 it will lead to additional yearly expenditures of US$550 million to mitigate freshwater deficiency in CA (CAN, 2014).

The negative effects of climate change are spread unevenly throughout Kazakhstan with more precipitation in the north and increasingly less precipitation in the south which can cause substantial damage to both the population's health and to local agriculture. Like many other places, Kazakhstan is likely to suffer from changes in the 'transmission of infectious diseases, increased mortality and morbidity from extreme weather events and reduced availability of clean water' (WHO, 2009). Indeed, Kazakhstan is already suffering from the increased frequency and intensity of floods, mudflows, heatwaves (e.g. heatwaves in 2010 and 2014), forest and steppe fires, and sudden changes in temperature. Extreme weather events (associated with climate change) have been seen to destroy people's houses, and damage existing utility infrastructure (interview 5). These problems also jeopardise Kazakhstan's agricultural industry (it is one of the world's largest wheat producers), and it has already noticed 'reduced crop yields from drought and fires' (WHO, 2009). For instance, in 2012 and 2014 the country's crops were severely damaged or destroyed (15% and 8% respectively). It is estimated that if farming practices remain the same, the decrease in annual harvests may reach 49% due to climate change (Ministry of Energy of the RK, 2017). Arguably, climate change also contributes to man-made disasters, for instance, a collapse of the dam wall of Sardoba reservoir which, whilst located in Uzbekistan, affected neighbouring Kazakhstan by destroying properties and causing US$10 million in damage in the agricultural sector (Simonov, 2020). All these problems can potentially threaten the social stability of the country as 'one sixth of the work force in Kazakhstan works in the agriculture, forestry and fishery sectors' (Ministry of Energy of the RK, 2017). Kazakhstan's vulnerability also comes from its over reliance on the extraction of natural resources which (as discussed at length below) serves as a foundation for the country's economic growth.

Due to CA's socio-economic and political problems, scholars point to its potentially low levels of adaptation abilities (Deng & Chen, 2017; Fay et al., 2010). This includes limited climate change awareness and a great disparity in available resources for economic development (World Bank, 2015). Existing problems with the transparency and openness of local governments, a lack of freedom of speech and restricted 'citizen dialogue' further hinder regional climate change adaptation (Stan Radar, 2016). Both climate change mitigation and adaptation struggles could also be explained by consistent prioritisation of seemingly more important issues (e.g. economic and political stability). Additionally, climate change policies in Kazakhstan must survive constant institutional change. For example, Kazakhstan numerously modified its environmental governance structure, the first institutional formation being a Ministry of Ecology and Bioresources which was established in 1992, and its most recent reincarnation being the Ministry of Ecology, Geology and Natural Resources which was officially formed in 2019 (in between there were four other Ministries that governed similar areas under different names). The latter now hosts the Department of Climate Policy and Green Technology (www.gov.kz). At the regional level, climate action is restrained by the lack of cooperation between neighbouring states, which rather see the issue as a reason for conflicts rather than an opportunity for cooperation (International Crisis Group, 2011). For instance, a struggle over freshwater and energy resources has already become a source of regional tension.

In sum, Kazakhstan's vulnerability comes from its specific geographical characteristics, and its unique economic, social and political situation where semi-authoritarian rule co-exists with a carbon-intensive economy. We argue that Kazakhstan's political history as well as its current foreign policy significantly contribute to the state's identity and subsequently, shape its climate change-related policies and processes.

Theory

Viewing the Soviet Union (SU) as an empire and its former members as postcolonial states, can be useful in understanding Kazakhstan's national identity and its environmental rhetoric. Heathershaw (2010) argues that 'the post-coloniality of Central Asian states is an integral dimension of their continuance today' (p. 10), and postcolonial theory is a key to understanding state discourses and their effects. Dubuisson (2020, p. 9) notices that in Kazakhstan, the discourses of the former Soviet space still shape both environmental decision-making and public responses to the issues of land protection, conservation and natural resources.

Postcolonial theory is concerned with the 'forces of oppression and coercive domination that operate in the contemporary world' (Young, 2001, p. 11) where current discourses of colonised countries are shaped by their historical past. Heathershaw (2010, p. 8) identifies three conceptual tools of postcolonial theory: hybridity, subalternity, orientalism. Hybridity – or inbetweenness – refers to transcultural forms of politics where new nationalist goals are underpinned by colonial thinking. Soviet states were constructed as colonial entities by the nation-builder (Smith et al., 1998); hence, postcolonial self-image underpins the political discourse of the post-Soviet landscape. In the case of Kazakhstan, it is still legitimising presidential rhetoric (Kudaibergenova, 2016a, p. 920). 'Subalternity' means control imposed by the ruling elites. The Soviet leaders distributed control through the local communist elites, and this allowed certain Kazakh officials to retain their status after the regime's collapse (Dave, 2007, p. 95). Shakhanova (2017) argues that the influence of Russia as Kazakhstan's 'historical other' still influences in some way national decision-making processes. Lastly, 'orientalism' signifies the production of knowledge through power – construction of national identity and culture through the discourse of the coloniser (Said, 1978). Soviet power produced knowledge both about and for the CA states – it created them as subjects to empire, and arguably it continues to affect current generations (Adams, 2008; Heathershaw, 2010).

Beissinger and Young (2002, p. 24) highlight an important role of postcolonial image in independent Kazakhstan characterising its political discourse by the 'silent incorporation of its colonial origins'. However, the 'struggle over identity' is a key feature in Kazakhstan's national discourse as the state faces the challenge of the reinvention of itself both nationally and internationally (Dave, 2007; Fierman, 2009). The presence of postcolonial rhetoric can also be seen in omissions. For instance, by not creating a robust state ideology, the elites adopted the language of former oppressor to re-legitimatise authority in the post-Soviet era (Kudaibergenova, 2016a). As a result, modern Kazakh postcolonialism comes as 'a purely political and nationalising discourse' (ibid, p. 921) that constructs and maintains the state's identity.

The issue of identity is also prominent in 'green' postcolonial scholarship as it focuses on the issues of power dynamics, the colonisation of nature and displacement of environmental practices (Grove & Grove, 1996; Plumwood, 2006). This is particularly relevant to the context of the former SU with its anthropocentric policies exported from Moscow to the republics (Sharipova, 2019). Likewise, postcolonial rhetoric penetrates the discourse of climate change, which is shaped by social problems, power relations, economic interests and the (inter-)national image of the state (Dubuisson, 2020). As Huggan (2004, p. 702) notes, the rise of 'green' postcolonial studies was in effect to understand that colonialism and imperialism cannot be explained without 'engaging with the massive scale of environmental devastation that they entail'. Providing the ground for 'struggles over resources, legitimacy, and meaning' (Kandiyoti, 2002, p. 295), the postcolonial context applied to climate change politics enforces a critical view of the discourses encountered with the use of natural resources, mitigation practices and the negative effects of climate change.

To date, Kazakhstan, as well as the whole CA region, has been largely overlooked in postcolonial studies (Moore, 2001) and there are two main reasons for this. First, the SU was never recognised as a traditional colonial power (Edgar, 2006, p. 255) because of its 'modernisation' projects and nativization policy ('korenizatsia'), and the combination of imperial and state modernising practices (Adams, 2008). Chernetsky et al. (2006) describe the Soviet power as 'expressly internationalist yet zealously territorial and expansionist' (p. 832) – such an image makes one see Kazakhstan primarily in post-socialist and post-Soviet rather than in postcolonial terms. Second, there is a lack of postcolonial thought inside the region as most local scholars avoid rhetoric associated with oppression and third world countries (Abashin, 2014). But as 'the arrival of post-colonialism in Central Asian studies is long over-due' (Heathershaw, 2010, p. 1), recently one can observe a growing body of this type of research (e.g. Beissinger & Young, 2002; Edgar, 2006; Kandiyoti, 2002; Khalid, 2006) as well as specific application of post-colonialism to environmental issues in the region (Adams, 2008; Dubuisson, 2020; Kudaibergenova, 2016b; Sharipova, 2019). Inspired by this theoretical discussion, we look at how Kazakh political elites construct the image of the country within climate change discourse and whether the country's postcolonial past is affecting its current responses to climate change.

Methodological considerations

Van Dijk (2001, p. 357) argues that control over public discourse is 'a first major form of power', thus discourse analysis can be seen as a key tool in understanding policymaking process (Leipold et al., 2019), including the one revolving around climate change-related issues (Bäckstrand & Lövbrand, 2019; Wilson Rowe, 2013). Therefore, for this qualitative study, we employ discourse analysis of Kazakhstan's official documents and expert interviews. Specifically, we applied political discourse analysis (PDA) which looks at how political actors construct beliefs and actions of broader society through language. The collected data were analysed by the means of the toolkit adopted from Van Dijk (2013, pp. 175–196) which allowed us to explore six analytical categories: membership, typical activities, aims, norms, position, and resources involved. Membership criteria points to the speaker's self-identity and attachment to a certain social group; typical activities criteria describe the actor's common action; aims point to what the actor wants and how this is reasoned; norms define what is good or bad in the actor's opinion; position indicates relationships with others; resources show what the actor has or does not have (*ibid*). The texts were coded with the software NVIVO-12. Further interpretations were done manually as computer-based analytics may limit and confuse the findings (Charmaz, 2000, p. 520).

We analysed five official documents (see Table 1 for the list) which serve as a foundation for Kazakhstan's climate policy (as claimed in the 7th national communication of the Republic of Kazakhstan (RK) to the UNFCCC (Ministry of Energy of the RK, 2017, pp. 75–77)). The importance of these documents was also highlighted through interviews: 'in Kazakhstan we have a hierarchical state management with a unified system of state planning' with 'Strategy-2050' being the most important one whilst everything else complies with it (interview 6). Thus, even if climate change is not featured in these

Table 1. Analysed documents.

Document	Released date	Description	Relation to climate change
Strategy Kazakhstan 2050: A New Political Course of the Established State	14 December 2012	Provides a long-term vision for strategic development of the state	Transition to a low carbon economy; Natural resource management
Concept for Transition of the RK to a Green Economy	30 May 2013	Sets the ground for systemic transformations to a green economy	Transition to a low carbon economy;
Strategic Plan for Development of the RK until 2020	1 February 2010	Sets a strategic plan for national development for a 10-year period	Transition to a low carbon economy;
Concept of Innovative Development of the RK until 2020	4 June 2013	Sets a strategic plan for transition to innovative economy	Developing RES and energy-saving technologies
Plan of the Nation – 100 Concrete Steps	6 May 2015	Sets a response to global socio-economic challenges and a strategy for economic growth	Developing energy-saving technologies and attracting foreign investors

documents, climate-related policies must correlate with the state's outlined goals, visions and plans.

Moreover, we interviewed Kazakhstan's policymakers and experts who contributed to domestic climate change adaptation and mitigation strategies, environmental legislation, the national Emissions Trading Scheme (ETS), communications to the UNFCCC and so forth. We also consulted national and international NGOs' members and scientists who directly affect policy-making decisions. The participants were asked open-ended questions guided by a topic list, which was adjusted depending on the participant's area of expertise. While most of the interviews were held as conversations of 40–60 minutes in length, two experts shared their thoughts in writing. We interviewed 13 experts in the period of February–March 2021.

Analysis

The analysis of the collected data showed that overall climate change is underrepresented within the state's official discourse. Even when the discussed policies directly affect GHG emissions in the country, there are often no explicit connections with climate change (e.g. the 'Green Economy Concept'). It is only in the 'Strategy to 2020' that climate change is discussed in alarming terms to ensure the advancement of rational resource use. The lukewarm attitude towards the problem among state officials was also voiced by interviewees who indicated that even the policy of decarbonisation or development of renewable energy sources (RES) often do not have climate change links, negatively impacting awareness of the problem (e.g. interview 6). The analysis showed that climate change policy is affected by three discursive categories: national strength, development of a green economy and international cooperation (see Table 2). It is within those discursive dimensions that we present our findings.

Climate change and national strength

Kazakhstan has been engaged with the global climate change policy framework since 1995 (Ministry of Energy of the RK, 2017); however, it has been slow with regard to national

Table 2. Discursive categories with examples.

	Identity	Activity	Aims	Norms	Relationship	Resources
National strength	Strong state	Progress made after the end of the Soviet era	TOP-30 global economy, national security	Strong and stable economy, social welfare	Emphasis on national unity	Natural resources
Green Economy	Sustainable economy	Developing RES and energy-saving technologies	Continuing economic growth & looking after the environment	Green economy, a 'win-win' approach	Regional leader & reliable international partner	Energy efficiency potential
International cooperation	Key global player	International cooperation	Foreign investments, global & regional recognition	Global standards, international cooperation, global influence	Multi-vector policy	Geolocation; natural resources

commitments. For instance, the Kyoto Protocol was ratified only in 2009. Just throughout the last decade related policies started to be included in the key national documents, for instance, transition of all mining companies to environmentally friendly production ('Strategy-2050'), privatising agricultural lands to encourage their efficient use, and replacing outdated construction standards with the 'eurocodes' ('100 Concrete Steps'). In 2010, Kazakhstan adopted a law 'on Amendments to Certain Legislative Acts of the Republic of Kazakhstan Relating to Environmental Issues' which allowed the country to start trading emissions and to encourage Joint Implementation (JI) projects. This led to the establishment of the Emissions Trading Scheme (ETS) in Kazakhstan, the only project of its kind in the Post-Soviet space. The pilot stage launched in 2013 and included 178 companies representing extractive industries (responsible for 55% of the state's GHG emissions) with the requirement to keep emissions levels at the base line year of 2010 (Ministry of Energy of the RK, 2017). Subsequent phases had more ambitious targets and included a wider range of participants positively contributing to the switch towards a greener economy. It should be noted that the first two rounds of the ETS were not successful in encouraging participants to cut GHG emissions (because of loose rules on access to quotas) whilst after the suspension of the scheme in 2016 adjustments were made to motivate industries to start lowering their emissions (interview 9). Despite some industrial lobbying against the ETS's existence (*ibid*), the scheme resumed in 2018. The ETS was meant to be an economic mechanism to regulate carbon emissions, but our analysis showed that it also became another proud moment in Kazakhstan's national politics (interview 4):

> When we were in full swing trading quotas, in Moscow there was still almost no talk about it [...] Moreover, I think that it is not only Russia, but Kazakhstan occupies a leading position among all CIS [Commonwealth of Independent States] countries.

Overall, national climate policy contributes to a persistent narrative of Kazakhstan being a 'strong state' which can deal with various risks, including climate change. In fact, climate change is not only a challenge, but an opportunity to switch towards sustainable development to further improve the country's domestic stability and its international position. In the 'Strategy-2050', former President Nazarbayev proclaimed Kazakhstan's objective 'to be among the top 30 global economies by 2050' which developed into an extensive concept of national strength and prosperity (see also '100 Concrete Steps'). The idealistic portrayal of Kazakhstan's bright future includes all aspects of its development: economic modernisation, education, health, women's rights and so on. Moreover, 'Strategy-2050' presents an interesting example of how Nazarbayev identifies himself with Kazakhstan as the strategy looks a lot like a personal letter from a father figure rather than a state leader:

> I call on all people to arm themselves with eternal qualities - diligence, hard work and dedication, which will help us to resist and create a worthy future for our Motherland. I believe in you. I believe that we will not miss a new historic chance.

This personification of politics became evident also during our interviews. For instance, some experts noted that the whole idea of sustainable development and green economy could be attributed to Nazarbayev's personal desire to earn international recognition[4] (e.g. interview 1). Furthermore, several interviewees pointed to current President Tokayev's professional background (specifically, his former role as a Director-General at the UN's Geneva office) which allows him to understand international positions on major issues and how to attract positive attention and investments to address sustainable development and climate change problems in the country (interviews 3 & 4). This is particularly important as in Kazakhstan's climate policy the president is considered to be the main decision-maker (interview 4).

The presentation of Kazakhstan as a strong state is also solidified against the troublesome historical background with the emphasis on the challenging post-Soviet period (rather than the Soviet one). For example, despite 'the post-Soviet chaos' the state's leadership through the 'right' political strategy and 'hard work' has managed to improve Kazakhstan's politics and economy ('Strategy-2050'). Climate politics emerging in Kazakhstan during this post-Soviet period appear to be a response to global trends or even 'as a tribute of fashion because everyone talked about the climate, which means that we [Kazakhstan] also needed to talk about it' (interview 11).

However, there are obvious limitations with the national climate change policy that are evident through a lack of coherency with existing mitigation and adaptation efforts, limited coordination among involved stakeholders and the lack of a national strategy/programme specifically dedicated to climate change which would bring together a range of measures and actions (Ministry of Energy of the RK, 2017). This sentiment of institutional incoherency was echoed by our interviewees, as several of them highlighted that the complexity of climate change requires coordination between various state and private institutions which is currently limited. The problem translates into mutually exclusive policy decisions and steps, as one of the NGO representatives (interview 6) sharply noted 'it is impossible to increase livestock breeding and at the same time reduce [GHG] emissions.'

Kazakhstan's climate policy is further weakened by constant institutional change (as mentioned above) where the accumulation of knowledge on complex environmental problems 'thins out' as people go in and out of their ministerial positions or switch between various institutions (interviews 1 & 13). The problem is then complicated by the limitations of climate science development in the country. Whilst important work has been done by the local scientific institutions (e.g. 'Kazhydromet', Scientific and Educational Centre 'Green Academy', Nazarbayev University and KazNU research groups) and they are able to advise the state's climate policy (along with the relevant NGOs), there is a 'lack of policy to build the capacity of young scientists and maintain a continuity [of climate knowledge]' (interview 8). Furthermore, despite Kazakhstan's commitment to develop national science ('Concept of ID to 2020'), there is a lack of skilled ecologists in Kazakhstan, and the average wage in academia remains quite low (interview 11).

To sum up, the discursive representation of national strength and pride where even climate change threats are seen as an opportunity rather than a constraint is weakened by the reality of Kazakhstan's climate policies that require a more consistent national effort.

Climate change and green economy
The most popular narrative in all analysed documents is the discussion of 'green economy' and 'sustainable development' which suggests that the government seeks to resolve existing environmental problems, including climate change, without economic loss and abandonment of its resource driven economy. Here, sustainable development includes energy efficiency, diversification of the economy, and contribution to social and economic stability with the creation of new employment opportunities (for example, by 2050, it is expected that more than 500,000 jobs will be created) ('Green Economy Concept'). Thus, it is seen as an opportunity 'to find money for decarbonisation' and to follow global trends where tightening international carbon regulations leads to the same processes inside the country (interview 3). For example, as more countries, including the USA, Canada and China, are about to introduce the carbon tax, it is reasonable for Kazakhstan to enforce domestic regulations on businesses rather than to face budget losses (interview 9). Changes in the international market already led to some positive developments in Kazakhstan's national climate policy – for example, the requirement to disclose annual GHG emissions (World Bank, 2018) which concerns organisations/businesses emitting more than 20,000 tons a year (interview 6).

The analysed texts also demonstrate a presence of 'resource nationalism', where Kazakhstan's fossil fuel reserves are presented as 'the powerhouse of our economy' ('Strategy-2050'). Interestingly, the discourse of sustainable development and economic modernisation does not clash with the notion of national pride in the extractive industry which is explained by the fact that GHG emissions from fossil fuel extraction are relatively low (interviews 10, 11 & 13) while the majority of extracted resources are exported. Hence, it is not the state's concern what happens with fossil fuels once they are exported: 'we drove it [oil] into the pipeline, and it went on, and what happens next is not important. We extract – we sell, that is it' (interview 10). On the other hand, it is stated that success in the oil and gas industries will help to build a new economy for the future as well as to strengthen Kazakhstan's role in international affairs dealing with global problems, including environmental ones. For example, the 'Strategy-2050' claims: 'we have been blessed with abundant natural resources and other countries will need to rely on us for their resource needs'. Poberezhskaya and Danilova (2021) argue that in Kazakhstan's official discourse even climate change is presented as another 'resource' that is utilised to bring benefits to the state, for instance, to present itself as an active participant of the international community.

Interestingly, climate change also appears as an opportunity to embrace innovation: 'the threat of climate change and limited natural resources have led to a scientific and technological breakthrough' ('Concept of ID to 2020'). The majority of Kazakhstan's own GHG emissions comes from over reliance on coal and oil for the domestic market which is exacerbated by the infrastructure, technology, and standards inherited from the Soviet period: about 50% of energy-related infrastructure in the country is older than 30 years, some 50–60 years old (ADB, 2013). In the Environmental Performance Index (EPI), Kazakhstan's carbon intensity is behind even developing nations including fellow former Soviet republics like Russia, Belarus, Armenia and Turkmenistan (UNECE, 2019). Therefore, Kazakhstan has strong capacity to reduce GHG emissions through improvements in energy efficiency as well as switching to RES (Karatayev & Clarke, 2016).

Indeed, Kazakhstan has necessary natural, climatic, and economic conditions to develop sustainable energy solutions, being the only country in CA which has both significant solar and wind energy capacity (Samruk-Kazyna, 2018). Relatively speaking, the country has already achieved some positive results given the steady growth of RES productivity over the past decade (see Figure 1). Furthermore, the data on solar capacities has become publicly accessible (AtlasSolar, 2017), financing of renewable energy increased from US$1.33 million in 2010 to US$93 million in 2018 (IRENA, 2019), and the sector has attracted foreign financial and technical support (e.g. EUR 300 million from the European Bank for Reconstruction and Development (EBRD); and US$107.8 million from the Clean Technology Fund) (Ministry of Energy of the RK, 2017).

As a result Kazakhstan has achieved its goal of reaching 3% of RES in energy mix by 2020 as stated by the Minister of Energy (Sabekov, 2021). However, there is a widespread opinion that the 2030 target of 35% and the 2050 target of 50% will be missed (interviews 3, 6, 9 & 11). In fact, the renewable energy sector continues to suffer from various barriers including limited regulatory components and the lack of a feed-in tariff system (Koch & Tynkkynen, 2021). Without this, renewable energy producers could not realistically be

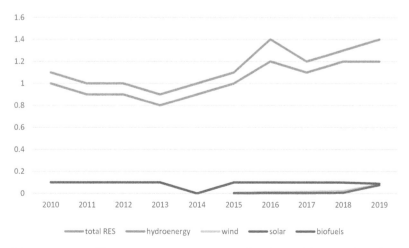

Figure 1. RES sector in Kazakhstan, 2010–2019. Source: Authors' own elaboration based on data from KazStat (2021).

expected to compete with traditional fuel supplies, which have long been (and continue to be) aided by artificially low electricity prices supported by state subsidies (Wheeler, 2017). Interestingly, along with the RES, nuclear energy is also seen as one of the ways to reduce GHG emissions and contribute to climate change mitigation (Ministry of Energy of the RK, 2017). However, due to the country's difficult past (e.g. nuclear pollution caused by the Semipalatinsk testing site) nuclear energy, as in many other parts of the world, is a contested topic (interview 9) (see also Howie et al., 2020).

The narrative of 'modernisation' and economic prosperity is persistent not only through all the documents that impact the state's climate change strategy but also in Nazarbayev's overall official rethoric (Kudaibergenova, 2015; Seydullayeva et al., 2015). Unsurprisingly, within the discourse of 'green economy', the 'economy' part takes clear priority over the 'green' one. Thus, the aim of sustainable development is to strengthen Kazakhstan's political and economic stance rather than deal with the climate crisis as the 'initiatives that not only improve the environmental situation but also result in increased economic benefits will be prioritised' ('Green Economy Concept').

Climate change and international cooperation
Our data demonstrate that Kazakhstan is presented as a 'responsible and reliable partner with significant influence in the international arena' ('Strategy–2050'). This image is supported by Kazakhstan's role as a contributor to global energy security; a cultural 'bridge' connecting the Islamic and Christian worlds, the East and the West; a guarantor of regional security in CA; and a global ambassador ('Strategy to 2020'). The global environmental crisis in this regard is seen as an opportunity to solidify this image. Furthermore, there is a clear discursive alignment with international actors and practices that serve as examples of successful sustainable development and economic diversification (e.g. 'Concept to ID'). For example, the international exposition 'Future Energy' (EXPO-2017) held in Kazakhstan became a symbol of national pride (e.g. 'Concept to ID'; 'Strategy–2050') contributing to all identified narratives: advancing the image of the strong state for Kazakhstan and of a powerful leader for President Nazarbayev (interview 1), as well as bringing attention to the green economy and Kazakhstan's international commitments (Poberezhskaya & Danilova, 2021). This desire to match expectations of the global community (mostly the EU and the OECD members) correlates with Kazakhstan's persistent interest in gaining Western approval since its independence in 1991 (Koch, 2018; Schatz, 2006) and perseverance of the 'multi-vector policy' which is described in the 'Strategy to 2020' as 'friendly relations of equal cooperation with all states'.

Against this backdrop, Kazakhstan's GHG emissions reduction goals present an interesting case. Whilst in 1990 emissions were relatively high, following the economic collapse caused by the dissolution of the SU and political and social instability throughout the 1990s (Bolesta, 2019), Kazakhstan unintentionally almost halved its emissions from the base-line year (see Figure 2). As the country stabilised economically from 2000 onwards, emissions have been steadily increasing, though they remained below the 1990 base level at least until 2018[5] (Figure 2). Therefore, Kazakhstan was able to make reduction commitments without economic sacrifice. Indeed, under the Paris Agreement, Kazakhstan aims to keep GHG emissions 15% below the 1990 level by 2030 (an unconditional target). However, unlike many countries, Kazakhstan also has a 'conditional target' of 25% GHG

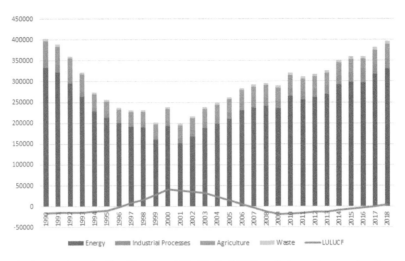

Figure 2. GHG emissions in Kazakhstan, 1990–2018. *GHG emissions, thousands of tons of CO2 equivalent. Source: Authors' own elaboration based on data from the Ministry of Ecology, Geology and Natural Resources of the RK (2020, pp. 37–38).

emissions reduction by 2030: the condition requires 'additional international investments, access to low carbon technology transfer mechanisms, green climate funds and flexible mechanisms for countries in economic transition' (Government of the RK, 2015). Experts argue that even despite the economic recession of the 1990s, if Kazakhstan continues a 'business as usual' approach without introducing robust punitive measures, it will not reach the GHG emissions reduction targets (interviews 3, 4 & 9) with some suggesting that emissions already exceed the base line (interview 11) (although there are no official data yet). There is still a possibility to achieve carbon neutrality by 2060 (as announced by the president in September 2020) by offsetting emissions via various projects, but that would require the state's commitment and substantial investments (interviews 9 & 13).

The paradox of relatively ambitious goals despite a lack of aspiration to give up its fossil fuel driven economy is explained by Kazakhstan's desire to impress international partners; Nazarbayev's personal drive to be seen as a modern leader committed to global sustainable development; limited understanding of how those commitments will be practically transferred into economic and industrial changes; and the above mentioned interest in foreign investments[6] (interview 4 & 3).

Indeed, Kazakhstan has been quite successful in attracting global attention to its climate change mitigation and adaptation efforts. In 2015, US$416.3 million were allocated to climate-related projects with 97% coming from 'loans' and 3% as 'grant assistance' (in addition to the EBRD, funding was also provided by the Global Environment Facility (US$9.66 million), USA (US$1.83 million), Japan (US$30,000) and South Korea (US$22,000)) (Ministry of Energy of the RK, 2017). Furthermore, that same year, the World Bank (2015) committed US$38 million 'from the International Development Association to finance the first phase of the Climate Adaptation and Mitigation Program for Aral Sea Basin (CAMP4ASB)'. Among other investors and lenders are the European Investment Bank (EIB), the Climate Investment Funds (CIF), European Union, World Health Organization (WHO), UNDP and USAID.

We argue that Kazakhstan's relations with foreign investors and Western partners is potentially the most evident manifestation of post-colonial rhetoric. Interestingly, whilst the blame is not allocated to the former 'colonial power' (the SU), it is occasionally attributed to the 'developed economies' and in particular Europe, for example:

> the economy of Kazakhstan during the years of independence has developed mainly due to the extractive sectors that were attractive to foreign investors. And since in Europe, they were already greening, they naturally invested mainly in dirty production [...] the extraction of raw materials and the production of energy-intensive products (interview 6).

Kazakhstan's international image is also supported through its pride in leading the way among developing countries. For instance, it committed to the Africa–Kazakhstan Partnership for the Sustainable Development Goals which aimed to assist 45 African states (budgeted at US$2 million). A similar agreement has been signed with the Caribbean Community, with Kazakhstan committing US$770,000 to help the region with their sustainability and climate change efforts. Kazakhstan has also initiated the inter-regional 'Green Bridge' partnership which is meant to stimulate a transition towards more sustainable economies (by 2019 the initiative included 15 countries and 12 NGOs) (Kozhanova, 2019). Kazakhstan's leadership is particularly stressed with regard to CA:

> Kazakhstan has a leading role [...] Others [CA countries] - yes, they have concerns, but they are concerned, that's all. They may discuss, but they do not really do anything. And we [in Kazakhstan] can see the direction, development (interview 4).

> Yes, so far Kazakhstan has been ahead of other states in the region [CA], mostly because it started first [working with climate change issues] (interview 3).

The international dimension of Kazakhstan's climate change policy presents a number of opportunities for the interested stakeholders who can benefit from the state's openness to financial investments but also its ambitions to be seen as an active global player. However, there is a danger of contributing to Kazakhstan's policy of 'greenwashing' (Koch & Tynkkynen, 2021). Whilst the narratives of sustainable development and commitment to the global fight against climate change strengthen the image of the progressive state, arguably, the green rhetoric is also used as a tool of political control, promoting certain types of environmental behaviour among stakeholders, local policymakers and citizens (Domjan & Stone, 2010) that does not question the state's reliance on fossil fuels.

Discussion

Our analysis demonstrates the limited presence of postcolonialism in Kazakhstan's political discourse of climate change. There is some evidence of the 'non-responsibility' rhetoric, a common characteristic of postcolonial narratives (Said, 1987), where the blame is allocated to advanced economies for investing primarily in 'brown' industries and moving carbon intensive facilities to developing countries, like Kazakhstan (interviews 4 & 9). Also, oil production is not seen as an environmental harm as it is mostly exported to the EU countries – hence, 'they are the real polluters' (interview 10). Such rhetoric is common for postcolonial states during climate change negotiations, where greater carbon reduction commitments are expected from the developed countries (Dubash, 2012; Rajao & Duarte, 2018).

Despite relative silence over climate change issues, the studied documents do acknowledge some associated problems. Climate change is seen as one of the threats to Kazakhstan's water security (e.g. 'Green Economy Concept'), which is then linked with other potential issues, including deteriorating agriculture, negative impacts on trade and national finances, and overall state stability ('Strategy 2020'). In these rare signs of vulnerability, we saw some allusions to the Soviet past where Kazakhstan became a victim of nature mismanagement (e.g. the Aral Sea). Dubuisson (2020) argues that environmental protection discourse is a responsibility discourse, and 'any conceptualisation of "land and environmental protection" is a multiply discursive perspective in which different models of responsibility are invoked' (p. 10). However, as the SU does not exist anymore, any attempts to blame it lose their value, especially, when considering that modern Kazakhstan continues to pursue similar approaches to nature (Kopack, 2019). Unsurprisingly, with regards to climate change we have not observed any explicit blame allocation (similar arguments can be seen in Poberezhskaya & Danilova, 2021). The finding is also supported by the conducted interviews, where acknowledgement of environmental problems caused by the SU go hand in hand with recollection of the benefits that the country used to enjoy:

> during the SU, indeed, there were such dangerous industries [...] But, nevertheless, there were many good things, for example, the capital of Almaty was a very green city (interview 5).

> people, of course, are very concerned about all of this [pollution accumulated during the Soviet time] [...] huge consequences, we still see now [...][but people talk about the USSR] not in a negative way, rather like this: [...] 'What do we do with this? [...] mostly people speak well of the past [...] the social privileges that there were (interview 4).

The Soviet past is reflected in the technocratic approach to environmental protection which is still evident in Kazakhstan. In this view, techno-scientific progress can resolve any environmental problems with no need to sacrifice economic advancement: 'we need to learn how to properly manage it [natural resources], saving our export revenues and, most importantly, transforming our natural resources into an efficient and sustainable vehicle for economic growth' ('Strategy-2050'). Indeed, the principle of prioritising the economy over the environment is strongly embedded in the state's policies: 'it is reported everywhere that we have "heavy" Soviet heritage when the economy was first, and environment last [...], but professional environmentalists see it is still the same' (interview 9). Furthermore, the experts argue that environmental policies have not seen any significant progress since the time of the SU as the state has been moving by inertia: with almost all environmental legislation and emission norms remaining unchanged (interview 11).

While the Soviet-inspired attitude towards the environment looks irrational in the light of the current environmental agenda and 'green' political efforts, the 'Soviet legacy' here can be explained by the struggle with national identity (Sakal, 2015). As one of the experts mentioned, the country is still under recognized abroad, and it is difficult to explain what Kazakhstan is without referring to its Soviet past (interview 3). Although environmental rhetoric contributes to the state's image and recognition at the international level (Weinthal & Watters, 2010), it is doubtful that such discourse brings a real change – as the approach to nature has not evolved.

Notably, within the ambiguous Kazakh national discourse, the image of the 'strong state' intertwines with the claims for international aid (Kudaibergenova, 2016a, p. 921).

Figure 3. Economic Growth in Kazakhstan, %GDP, 1991–2019. Source: Authors' own elaboration based on data from the World Bank group (n.d.).

For example, Kazakhstan is shown as a key geographical hotspot, the owner of abundant resources which may gain additional value in the face of environmental changes, and as a responsible state contributing to the global agenda. Meanwhile, the identity of a developing state is supported through emphasis on foreign investments and need for financial support. In line with Schatz (2006), we explain this conundrum as a reassertion of Kazakhstan's postcolonial status. While the national economy is experiencing steady growth (see Figure 3), there are too many issues to touch upon regarding sustainable development, and it is hardly possible to achieve the proclaimed GHG emission reduction targets without external help (interview 3).

The alignment with international discourse invites financial support from international donors – thus there is little financial sense in climate denialism or scepticism (Poberezhskaya & Danilova, 2021) but instead the state presents climate policy as a policy of opportunities. Isaksen and Stokke (2014) identify a similar discursive turn in India's political discourse: the 'third world' rhetoric is currently being replaced by a 'win-win' discourse (p. 114). Remarkably, Kazakhstan's fossil fuel industries are not seen as a threat or a problem for sustainable development but in fact as 'a guarantee of safety for present and future generations' where 'the oil and gas complex' acts as 'a locomotive for the entire economy' ('Strategy-2050'). Hence, national and international policies and rhetoric hardly match: the positive global image that is being promoted and investments in the renewable sector are overshadowed by energy inefficiencies, inconsistent policies and a lack of experts in the country.

Conclusion

In 'Strategy-2050' Nazarbayev firmly stated that the 'economy is first, then politics' which of course includes environmental politics. This approach is evident in the way climate change is often framed within both discussions of economic benefits (e.g. increasing energy efficiency, receiving foreign investments) or potential economic losses (e.g. introduction of the carbon tax). Kazakhstan's commitments to the fossil fuel industry prevents a more sophisticated climate change mitigation policy. At the same time, policy processes and initiatives that do exist in the country are constrained by limited support for climate science and the low level of public awareness. This is further exacerbated by problems with the institutionalisation and formalisation of the process, where decisions are impacted by those in the posts and/or their informal relations with interested parties (interview 2). Connected to this is the limited transparency of how decisions are made and the rationale behind them (ibid). Lastly, it does not help that the relevant state institutions tend to shift responsibility to one another rather than solving the issues collectively which is 'very much a Soviet way' of policymaking (interview 9, see also Mouraviev, 2021). The Soviet past also shows via instrumental attitudes towards the environment and the personification of the policy making process as well as its top-down approach. However, it did not manifest itself as part of the post-colonial rhetoric in Kazakhstan.

Based on the outlined findings, we suggest that relevant national and international policymakers should consider the following factors to advance climate change policy in Kazakhstan. Firstly, even if Kazakhstan's government decides to part with its resource-intensive industries and move away from dependency on fossil fuel exports, it will not be able to do so in a short period of time and without external support. As such, a move could potentially result in serious social and political problems (e.g. leading to destabilisation in the regions where extractive industries are essential to people's employment and/or to regional budgets) which is also an outcome of the Soviet legacy Kazakhstan has to deal with.[7] Therefore, sustainable climate change mitigation policy should consider not only economic but also social implications. Secondly, despite the large volume of oil, gas, and coal reserves in Kazakhstan, there is an ongoing discussion of the nation's energy security (Koulouri & Mouraviev, 2019) which presents an opportunity for highlighting the role of RES. Thirdly, the importance of Kazakhstan's interest in its national and international image-building should be used to the advantage of climate change policy. As Kazakhstan stays faithful to its 'multi-vector policy' and a desire to be seen as an important global actor, it will not be able to disengage from the global climate regime. Fourthly, a sound climate policy requires extensive support of national climate science as well as engagement with other important actors, such as NGOs, media and business communities.

Whilst this article offers a comprehensive overview of the official discourse on climate change in Kazakhstan (contributing to climate change discussions in the post-Communist space (e.g. Martus, 2019; Poberezhskaya, 2016, 2018; Poberezhskaya & Ashe, 2018)), future research endeavours would benefit from a combination of quantitative and qualitative analysis of media, science, activists and business discourses to see how they impact climate change politics in Kazakhstan. Furthermore, considering the importance of the international dimension of Kazakhstan's climate politics, the role of international organisations needs to be explored in greater detail with particular focus on engagement (or a lack of it) by regional organisations (Ambrosio, 2008; Izotov & Obydenkova, 2021; Libman & Obydenkova, 2013, 2018a, 2018b). Lastly, following our findings on the impact of the political regime and the head of the state over climate change politics in Kazakhstan, a nuanced study of authoritarianism and its effect on environmental policies in CA would also be beneficial.[8]

To conclude, the above analysis shows a mismatch between the representation of Kazakhstan's sustainable commitments and the real climate policy steps, in fact even the state's proud regional leadership is questioned: 'Kazakhstan is the leader in CA in terms of GHG emissions. What example can we set? Our emissions are growing, not decreasing [...] Maybe it is more an example in words, but in practice we didn't show it' (interview 11). Unfortunately, Kazakhstan is by far not the only country found in this predicament, where rhetorical change is not met by adequate policy responses. Therefore, it is important for the stakeholders interested in advancing climate change policy in Kazakhstan to have a full understanding of the outlined objective and subjective factors impacting the state's position on this environmental problem.

Notes

1. For instance, in China, Kazakhstan's key strategic energy sector partner and the world's leading coal producer, the share of coal in its energy mix dropped by 66% and renewables' share reached 15% in 2020 (The Oxford Institute for Energy Studies, 2020).
2. Partly due to the Covid-19 pandemic (Climate Action Tracker, 2020).
3. See Figure 2 for Kazakhstan's GHG emissions' trajectory.
4. Weinthal and Watters (2010) notice that Nazarbayev was using the rhetoric of environmental concern as a tool for building his image and legitimacy both in the domestic and international arenas during his first years of leadership.
5. The base level is 401.87 million tons/year, and it was 396.57 in 2018
6. The concern over investments also underpins the recent silencing of coal production as the foreign sponsors (even China) are less motivated to support 'brown' industries (interview 10).
7. Like many other post-Communist countries (see: Kudaibergenova, 2016b; Lankina et al., 2016a; Libman & Obydenkova, 2019; Nazarov & Obydenkova, 2020; Pop-Eleches & Tucker, 2017) Kazakhstan has been and still is dealing with a diverse range of Soviet legacies, such as corruption, its dependence on Soviet trade ties and misinformation.
8. The importance of democracy (associated with decentralisation, transparency, and lower corruption) for environmental policy and agenda has been studied in Payne 1995; Fredriksson and Wollscheid (2007); Libman and Obydenkova (2014), Obydenkova and Salahodjaev (2016, 2017), Obydenkova et al. (2016); Fredriksson and Neumayer (2013)

Acknowledgements

We would like to thank Dr Imad El-Anis, our interviewees and two anonymous reviewers for their invaluable contributions.

Disclosure statement

No potential conflict of interest was reported by the author(s).

ORCID

Marianna Poberezhskaya http://orcid.org/0000-0001-6442-5292
Alina Bychkova http://orcid.org/0000-0002-3303-9150

References

Abashin, S. (2014). Nations and post-colonialism in central Asia: Twenty years later. In: Hohmann, S., Mouradian, C., & Serrano, S. (Eds.) *Development in Central Asia and the Caucasus: Migration, Democratisation and Inequality in the Post-Soviet Era* (pp.80-98). Bloomsbury Publishing.
Adams, L. (2008). Can we apply postcolonial theory to Central Eurasia? *Central Eurasian Studies Review*, 7(1), 2–7. https://centraleurasia.org/wp-content/uploads/2018/04/Vol.7_no.1_fulljournal_CESR.pdf

ADB. (2013). *Asian Development Bank and Kazakhstan – Fact sheet* [Fact sheet]. https://think-asia.org/bitstream/handle/11540/359/KAZ.pdf?sequence=1

Ambrosio, T. (2008). Catching the 'Shanghai Spirit': How the Shanghai cooperation organization promotes authoritarian norms in Central Asia. *Europe-Asia Studies, 60*(8), 1321–1344. https://doi.org/10.1080/09668130802292143

AtlasSolar. (2017). (Retrieved April 24, 2021), from http://atlassolar.kz/

Bäckstrand, K., & Lövbrand, E. (2019). The road to Paris: Contending climate governance discourses in the post-Copenhagen era. *Journal of Environmental Policy & Planning, 21*(5), 519–532. https://doi.org/10.1080/1523908X.2016.1150777

Beissinger, M., & Young, M. C. (Eds.). (2002). *Beyond state crisis?: Post-colonial Africa and post-Soviet Eurasia in comparative perspective.* Woodrow Wilson Center Press.

Bernauer, T., & Siegfried, T. (2012). Climate change and international water conflict in Central Asia. *Journal of Peace Research, 49*(1), 227–239. https://doi.org/10.1177/0022343311425843

Bolesta, A. (2019). From socialism to capitalism with communist characteristics: The building of a post-socialist developmental state in Central Asia. *Post-Communist Economies*, 1–28. https://doi.org/10.1080/14631377.2019.1694350

CAN. (2014) *Prognoz po izmeneniyu klimata v Tsentral'noi Azii (Climate change forecast in Central Asia)*. Climate Action Network Eastern Europe, Caucasus and Central Asia. https://infoclimate.org/prognoz-po-izmeneniyu-klimata-v-tsentralnoy-azii/

Charmaz, K. (2000). Grounded theory: Objectivist and constructivist methods. In Lincoln, Y. S. & Denzin, N. K. (Eds.), *Handbook of qualitative research*. (2nd.). (pp. 509-535). Sage Publications.

CIA.gov. (2021). *Kazakhstan. CIA The World Factbook.* (Retrieved 2021, April, 20), from https://www.cia.gov/the-world-factbook/countries/kazakhstan/#economy

Climate Analytics. (2019). *Global and regional coal phase-out requirements of the Paris Agreement: Insights from the IPCC Special Report on 1.5°C.* (Retrieved March 21, 2021), from. https://climateanalytics.org/media/report_coal_phase_out_2019.pdf

Dave, B. (2007). *Kazakhstan: Ethnicity, language and power.* Routledge.

Deng, H., & Chen, Y. (2017). Influences of recent climate change and human activities on water storage variations in Central Asia. *Journal of Hydrology, 544*, 46–57. https://doi.org/10.1016/j.jhydrol.2016.11.006

Domjan, P., & Stone, M. (2010). A comparative study of resource nationalism in Russia and Kazakhstan 2004–2008. *Europe-Asia Studies, 62*(1), 35–62. https://doi.org/10.1080/09668130903385374

Dubash, N. .(2012). Climate politics in India: Three narratives, N. K. Dubash Ed., *Handbook of climate change and India. Development, politics and governance*. Ed. 197–207. Routledge

Dubuisson, E. M. (2020). Whose World? Discourses of protection for land, environment, and natural resources in Kazakhstan. *Problems of Post-Communism*, 1–13. https://doi.org/10.1080/10758216.2020.1788398

Edgar, A. (2006). Bolshevism, patriarchy, and the nation: The Soviet" emancipation" of Muslim women in pan-Islamic perspective. *Slavic Review, 65*(2), 252–272. https://doi.org/10.2307/4148592

Fay, M., Block, R., & Ebinger, J. (eds.). (2010). *Adapting to climate change in Eastern Europe and Central Asia.* Europe and Central Asia reports. World Bank Group.

Fierman, W. (2009). Identity, symbolism, and the politics of language in Central Asia. *Europe-Asia Studies, 61*(7), 1207–1228. https://doi.org/10.1080/09668130903068731

Fredriksson, P. G., & Neumayer, E. (2013). Democracy and climate change policies: Is history important? *Ecological Economics, 95*, 11–19. https://doi.org/10.1016/j.ecolecon.2013.08.002

Fredriksson, P. G., & Wollscheid, J. R. (2007). Democratic institutions versus autocratic regimes: The case of environmental policy. *Public Choice, 130*(3–4), 381–393. https://doi.org/10.1007/s11127-006-9093-1

Government of the RK. (2015). *Intended nationally determined contribution - Submission of the Republic of Kazakhstan*, Government of Kazakhstan, 4. http://www4.unfccc.int/submissions/INDC/Published%20Documents/Kazakhstan/1/INDC%20Kz_eng.pdf

Grove, R., & Grove, R. H. (1996). *Green imperialism: Colonial expansion, tropical island Edens and the origins of environmentalism, 1600-1860*. Cambridge University Press.

Heathershaw, J. (2010). *Central Asian statehood in post-colonial perspective*. Ashgate.

Howie, P., Yesdauletov, I., & Dyussenov, Y. (2020). Support for nuclear power in Central Asia: Examining historical and spatial separation. *Post-Communist Economies, 32*(7), 947–968. https://doi.org/10.1080/14631377.2020.1722581

Huggan, G. (2004). "Greening" postcolonialism: Ecocritical perspectives. *MFS Modern Fiction Studies, 50*(3), 701–733. https://doi.org/10.1353/mfs.2004.0067

IEA. (2020). *Kazakhstan energy profile*. IEA, Paris. Retrieved April, 24, 2021, from https://www.iea.org/reports/kazakhstan-energy-profile

International Crisis Group. (2011). *Central Asia: Decay and decline (Asia Report N°201)*. https://d2071andvip0wj.cloudfront.net/201-central-asia-decay-and-decline.pdf

IRENA. (2019). *Renewable capacity statistics 2019*.

IRENA. (n.d.). *Country Rankings – Kazakhstan*. Retrieved 2021, April, 21, from https://www.irena.org/Statistics/View-Data-by-Topic/Capacity-and-Generation/Country-Rankings

Isaksen, K. A., & Stokke, K. (2014). Changing climate discourse and politics in India. Climate change as challenge and opportunity for diplomacy and development. *Geoforum, 57*, 110–119. https://doi.org/10.1016/j.geoforum.2014.08.019

Izotov, V., & Obydenkova, A. (2021). Geopolitical games in Eurasian regionalism: Ideational interactions and regional international organisations. *Post-Communist Economies, 33*(2–3), 150–174. https://doi.org/10.1080/14631377.2020.1793584

Kandiyoti, D. (2002). Post-colonialism compared: Potentials and limitations in the Middle East and Central Asia. *International Journal of Middle East Studies, 34*(2), 279–297. https://doi.org/10.1017/S0020743802002076

Karatayev, M., & Clarke, M. L. (2016). A review of current energy systems and green energy potential in Kazakhstan. *Renewable and Sustainable Energy Reviews, 55*, 491–504. https://doi.org/10.1016/j.rser.2015.10.078

KazStat. (2021) . *Renewable Energy Supply*. Agency for Strategic planning and reforms of the Republic of Kazakhstan Bureau of National statistics.

Khalid, A. (2006). Backwardness and the quest for civilization: Early Soviet Central Asia in comparative perspective. *Slavic Review, 65*(2), 231–251. https://doi.org/10.2307/4148591

Koch, N. (2018). *The geopolitics of spectacle: Space, synecdoche, and the new capitals of Asia*. Cornell University Press.

Koch, N., & Tynkkynen, V. P. (2021). The geopolitics of renewables in Kazakhstan and Russia. *Geopolitics, 26*(2), 521-540. https://doi.org/10.1080/14650045.2019.1583214

Kopack, R. A. (2019). Rocket wastelands in Kazakhstan: Scientific authoritarianism and the Baikonur Cosmodrome. *Annals of the American Association of Geographers, 109*(2), 556–567. https://doi.org/10.1080/24694452.2018.1507817

Kopra, S. (2018). *China and great power responsibility for climate change*. Taylor & Francis.

Korppoo, A. (2016). Who is driving Russian climate policy? applying and adjusting veto players theory to a non-democracy. *International Environmental Agreements: Politics, Law and Economics, 16*(5), 639–653. https://doi.org/10.1007/s10784-015-9286-5

Koulouri, A., & Mouraviev, N., Eds. (2019). Energy security through the lens of renewable energy sources and resource efficiency. In *Energy security: policy challenges and solutions for resource efficiency* (pp. 9-35). Palgrave Macmillan.

Kozhanova, N. (2019). Fifteen countries join Green Bridge initiative, sharing ideas and learning with Kazakhstan. *The Astana Times, 15*(October), 2019. https://astanatimes.com/2019/10/fifteen-countries-join-green-bridge-initiative-sharing-ideas-and-learning-with-kazakhstan/

Kudaibergenova, D. (2015). The ideology of development and legitimation: Beyond 'Kazakhstan 2030'. *Central Asian Survey, 34*(4), 440–455. https://doi.org/10.1080/02634937.2015.1115275

Kudaibergenova, D. (2016a). The use and abuse of postcolonial discourses in post-independent Kazakhstan. *Europe-Asia Studies, 68*(5), 917–935. https://doi.org/10.1080/09668136.2016.1194967

Kudaibergenova, D. (2016b). Eurasian Economic union integration in Kazakhstan and Kyrgyzstan. *European Politics and Society*, *17*(sup1), 97–112. https://doi.org/10.1080/23745118.2016.1171286

Lankina, T., Libman, A., & Obydenkova, A. (2016). Authoritarian and democratic diffusion in post-Soviet regions. *Comparative Political Studies*, *49*(12), 1599–1629. https://doi.org/10.1177/0010414016628270

Leipold, S., Feindt, P., Winkel, G., & Keller, R. (2019). Discourse analysis of environmental policy revisited: Traditions, trends, perspectives. *Journal of Environmental Policy & Planning*, *21*(5), 445–463. https://doi.org/10.1080/1523908X.2019.1660462

Libman, A., & Obydenkova, A. (2014). Governance of commons in a large nondemocratic country: The case of forestry in the Russian Federation. *Publius: The Journal of Federalism*, *44*(2), 298–323. https://doi.org/10.1093/publius/pjt065

Libman, A., & Obydenkova, A. (2019). Inequality and historical legacies: Evidence from post-communist regions. *Post-Communist Economies*, *31*(6), 699–724. https://doi.org/10.1080/14631377.2019.1607440

Libman, A., & Obydenkova, A. V. (2013). Informal governance and participation in nondemocratic international organizations. *The Review of International Organizations*, *8*(2), 221–245. https://doi.org/10.1007/s11558-012-9160-y

Libman, A., & Obydenkova, A. V. (2018a). Understanding Authoritarian Regionalism. *Journal of Democracy*, *29*(4), 151–165. https://doi.org/10.1353/jod.2018.0070

Libman, A., & Obydenkova, A. V. (2018b). Regional international organizations as a strategy of autocracy: The Eurasian Economic Union and Russian foreign policy. *International Affairs*, *94*(5), 1037–1058. https://doi.org/10.1093/ia/iiy147

Martus, E. (2019). Russian industry responses to climate change: The case of the metals and mining sector. *Climate Policy*, *19*(1), 17–29. https://doi.org/10.1080/14693062.2018.1448254

Ministry of Ecology, Geology and Natural Resources of the RK, (2020). *National report of the Republic of Kazakhstan on the inventory of anthropogenic emissions from sources and removals by sinks of GHG not regulated by the Montreal Protocol for 1990-2018*, Nur-Sultan, (Retrieved April 22, 2021), from https://unfccc.int/documents/253715.

Ministry of Energy of the RK. (2017). *Seventh national communication and third biennial report of the republic of Kazakhstan to the UN framework on climate change*. Astana. https://unfccc.int/sites/default/files/resource/20963851_Kazakhstan-NC7-BR3-1-ENG_Saulet_Report_12-2017_ENG.pdf.

Moore, D. (2001). Is the Post- in Postcolonial the Post- in Post-Soviet? Toward a Global Postcolonial Critique. *PMLA/Publications of the Modern Language Association of America*, *116*(1), 111-128. https://doi.org/10.1632/pmla.2001.116.1.111

Mouraviev, N. (2021). Renewable energy in Kazakhstan: Challenges to policy and governance. *Energy Policy*, *149*, 112051. https://doi.org/10.1016/j.enpol.2020.112051

Nazarov, Z., & Obydenkova, A. V. (2020). Democratization and firm innovation: Evidence from European and Central Asian post-communist states. *Post-Communist Economies*, *32*(7), 833–859. https://doi.org/10.1080/14631377.2020.1745565

Obydenkova, A., Nazarov, Z., & Salahodjaev, R. (2016). The process of deforestation in weak democracies and the role of intelligence. *Environmental Research*, *148*, 484–490. https://doi.org/10.1016/j.envres.2016.03.039

Obydenkova, A. V., & Salahodjaev, R. (2016). Intelligence, democracy, and international environmental commitment. *Environmental Research*, *147*, 82–88. https://doi.org/10.1016/j.envres.2016.01.042

Obydenkova, A. V., & Salahodjaev, R. (2017). *Climate change policies: The role of democracy and social cognitive capital*. *Environmental research*, *157*, 182–189. http://dx.doi.org/10.1016/j.envres.2017.05.009.

OECD. (2016). *Financing climate action in Kazakhstan, country study*. https://www.oecd.org/environment/outreach/Kazakhstan_Financing_Climate_Action.Nov2016.pdf

Plumwood, V. (2006). Decolonising relationship with nature. In B. Ashcroft, G. Griffiths, & H. Tiffin (Eds.), *The post-colonial studies reader* (pp. 503–508). Routledge.

Poberezhskaya, M. (2016). *Communicating climate change in Russia: State and propaganda*. Routledge.

Poberezhskaya, M. (2018). Blogging about climate change in Russia: Activism, scepticism and conspiracies. *Environmental Communication, 12*(7), 942–955. https://doi.org/10.1080/17524032.2017.1308406

Poberezhskaya, M., & Ashe, T. (eds.). (2018). *Climate change discourse in Russia*. Routledge Focus.

Poberezhskaya, M., & Danilova, N. (2021). Reconciling climate change leadership with resource nationalism and regional vulnerabilities: A case-study of Kazakhstan. *Environmental Politics*, 1–24. https://doi.org/10.1080/09644016.2021.1920768

Pop-Eleches, G., & Tucker, J. A. (2017). *Communism's shadow: Historical legacies and contemporary political attitudes*. Princeton University Press.

Rajao, R., & Duarte, T. (2018). Performing postcolonial identities at the United Nations' climate negotiations. *Postcolonial Studies, 21*(3), 364–378. https://doi.org/10.1080/13688790.2018.1482597

Sabekov, S. (2021, February 9) Nurlan Nogayev told about the development of renewable energy sources in Kazakhstan. Kazinform. https://www.inform.kz/ru/kak-prohodit-razvitie-vie-v-kazahstane-rasskazal-nurlan-nogaev_a3750921

Said, E. W. (Ed). (1978). *Orientalism*. Vintage.

Sakal, H. B. (2015). Natural resource policies and standard of living in Kazakhstan. *Central Asian Survey, 34*(2), 237–254. https://doi.org/10.1080/02634937.2014.987970

Samruk-Kazyna. (2018). *Green economy: Realities and prospects in Kazakhstan*. https://www.sk.kz/upload/iblock/8d9/8d97878e7ec2466e04ab62e5d8f4c3a3.pdf

Schatz, E. (2006). Access by accident: Legitimacy claims and democracy promotion in authoritarian Central Asia. *International Political Science Review, 27*(3), 263–284. https://doi.org/10.1177/0192512106064463

Schreurs, M. A. (2011). Climate change politics in an authoritarian state: the ambivalent case of China. In: Dryzek, J., Norgaard, R., & Scholsberg, D. (Eds.) *The Oxford handbook of climate change and society*. (pp. 449-463). Oxford University Press.

Seydullayeva, G. A., Orynkhanova, G. A., & Tazhibayeva, S. A. (2015). Concept of "modernization" in a political discourse of modern Kazakhstan: On the example of messages of the President of the Republic of Kazakhstan to the people of Kazakhstan. *Procedia Economics and Finance, 26*, 72–76. https://doi.org/10.1016/S2212-5671(15)00840-0

Shakhanova, G. (2017). *Postcolonial Identity of Kazakhstan: Subalternity and Empire in the Russian-Kazakh Relations* [Doctoral dissertation, Vysoká škola ekonomická v Praze].

Sharipova, D. (2019). The decolonization of the environment in Kazakhstan: The Novel final respects by Abdi-Jamil Nurpeisov. *Nationalities Papers, 47*(2), 296–309. https://doi.org/10.1017/nps.2018.24

Simonov, E. (2020, June 23). *Uzbekistan dam collapse was a disaster waiting to happen*. The Third Pole. https://www.thethirdpole.net/en/regional-cooperation/uzbekistan-dam-collapse/

Smith, G., Law, V., Wilson, A., Bohr, A., & Allworth, E. (1998). *Nation-building in the post-Soviet borderlands: The politics of national identities*. Cambridge University Press.

Spivak, G., Condee, N., Ram, H., & Chernetsky, V. (2006). Are We Postcolonial? Post-Soviet Space. *PMLA*,121(3), 828–836. http://www.jstor.org/stable/25486358

Stan Radar (2016). *Izmeneniya klimata v Tsentral'noi Azii: Kakovy posledstviya? (Climate change in Central Asia: What are the consequences?)*, Stan Radar, 30 November 2016. https://stanradar.com/news/full/23109-izmenenija-klimata-v-tsentralnoj-azii-kakovy-posledstvija.html

The Oxford Institute for Energy Studies. (2020). *Current direction for renewable energy in China: Oxford Energy Comment*. University of Oxford. https://www.oxfordenergy.org/wpcms/wp-content/uploads/2020/06/Current-direction-for-renewable-energy-in-China.pdf

UNECE. (2019). *Environmental performance reviews: Kazakhstan: Third review. Environmental Performance Reviews Series, 50*. https://unece.org/DAM/env/epr/epr_studies/ECE_CEP_185_Eng.pdf

Van Dijk, T. A. (2001). Critical discourse analysis. In: Schiffrin, D., Tannen, D., Hamilton, H. E. (Eds.) *The handbook of critical discourse analysis* (pp. 352-372). Blackwell Publishes.

Van Dijk, T. A. (2013). Ideology and discourse. In: Freeden, M., Sargent, L. T. & Stears, M. *The Oxford handbook of political ideologies* (pp. 175-196). Oxford University Press. http://dx.doi.org/10.1093/oxfordhb/9780199585977.013.007

Weinthal, E., & Watters, K. (2010). Transnational environmental activism in Central Asia: The coupling of domestic law and international conventions. *Environmental Politics*, *19*(5), 782–807. https://doi.org/10.1080/09644016.2010.508311

Wheeler, E. (2017, May 2). *Kazakhstan's renewable energy quest*. The Diplomat, https://thediplomat.com/2017/05/kazakhstans-renewable-energy-quest/

WHO (2009). *Protecting health from climate change – Kazakhstan*. World Health Organisation. https://www.euro.who.int/__data/assets/pdf_file/0010/132949/Protecting_health_KZH.pdf.

Wilson Rowe, E. (2013). Climate science, Russian politics, and the framing of climate change. *Wiley Interdisciplinary Reviews. Climate Change*, *4*(5), 457–465. https://doi.org/10.1002/wcc.235

World Bank. (2014) *Turn Down the Heat. Confronting the New Climate Normal: The Climate Challenge for Central Asia*. (Report 98222), http://documents.worldbank.org/curated/en/294131467991967756/pdf/98222-WP-P148173-PUBLIC-ADDSERIES-Turn-down-the-heat-doc-date-6-1-2015-Box393168B.pdf

World Bank. (2015). *World Bank Supports Climate Resilience in Central Asia*. [Press release]. (Retrieved April 12, 2021), from https://www.worldbank.org/en/news/press-release/2015/11/03/world-bank-supports-climate-resilience-in-central-asia

World Bank. (2018). *The challenge of economic diversification amidst productivity stagnation: Kazakhstan*. CEU - Country Economic Update. https://pubdocs.worldbank.org/en/265701543402099127/Kazakhstan-Economic-Update-Fall-2018-en.pdf

World Bank. (n.d.) *The World Bank in Kazakhstan*. (Retrieved April 18, 2021, from).https://www.worldbank.org/en/country/kazakhstan/overview#3

Xenarios, S., Gafurov, A., & Schmidt-Vogt, D. et al. (2019). Climate change and adaptation of mountain societies in Central Asia: uncertainties, knowledge gaps, and data constraints. *Regional Environmental Change*, *19*, 1339–1352. https://doi.org/10.1007/s10113-018-1384-9 https://doi.org/10.1007/s10113-018-1384-9

Young, R. J. C. (2001). *Postcolonialism: An Historical Introduction*. Blackwell.

Greenhouse gas emissions regulation in fossil fuels exporting countries: opportunities and challenges for Russia

Ilya A. Stepanov and Igor A. Makarov

ABSTRACT
A carbon price is considered the most cost-efficient greenhouse gas emissions reduction tool often used as part of a climate policy. However, Russia and the other countries rich in fossil fuels tend to have weak incentives for proactive climate policies including carbon pricing which may lead to falling revenues in emitting industries. Can the carbon price be implemented as part of the development strategy in fossil fuel exporting countries, including Russia? The paper analyzes the variety of existing approaches to applying the carbon price across various energy exporting economies. The paper contributes to the existing literature with the analysis of challenges and opportunities of carbon pricing in these countries and proposes key principles of a viable carbon pricing system in Russia. These principles are (a) balanced emissions coverage and support of vulnerable industries and social groups, (b) fiscal neutrality, (c) gradualness of implementation and (d) use of carbon offsets.

Introduction

Despite the growing attention to climate change and the strengthening national climate policies, at the global scale, the economic growth is still accompanied by an increase in greenhouse gas emissions (GHG). Since the beginning of the century, global GDP has grown by 41.2% in real terms, while emissions have increased by 30.7%.[1] Developed countries that import significant amount of energy and carbon-intensive goods have experienced a gradual reduction in emissions; however, in developing countries emissions continue to grow.[2]

Mitigation of climate change as well as other environmental challenges is especially difficult in countries with large reserves of fossil fuels, transitional economies, states in political regime transition, and unconsolidated democratic institutions (Fredriksson & Neumayer, 2013; Johnsson et al., 2019; Libman & Obydenkova, 2014; Obydenkova et al., 2016; Obydenkova & Salahodjaev, 2016, 2017; Payne, 1995). It is energy-rich countries that pursue less active climate policies and set less ambitious goals for reducing emissions in comparison to energy-deficient countries (Ide, 2020; Tørstad et al., 2020).

Conventionally, in academic literature, public and political discussions on climate policy, a special role is attributed to incentive-based instruments of GHG emissions regulation (Hoel & Karp, 2001; Pizer, 2002; Fan et al., 2017; Mascher, 2018; Narassimhan 2018). They imply introduction of a carbon price, which can be introduced in the form of a carbon tax, an emissions trading system (ETS), or a hybrid instrument that combines both (Goulder & Parry, 2008). The carbon price makes it possible to reduce emissions in the least costly way and at most appropriate facilities (Makarov & Stepanov, 2017). Currently, a carbon price in one form or another is already used in 60 countries and regions of the world (World Bank, 2020).

The majority of emissions regulation systems which involve carbon pricing have been introduced in countries and regions which do not have significant reserves of fossil fuels and rely on energy imports (World Bank, 2020). It is often difficult to introduce carbon price in a country that specialises in production and exports of fossil fuels and energy-intensive products. For such a country, an active emissions reduction policy, including the introduction of a carbon price, is associated with high opportunity costs for the energy sector as well as for the related industries and could be fraught with a weakening international competitiveness of national business (Peszko et al., 2020).

The introduction of a carbon price, especially in developing countries and countries under political and economic transition which export energy resources and energy-intensive products, may conflict with other developmental priorities, such as poverty alleviation and accelerated economic growth (Arlinghaus, 2015; Grainger & Kolstad, 2010; Grigoriev et al., 2020), which depend directly on the dynamics of energy consumption. Additionally, the transitional states with pronounced historical legacies of Communism may witness higher level of corruption, low public accountability, misinformation, specific public attitudes and patterns of behaviour, manipulated official mass media and lack of transparency in implementation of political and economic goals, including but not limited to environmental agenda (Lankina et al., 2016a, 2016b; Libman & Obydenkova, 2019; Nazarov & Obydenkova, 2020; A. Obydenkova & Bruno, 2018; Pop-Eleches & Tucker 2017). As these studies demonstrated, these historical legacies are associated with socio-political and economic consequences and may all lead to poor outcomes in public resource management (such as deforestation, for example), lower commitment to international environmental agreements, rhetorical support to environment in the absence of effective policy strategies, increase of environmental conflicts and decreased public interest and environmental movements – the aspects addressed to some extent in this Special Issue.

Most of the existing studies on carbon pricing either focus on the assessment of its performance in energy-deficient countries and regions (Brink et al., 2016; Green, 2021; Hájek et al., 2019) or depict broader decarbonisation policy issues (Peszko et al., 2020) not touching upon the specifics of carbon pricing in fossil-fuel exporting countries. Some of the studies indicate that in emerging economies, including those specialising in fossil fuels exports, carbon pricing may not be an appropriate part of the climate policy toolkit because of political economy constraints (Finon, 2019). But could the carbon pricing generally be a viable policy tool in the fossil-fuel exporting economies, including Russia, and what it depends on?

The present paper contributes to the existing literature on historical legacies of Communism and their challenges in implementation of agenda of sustainable development with the analysis of carbon pricing systems in place in the countries and subnational entities which export fossil fuel energy resources and may face above mentioned dilemmas in the domains of economic and energy policy. Based on international practices of carbon regulation in energy-exporting countries and regions, we investigate decarbonisation and emissions regulation opportunities in Russia – one of the world's largest exporter of fossil fuels. Russia accounts for 4% of global GHG emissions,[3] but its importance for global efforts to combat climate change is significantly higher due to the high volumes of exports of fossil fuels and carbon-intensive goods to developed countries (Makarov & Sokolova, 2017).

After joining the Paris Agreement in 2019, the discussion on the approaches to GHG emissions regulation in Russia, including in the form of carbon price, has intensified. However, the possible introduction of such regulation scheme faces strong opposition from business that fears the increase in the fiscal burden undermining its competitiveness, as well as from part of the government agencies concerned for the rising heat and electricity prices and significant negative social consequences. Given the dominance of fossil fuels in the economy, the pace of economic growth and population well-being heavily depend on the use of fossil fuels which account more than four-fifth of total GHG emissions in Russia.[4]

As part of the analysis, this study aims to formulate the basic principles of a consistent form of emissions regulation in Russia, which, on the one hand, would create greater incentives to reduce emissions, and, on the other, would minimise risks for the economy and society. These principles are based on the analysis of the best international practices of emissions regulation in the countries exporting fossil fuels as well as on the analysis of the specifics of taxation in Russian energy sector.

This paper has the following structure. The second section provides a brief description of Russia's climate policy. The third section presents risks associated with the global low-carbon transition for the Russian economy. The fourth section presents an analysis of the existing emissions regulation schemes in energy exporting countries and regions of the world, including a description of their key attributes. The fifth section illustrates the role of fossil fuels in the Russian economy and their contribution to the GHG emissions. The sixth section describes the key elements of a possible emissions regulation system in the Russian energy sector. The final section draws conclusion and outlines the limitation of our study as well as the agenda for further investigation.

Overview of the Russian climate policy

Officially, Russia's climate policy began to form in 2009, when the Climate Doctrine of the Russian Federation was adopted (Climate Doctrine of the Russian Federation, 2009). In 2008–2012 Russia took part in the first commitment period of the Kyoto Protocol, according to which it was obliged not to increase the volume of GHG emissions relative to the basic year 1990 (e.g. Andonova & Alexieva, 2012; L. B. Andonova, 2008; L.B. Andonova, 2003). In 2019, Russia joined the Paris Agreement and later submitted its NDC with the emissions target for 2030 at the level of 70 against 1990 level, 'subject to the maximum possible account of absorbing capacity of forests and other ecosystems'.[5] At the national level, by 2030, the Presidential Decree 2020 sets the goal of reducing emissions to 70% of the 1990 level (Presidential Decree on GHG Emissions Reduction, 2020). The Law on GHG emissions regulation and absorption is under consideration of the

State Duma in the time of writing. According to the project of the Strategy for the long-termlow-carbon development strategy, according to the baseline scenario, it is planned to reduce emissions by 33.3% by 2030, and by 36.0% by 2050 compared to 1990 (The project of the strategy of the long-term development of Russia with low greenhouse gas emissions 2050, 2020).

The goals in sustainable development agenda set by Russia in terms of reducing greenhouse gas emissions are not very ambitious. It is likely that they will be achieved even without any additional effort (I. A. Makarov et al., 2020; Kokorin & Korppoo, 2014; Makarov, 2016; Makarov & Stepanov, 2017). The draft of the Law on GHG emissions regulation and absorption does not imply any requirements for the business except for monitoring and verification of GHG emissions. It also suggests no carbon price in Russia.[6]

The reduction of emissions to 70–75% of the 1990 level technically means a significant increase of emissions in comparison with current level. In the period of 1990–2018 Russian GHG emissions decreased by 30.4% excluding emissions from land use, land-use change and forestry (LULUCF) and by 47.6% taking LULUCF into account.[7] At the moment, the GHG emissions in Russia are already at the level of the 2030 target, excluding LULUCF, and 27.6 percentage points (p.p.) below the target if LULUCF is taken into account (Figure 1). The goals set out in the project of the Strategy (within a baseline scenario) technically imply an increase in emissions by 27.3% by 2030 and by 22.1% by 2050 compared to the 2018 level (The project of the strategy …, 2021).

The important factor having an impact on the debate about climate policy in Russia is the initiative of the EU to introduce carbon border adjustment mechanism starting from 2022 to 2023 (EU Parliament, 2021). Carbon border adjustment mechanism would impose

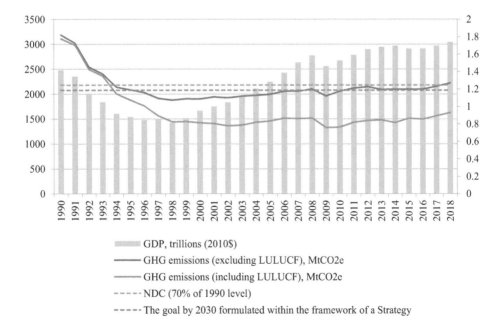

Figure 1. Dynamics of Russia's real GDP (right axis), GHG emissions with and without LULUCF (left axis). Sources: Composed by authors based on World Bank Open Data; UNFCCC. NDC registry.

an additional financial burden on the energy-intensive goods imported from countries with no carbon regulation. Russian goods delivered intensively on the European market are especially vulnerable (Makarov & Sokolova, 2017; BCG, 2020; KPMG, 2020; Marcu 2021). In the expert community as well as in the government, the prospects for introducing a national system of incentive-based emissions regulation are being discussed more and more often (Davydova, 2020; Edelgeriev, 2020). It is likely that a carbon price will appear in Russia in one form or another by the mid-2020s. The prerequisites, opportunities and limitations of its introduction are the subject of analysis in the subsequent sections.

Risks of energy transition for Russia

The global low-carbon transition is characterised by the expansion of the renewable energy capacities, energy efficiency improvement in industry, the announcement of national plans for carbon neutrality by a number of governments and the implementation of appropriate climate and energy policy measures at national and subnational levels (IEA, 2020a; I. A. Makarov et al., 2020; IDDRI, 2015). The main consequence of these processes is a slower growth in demand (and even the reduction in demand in most developed countries) for fossil fuel energy against the background of growing market competitiveness of carbon-free or low-carbon energy sources (I. A. Makarov et al., 2020). In the 2000s, the world demand for fossil fuels grew at an average rate of 2.4% per year, while in the 2010s a growth rate was just 1.4% annually (IEA, 2020b). Under such circumstances, countries which have large reserves of fossil fuels and specialise in their exports face a number of risks. Based on Peszko et al. (2020) and I. A. Makarov et al. (2020) we distinguish four interconnected categories of these risks, each of which is relevant for Russia.

The first one includes the risks of a decrease in the demand for energy exports at the foreign markets. According to the Global and Russian Energy Outlook 2019 (A. A. Makarov et al., 2019), no significant increase in Russian hydrocarbon exports is expected by 2040. A. A. Makarov et al. (2019) show that in the most favourable scenario for Russia, the volume of oil and gas exports by 2040 will exceed the level of 2018 by 1% in physical units and by 45% in value. In the scenario implying a quick transition to low-carbon and energy-saving technologies, exports will fall by 15% in physical units and by 17% in value terms (A. A. Makarov et al., 2019). Alternative estimates made using the EPPA (Emissions Prediction and Policy Analysis Model) show that if countries fulfil their INDCs under the Paris Agreement, Russian energy exports in energy units will decrease by about 20% compared to the baseline scenario, which would mean a loss of 0.2–0.3 p.p. of GDP growth rates by 2030 (I. A. Makarov et al., 2020). In case of transition along the 2 degrees trajectory after 2030, the losses may increase by another 0.3–0.5 p.p. of GDP growth rates per year (I. A. Makarov et al., 2020).

The second group includes the risks of decreased investment attractiveness of hydrocarbon assets and the associated economic activities. An increasing number of large investment and pension funds, insurance companies and other institutional investors indicate the plans to withdraw assets from coal, oil and even natural gas projects (Arabella Advisors, 2018). Thus, the development of new hydrocarbon deposits, which may last for 5–10 years (excluding shale projects with a short investment cycle of 2–3 years), becomes an increasingly risky activity, turning to be less and less attractive for private investors.

The third group of risks consists in the emergence of trade barriers in global markets for carbon-intensive manufactured goods, including carbon border adjustment mechanism in the European Union (EU) (Macru 2021). Russia is a major net exporter of CO_2 emissions embodied in trade. In terms of their net exports, the country ranks second in the world, after China. Russia also has the highest carbon intensity of its exports among the leading economies (Makarov & Sokolova, 2017).

In this regard, the introduction of a carbon border adjustment mechanism in the EU implies significant risks for the Russian exporters who deliver energy-intensive goods to the European market, including metals, chemicals and fertilisers (Marcu, 2021). The specific form of the carbon border adjustment mechanism is still under discussion. Nevertheless, a number of quantitative estimates of the possible losses of the Russian exporters due to the introduction of carbon border adjustment mechanism are already available. According to BCG (2020) estimates, potential losses will range from 3 to 4.7 billion dollars per year; according to KPMG (2020) estimates – from 4 to 8 billion euros per year. The Institute for Economic Forecasting of the Russian Academy of Sciences provides an estimate of 3.6 billion dollars losses a year (Shirov, 2021). According to the estimates of the European Roundtable on Climate Change and Sustainable Transition, annual damage will range from 61 million to 1.24 billion euros (Marcu, 2021).

Finally, the fourth group of risks includes technological risks, namely the risks of technological backwardness in the development of low-carbon sectors of the economy, which will play an increasingly significant role in the future (Kozlova et al., in press). The illustration of understanding these risks among Russian policy makers is the launch of the programme for support of renewables in 2013. This objective of this program is not to increase the share of renewables in the energy mix but to create a new sector of renewable energy equipment in Russia based on modern technologies and oriented to exports (Kozlova et al., in press).

Russia like other hydrocarbon-rich countries faces a development dilemma. On the one hand, there are economic, financial and technological risks associated with maintaining reliance on fossil fuels. On the other hand, there are risks of missed opportunities due to the non-use of the huge fossil-fuel related part of national natural wealth (Peszko et al., 2020). Over the past 50 years, fossil fuel reserves have been perceived as a key driver of economic growth, poverty alleviation and social problems solving. Active green policies would lead to the loss of a significant part of the resource rent in the form of corporate profits and tax revenues and which is, in fact, identical to the loss of the part of national wealth (Manley et al., 2017). Moreover, the political decision to launch ambitious climate policies is complicated by the fact that the risks associated with the global low-carbon transition are long-term, while the risks of domestic climate policies are mostly short-term. In such circumstances, the political elites have little incentive to force energy transition within the country. In fact, this is the main reason for the largely inactive climate policy in Russia.

Specifics of carbon pricing in the energy-exporting countries

In the very basic form, carbon price represents a levy per a unit of GHG emissions which is charged per ton of the actual emissions or per ton of the emissions associated with the volume of fossil fuels supplied by the energy company to market. Carbon price is considered to be the most cost-efficient climate policy tool, in other words, the carbon price allows reducing emissions in the less costly manner (Makarov & Stepanov, 2017). Its cost-efficiency stems from the fact that it allows the marginal cost of emission reductions to be equalised among all the emitters and emission sources included in the regulatory system (Goulder & Parry, 2008; Makarov & Stepanov, 2017).

Despite its growing popularity (so far, there have been already 60 carbon pricing initiatives launched worldwide, and their number is growing every year), the use of carbon price faces a number of difficulties that can be particularly noticeable in emerging economies with substantial fossil fuel reserves. For example, the introduction of a carbon price can undermine the competitiveness of some vulnerable and carbon-intensive industries, as well as lead to a regressive (in fiscal terms) redistribution of wealth between social groups (Arlinghaus, 2015). Empirical evidence suggests that the opportunity to overcome these and other difficulties depends on the possibility of the regulatory design to take into account the specifics of the country or individual industries where this regulation is introduced. This section presents and overview of a number of cases of fossil-fuel exporting countries which use carbon price as an instrument of GHG emissions reduction.

Energy-importing countries tend to set objectives and introduce measures to reduce emissions which are well integrated in a set of other energy policy priorities, such as strengthening energy security, supporting national renewable energy producers and reducing dependence on energy imports (European Commission, n.d.; Schmitz, 2017; World Bank, 2020). It contrasts to energy-exporting countries which have much less incentives to implement ambitious climate policy (Ide, 2020; Tørstad et al., 2020). The introduction of carbon price is an indirect indicator of the loyalty of most business and government circles to the introduction of direct economic restrictions on carbon-intensive activities in the country (Meckling et al., 2017). In this regard, it is not surprising that only 10 of the 60 existing carbon pricing initiatives are implemented in energy exporting countries or regions (World Bank, 2020).

This section examines the existing carbon pricing initiatives in countries or subnational entities where the ratio of net fossil fuel exports to primary energy consumption exceeds 15%.[8] These involve Canada, which has two parallel national carbon pricing initiatives in place, and its two provinces – British Columbia (which also use two systems at once) and Alberta, which have independent carbon pricing initiatives, as well as Norway, Australia, Kazakhstan, South Africa and Colombia. Table 1 provides basic information on carbon pricing in energy exporting countries and regions.

In Canada, two systems operate in parallel at the national level: the Canadian federal fuel charge – a carbon tax that applies to a number of industrial sectors of the economy, and the Output-Based Pricing System – ETS for the electricity generation sector. The latter sets an emissions cap for industry facilities in accordance with sectorial standards and allows trading and postponing allowances for subsequent rounds of regulation if the actual amount of a particular company's emissions is less than the baseline. The federal system of emissions pricing applies to all Canadian provinces, unless they have independent initiatives that meet federal standards.

British Columbia has a carbon tax, which, with some exceptions, covers all sectors, as well as an ETS for the LNG industry, which is de jure functioning, but in practice has not been launched yet due to the protracted process of building LNG plants. In Alberta, there is an ETS – Technology Innovation and Emissions Reduction (TIER), which is arranged in

Table 1. Carbon regulation in energy-exporting countries and subnational entities.

Country/Subnational Entity, type of Regulation	Year of Implementation	Coverage of Sectors and Sources of Emissions	Percentage of Emissions Covered by the System	Point of Regulation (Upstream, Midstream or Downstream)	Price Level	Exceptions, Compensation, Interaction with Other Climate Policy Instruments	Use of Carbon Revenues
Norway, carbon tax and ETS The carbon tax is split into an excise tax on mineral products and a separate law for petroleum activities on the continental shelf. Norway is also included into the EU Emissions trading system (EU ETS).	1991	All sectors with some exemptions for certain sectors; covers natural gas, liquid and gaseous fossil fuels.	62% (carbon tax only)	Producers, distributors and importers of the fossil fuels covered (upstream & midstream).	Upper: NOK545/t CO$_2$e (US $53/t CO$_2$e). Lower: NOK31/t CO$_2$e (US$3/t CO$_2$e)	Operators covered by the EU ETS are exempt from the carbon tax, except for offshore oil production activities that experience the highest tax rate in order to encourage the use of electricity generated onshore instead of electricity generated on the petroleum platforms. The use of fossil fuels in certain sectors and/ or for certain purposes is also (partially) exempt from the carbon tax, including international aviation and international shipping, export of the fuels covered, etc.	30%: 'green' subsidies (support for renewable energies, development of energy efficiency, and low-carbon R&D); 40%: general government funds; 30%: funding for reduction of corporate income tax ('capital tax').

(Continued)

Table 1. (Continued).

Country/Subnational Entity, type of Regulation	Year of Implementation	Coverage of Sectors and Sources of Emissions	Percentage of Emissions Covered by the System	Point of Regulation (Upstream, Midstream or Downstream)	Price Level	Exceptions, Compensation, Interaction with Other Climate Policy Instruments	Use of Carbon Revenues
South Africa, carbon tax with carbon tax allowances Emitters can receive tax deduction through the implementation of offset emissions reduction projects	2019	Applies to GHG from the industry, power, buildings and transport sectors irrespective of the fossil fuel used, with partial exemptions for all these sectors.	80%	Users of the fossil fuels (downstream).	R120/t CO_2e (US$7/t CO_2e)	Under the draft bill, for many sectors tax exemptions starting from 60% up to 95% will apply. The level of tax exemption depends on the presence of fugitive emissions, level of trade exposure, emission performance, offset use and participation in the carbon budget programme. Also, residential transport is exempt from the carbon tax. Under the draft legislation, companies may be eligible for either a 5 or 10% offset allowance to reduce their carbon tax liability.	The implementation of the carbon tax will be complemented by a package of tax incentives and revenue recycling measures to minimise potential adverse impacts on energy intensive sectors such as mining and iron and steel, from the introduction of the carbon tax. This will be achieved through a tax credit for the renewable energy premium built into the electricity tariffs and a credit for the existing electricity generation levy. Efforts will also be made to prioritise and enhance allocations for free basic electricity (or alternative energy) and funding for public transport and initiatives to move some freight from road to rail.

(*Continued*)

Table 1. (Continued).

Country/Subnational Entity, type of Regulation	Year of Implementation	Coverage of Sectors and Sources of Emissions	Percentage of Emissions Covered by the System	Point of Regulation (Upstream, Midstream or Downstream)	Price Level	Exceptions, Compensation, Interaction with Other Climate Policy Instruments	Use of Carbon Revenues
Australia ERF Safeguard Mechanism Operators do not have to pay for GHG emission up to their baseline emission level which is based on their historical emissions. Covered facilities receive tradable permits for emission reductions only in case of implementation of specific emission reduction projects.	2016	The ERF Safeguard Mechanism applies to GHG emissions from the industry and power sectors and includes industrial process emissions.	50%	Operators are liable for reporting the emissions covered under ERF Safeguard Mechanism at a facility level (upstream).	A$16/t CO_2e (US$10/t CO_2e)	Operators do not pay for emissions within acceptable limits. Small emitters are exempt from ERF Safeguard Mechanism.	-
Kazakhstan ETS Emission allowances under the cap are distributed via free allocation. Operators can choose whether to receive free allowances based on their historical emissions or benchmarks and their production levels.	2013, but during 2016–2017 it was frozen. Resumed its work in 2018	The Kazakhstan ETS applies to CO_2 emissions from the power sector and centralised heating as well as certain industry sectors.	50%	Operators are liable for reporting their covered emissions at a facility level and surrendering an equivalent amount of Kazakhstan emission allowances (upstream).	KZT500/t CO_2e (US$1/t CO_2e)	All operators receive their allowances (largely) for free. Also, small emitters are exempt from the Kazakhstan ETS.	-

(Continued)

Table 1. (Continued).

Country/Subnational Entity, type of Regulation	Year of Implementation	Coverage of Sectors and Sources of Emissions	Percentage of Emissions Covered by the System	Point of Regulation (Upstream, Midstream or Downstream)	Price Level	Exceptions, Compensation, Interaction with Other Climate Policy Instruments	Use of Carbon Revenues
Canada **Canada federal fuel charge, carbon tax** The federal regulatory system consists of two components: a Canada federal fuel charge, and ETS for carbon-intensive industries at risk of weakening international competition (Output-Based Pricing System (OBPS).	2019	The federal fuel charge applies to GHG emissions from all sectors with some exemptions for industry, agriculture and transport sectors. The tax covers 21 types of fuel delivered, transferred, used, produced, imported or brought into a province and territory where the federal fuel charge applies. It also applies on combustible waste that is burned for the purpose of producing heat or energy in those jurisdictions.	19%	Registered distributors of the fossil fuels covered are liable for payment of the tax as it is applied early in the supply chain in most cases. End users generally do not have direct compliance obligations as their purchased fuel already has the fuel charge embedded (midstream).	CAN$20/t CO_2e (US$17/t CO_2e)	Certain users of fossil fuels in industry, agriculture and transport are exempt from the federal fuel charge. In addition, fuels exported or removed from jurisdiction under the backstop system are also exempted from the fuel charge. There are also some exemptions from the fuel charge for farmers and remote off-grid communities.	The collected revenues remain in the province where they were collected. Provinces have the right to use them according to their needs, including to address impacts on vulnerable populations, sectors, and to support other climate policies. In previously non-climate regulated provinces (Ontario, New Brunswick, Manitoba, Saskatchewan and Alberta), the Canadian government returns approximately 90% of direct federal fuel charge revenues to individuals and families through the Climate Action Incentive programme. The remaining proceeds go to support municipalities, small and medium-sized businesses, schools, hospitals, universities and colleges, non-profit organisations and indigenous communities.

(*Continued*)

Table 1. (Continued).

Country/Subnational Entity, type of Regulation	Year of Implementation	Coverage of Sectors and Sources of Emissions	Percentage of Emissions Covered by the System	Point of Regulation (Upstream, Midstream or Downstream)	Price Level	Exceptions, Compensation, Interaction with Other Climate Policy Instruments	Use of Carbon Revenues
Canada Output-Based Pricing System (OBPS), ETS The federal OBPS sets emissions-intensity or output-based standards by sector. Facilities that emit less than their standard earn credits they can sell or bank for future use.	2019	The OBPS applies to GHG emissions of all electricity generation and industrial facilities that emit 50 kt CO_2e per year or more. Industrial facilities that emit above 10 kt CO_2e per year can opt in.	9%	Operators report emissions at a facility level. (upstream).	N/A	OBPS is form of soft regulation for carbon-intensive businesses at risk of carbon leakage that are exempt from paying the federal fuel charge. Businesses included in the system can use eligible offsets to cover their emissions through the implementation of third-party projects in segments of the economy that are not subject to carbon regulation.	
British Columbia, carbon tax	2008	The BC carbon tax applies to GHG emissions from all sectors with some exemptions for the industry, aviation, transport and agriculture sectors. The tax covers all fossil fuels combusted for heat or energy.	70%	Producers and importers of the fossil fuels covered are liable for payment of the tax (upstream).	CAN$40/t CO_2e (US$28/t CO_2e)	Various exemptions as rebates including exported fuels, fuel consumption by aviation and shipping travelling outside British Columbia, and coloured gasoline and coloured diesel purchased by farmers.	Carbon tax revenue is recycled back into the economy through various income tax reductions and tax credits.

(Continued)

Table 1. (Continued).

Country/Subnational Entity, type of Regulation	Year of Implementation	Coverage of Sectors and Sources of Emissions	Percentage of Emissions Covered by the System	Point of Regulation (Upstream, Midstream or Downstream)	Price Level	Exceptions, Compensation, Interaction with Other Climate Policy Instruments	Use of Carbon Revenues
British Columbia GGIRCA, ETS The BC GGIRCA enables a price to be put on emissions of industrial facilities or sectors exceeding a specific limit, in addition to the province's existing revenue neutral carbon tax. ETS covers liquefied natural gas (LNG) facilities currently under construction, once they become operational.	2016	The GGIRCA applies to GHG emissions from liquefied natural gas (LNG) facilities currently under construction, once they become operational.	0%	(businesses that the system should cover have not yet been launched)	Operators are liable for reporting the emissions covered under the BC GGIRCA at a facility level (upstream).	N/A	Operates in parallel with BC carbon tax.
Alberta TIER, ETS Within the system, the cap is set according to facility-specific benchmarks. Businesses can cover their emissions by purchasing permits on the market, implementing emission offsets or buying additional permits from the regulator at a fixed price.	2007	The Alberta TIER applies to GHG emissions from the industry and power sectors except for industrial process emissions. Covers enterprises that emit at least 100 kt CO_2 e per year.	48%	Operators report emissions at a facility level (upstream).	CAN$30/t CO_2e (US$21/t CO_2e)	Covered facilities only face compliance costs for the emissions above their baseline and facilities experiencing economic challenges due to the compliance costs can receive support from the Compliance Cost Containment Programme.	Investment in programmes and policies to reduce emissions as well as to reduce the government debt.

(Continued)

Table 1. (Continued).

Country/Subnational Entity, type of Regulation	Year of Implementation	Coverage of Sectors and Sources of Emissions	Percentage of Emissions Covered by the System	Point of Regulation (Upstream, Midstream or Downstream)	Price Level	Exceptions, Compensation, Interaction with Other Climate Policy Instruments	Use of Carbon Revenues
Colombia, carbon tax	2017	The Colombia carbon tax applies to GHG emissions from all sectors with some minor exemptions. The tax covers all liquid and gaseous fossil fuels used for combustion.	24%	Sellers and importers of the fossil fuels covered are liable for payment of the tax (upstream).		Tax exemptions apply to natural gas consumers that are not in the petrochemical and refinery sectors, and fossil fuel consumers that are certified to be carbon neutral. Income tax does not need to be paid over costs incurred as a result of the carbon tax. Emitters can achieve carbon neutrality through the use of offset credits generated from projects in Colombia.	Currently, all proceeds from this tax go to the Fund for Sustainable Environment and Sustainable Rural Development to support the peace process in areas affected by armed conflict.

Sources: Composed by authors based on Carl and Fedor (2016), IETA (2018), World Bank Carbon Pricing DashBoard, Retrieved 30 October 2020 from https://carbonpricingdashboard.worldbank.org/

the same way as the federal Canadian ETS, but allows emitters included in the system to reduce emissions through the implementation of third-party offset projects. A similar approach is used in the framework of the Australian ETS – Australia ERF Safeguard Mechanism. Emitters included in the system are also not required to buy allowances as long as their emissions are within the industry's acceptable limit, they can buy or sell unused allowances, and implement offset projects to reduce emissions. Finally, a similar ETS, but without the possibility of implementation of offset projects, has been operating in Kazakhstan.

With the exception of the Kazakh system (which covers only CO_2 emissions), the systems cover all major types of GHG. Carbon pricing can apply to different sectors of the economy, including industrial, construction, transport and energy, but the coverage of emissions varies greatly depending on the country: it ranges from 24% in Colombia to 80% in South Africa. The level of the carbon price itself varies significantly – it ranges from one in Kazakhstan to 53 dollars per ton of emissions in Norway.

A distinctive feature of the carbon pricing for most energy exporting countries is the regulation of emissions at the level of production or distribution of primary energy (upstream). In other words, even though emissions occur during the industrial production or electricity generation from fossil fuels, the carbon price is imposed on extractive companies or on primary energy suppliers, whose number is usually less than that of the direct emitters. This approach makes it possible to simplify the system of monitoring and verification of emissions and ultimately minimises the costs of administration of the carbon pricing system (Weisbach & Metcalf, 2009).

The analysis of the existing carbon pricing systems in energy exporting countries indicates a significant number of exceptions to the general rules of setting a carbon price. A large number of small or particularly vulnerable companies or entire industries enjoy privileges in the form of reduced carbon tax rates or are even excluded from the system. For example, in South Africa, the use of motor fuel by households in the transport industry is completely exempt from paying the carbon tax. In Canada, the federal ETS provides exceptions for the most carbon-intensive enterprises that are exposed to the risks of 'carbon leakage', meaning the loss of international competitiveness.

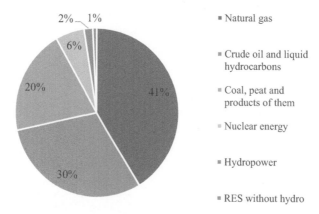

Figure 2. Structure of primary energy consumption in Russia in 2019. Source: Composed by authors based on IEA. World Energy Statistics and Balances.

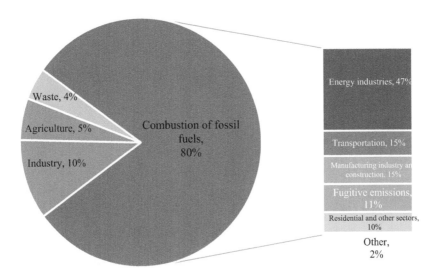

Figure 3. GHG emissions in Russia in 2018 by types of economic activity. Source: Composed by authors based on OECD (2020). Air and climate: Air emissions by source. Environment Statistics.

Finally, a number of systems provide compensatory mechanisms for the redistribution of revenue generated from the carbon tax or through the allocation of allowances under the ETS, aimed at mitigating the negative impact on vulnerable segments of the population or business. In particular, in British Columbia, the carbon tax is introduced on a fiscal-neutral basis: all carbon revenue is spent on reducing income and corporate tax rates; in

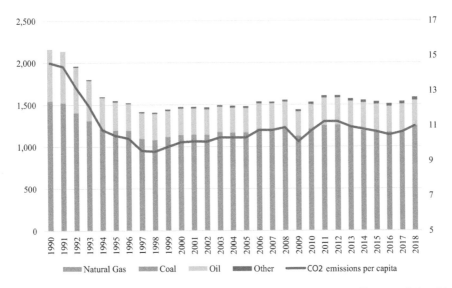

Figure 4. Dynamics of CO_2 emissions from fossil fuels combustion in Russia, million tons (left axis) and CO_2 emissions from fossil fuels combustion per capita, tons CO_2 per capita (right axis). Source: Composed by authors based on IEA (2019). CO2 Emissions from Fuel Combustion. Retrieved 19 =September 2020 from https://www.iea.org/subscribe-to-data-services/co2-emissions-statistics

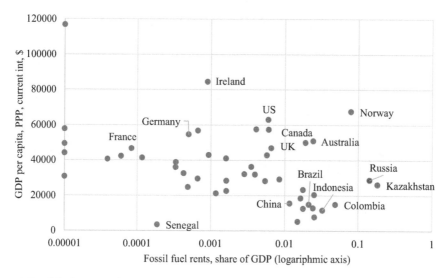

Figure 5. Fossil fuel rents and GDP per capita in Russia and countries that have carbon pricing systems implemented, scheduled for implementation or under consideration. Source: Composed by authors by authors based on World Development Indicators, World Bank (2020)

Norway, 30% of the collected revenue is spent on reducing corporate taxes for individual companies. In Canada, all funds collected under the federal and provincial systems are returned to the provincial budgets where they are collected, and among other things are used to finance special programmes to support vulnerable households and individuals.

Fossil fuels and their role in the Russian economy and GHG emissions

Russia is a net exporter of all types of fossil fuels. In energy units, crude oil and petroleum products are the most exported part of fossil-fuel production – 379.4 million toe per year. Exports of natural gas and coal amounts to 180.3 and 103.4 million toe, respectively. In total, the country exports about half (46%) of all energy produced.[9] The remaining part is consumed domestically, including for the manufacturing of carbon-intensive goods produced for exports.

Natural gas accounts for 41% of all primary energy consumption in Russia and 39% of its production. Thirty percentage of primary energy consumption in Russia is presented by oil and liquid hydrocarbons, 20% – by coal, 6% – by nuclear energy and 2% – by hydropower. Solar and wind energy generation still play a modest role (~1%) in primary energy consumption (Figure 2).

The fossil fuels combustion is responsible for 80% of all GHG emissions in Russia.[10] Almost half of them (47%) occur in energy sectors, including electricity and heat production, and 30% generated by the transport sector, the industrial production and construction (Figure 3).

Carbon dioxide accounts for 76% of all GHG emissions; methane accounts for 8%, nitrogen dioxide – 4%, hydrochlorofluorocarbons and other gases-less than 2% (OECD, 2020). More than a half (50.3%) of Russian CO_2 emissions from the fossil fuel combustion come from the production of electricity and heat. Other industrial sectors and construction account for 17.1% of emissions, transport – for 16% (OECD, 2020).

In 2018, the total amount of CO_2 emissions from fossil fuel combustion accounted for 1.59 billion tons. CO_2 emissions have remained roughly at the same level since the early 2000s. Since 2012 they have decreased by 4.4% (Figure 4). Emissions per capita also show a similar trend. Having peaked in 2012, they declined by 2.2% by 2018. The largest contribution to the total amount of CO_2 emissions from the burning of fossil fuels is made by natural gas – 52% of all CO_2 emissions, 25% come from oil and petroleum products combustion, and 21% – from coal combustion (Figure 4).

The hydrocarbon production and use sectors account for 25% of Russian GDP and 39% of federal budget revenues, 60% of export revenues, and almost a quarter of total fixed capital investment in Russia (Ministry of Energy, 2019; Ministry of Finance, 2020; Mitrova & Melnikov, 2019). These values are among the highest among all countries where carbon regulation is currently in effect (Figure 5).

Figure 5 shows similarities of Russia and Kazakhstan with regard to the levels of GDP per capita and the share of fossil fuel rents in the countries' GDP. Both countries are characterised by a high role of fossil fuels in the economy, post-Communist legacy in economic policy, underdevelopment of market institutions which may hinder socio-economic development (and, thus, lead to lower levels of per capita GDP). Countries which are yet to develop mature market institutions may face obstacles introducing carbon taxes or an ETS, including high costs of administration (costs for emission monitoring and verification) (Finon, 2019). In 2016, the Kazakhstan's ETS, being initially launched in 2013, was suspended until 2018, due to the lack of efficiency in the allowances' allocation methods and trading procedures (Carbon Pulse, 2016). The system was officially relaunched in 2018, however, the carbon price is still at the negligible level of 1 dollar per ton of CO_2-eq. (World Bank, 2020)

Under the circumstances of high fossil-fuel dependence and lack of institutional quality, thoughtless introduction of a carbon price in the Russian economy – without considering specifics of vulnerable sectors and the impacts for the low-income population groups – is fraught with serious shocks and is unlikely to be a politically feasible instrument of climate policy. Any additional fiscal burden (in the form of a tax or price of ETS) in the energy sector or carbon-intensive industries could be accompanied by a partial loss of their competitiveness in the foreign markets. The introduction of a carbon price on top of existing taxes could lead to an overall increase in prices in the economy and, as a result, a drop in real incomes of the population. In addition, the introduction of a carbon price can exacerbate inequality, in other words, lead to a relatively greater drop in the real incomes of the least affluent groups of the population, who spend most of their income on energy-intensive products. The possibilities of mitigating these and other negative consequences of the introduction of a carbon price lie in the development of a specific design of the carbon pricing system that takes into account the specifics of the Russian economy.

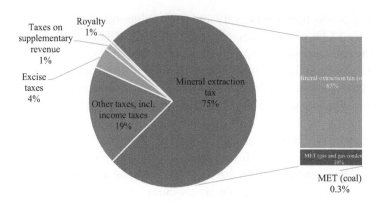

Figure 6. Structure of tax revenues from the energy sector to the Russian federal budget in 2019. Source: Composed by authors by the authors based on to the Federal Tax Service Data on the receipt of taxes and fees in the consolidated budget of the Russian FederationNote: the data are shown without export customs duties revenues and revenues from VAT

Key elements of the carbon pricing design in Russia

Balanced emission coverage and additional supportive measures for vulnerable industries and social groups

An analysis of the international experience of carbon regulation in energy exporting countries demonstrates that the negative effects of the introduction of a carbon price can be foreseen and minimised. This requires proper integration of the carbon price into the existing system of economic incentives in place in the economy. In order to avoid the negative consequences of fiscal-regressive nature of carbon prices, the system of economic regulation of emissions can either be a) fiscally neutral (e.g. be accompanied by a parallel decrease in the rates of other taxes) or b) suggest a mechanism for the redistribution of funds (in the form of tax revenues from a carbon tax or auctions under ETS) in favour of the most vulnerable groups of the population.

Even the gradual introduction of carbon price elements into the existing fiscal system will require a set of exemptions along with compensatory measures for the most vulnerable sectors of the economy. One of the most vulnerable sectors is the Russian coal industry, which performs an important socio-economic function. The coal industry itself provides 150 thousand jobs (and more than 1 million people are employed in related industries); coal accounts for about 22% of all energy production, and in some regions significantly more (in the Far Eastern Federal District – 42%) (Khokhlov & Melnikov, 2019; Ministry of Energy, 2019). In this regard, the introduction of a carbon price should be accompanied by the implementation of a set of measures to help coal industry workers, their retraining, material support for vulnerable households, etc.

Integration of the carbon price into the system of existing taxes in the energy sector

A careful and gradual integration of the carbon price into the existing fiscal system in the Russian energy sector, with an increase in the rates of some taxes accompanied by a decrease in others, can help mitigate the negative consequences for sensitive sectors of the economy. In other words, the alternative to a simple introduction of a carbon price in the form of a carbon tax or ETS may be a gradual transformation of the current energy tax system. The level of taxation in the Russian energy sector per unit of emissions is already at a fairly high level – at least 30 USD per ton of CO_2 emissions.[11] One can say that CO_2 emissions in Russia are already indirectly taxed.

But the current tax system in the energy sector largely performs a fiscal function and is limited in its ability to influence the dynamics of GHG emissions and the carbon intensity of domestic production. In 2019, 75.5% of tax revenues in the energy fuel sector were provided by the mineral extraction tax (MET), with the oil MET accounting for the largest share of 65.2%. The remaining part consists of corporate income tax, excise taxes on motor fuel, taxes on additional income from the extraction of hydrocarbons, as well as regular payments for the extraction of minerals (royalties) (Figure 6).

The analysis of the cases of other energy exporting countries shows that many of them regulate emissions at the production level, which significantly simplifies the process of emissions monitoring and verification and ultimately facilitates the administration of carbon pricing. The tax base in the Russian energy fuel sector is already mainly concentrated at the level of production. But taxation in the Russian energy sector does not yet take into account the carbon intensity of various sources of fossil energy, which significantly limits the possibility of mitigating risks associated with low-carbon transition in foreign markets. One of the possibilities of carbon regulation may be the gradual incorporation of elements of the carbon price in the Russian MET on a fiscal-neutral basis.

Gradual tightening of carbon pricing

International experience shows that carbon price is usually introduced gradually – phased development of the carbon pricing system involves the systematic growth in tax rates and the emissions coverage. In the coming decades, fossil fuels will continue to play a key role in the energy supply of the world economy (I. A. Makarov et al., 2020; BP, 2019; IEA, 2019). In this regard, the priority of the low-carbon development of the Russian economy is not the introduction of a high carbon price with a large coverage of emissions. Rather, the priority should be given to the creation of conditions for gradual transformation of the current system of economic incentives towards a more carbon-content focused one – the one which takes into account the carbon intensity of various energy sources and the production processes associated with their consumption.

When planning a carbon regulatory system in Russia, international experience can be useful in terms of using emissions trading systems with free allocation of allowances for emissions within established industry standards or in accordance with the historical emissions of certain issuing enterprises (see examples of the federal system of Canada, Alberta, Australia and Kazakhstan). This approach, on the one hand, will help avoid short-term damage from carbon pricing to the most vulnerable companies and, on the other hand, will send an unambiguous signal to growing companies that an increase in output will be accompanied by an additional carbon price aimed at adjusting their long-term business strategies.

Applying carbon offsets

The system of carbon offsets could play an important role in reducing emissions as well as in creating wider positive economic impacts. It implies that companies covered by the carbon pricing system may fulfil their emissions reduction commitments through investing in low-carbon projects that are not directly related to their production activities. It means that emissions may be reduced in the cheapest possible way even if the cheapest low-carbon projects fall within the economic sectors which are difficult to be regulated directly. Cases of other energy-exporting countries show that the implementation of the offset projects is possible both under the ETS (see case of Alberta) and the carbon tax (see case of South Africa).

In Russia, there are many opportunities to reduce emissions outside the large companies' facilities which may be easily included in carbon pricing scheme. These opportunities are especially large in the forestry sector. The potential of reforestation in Russia is estimated at 151 million ha with mitigation potentials of up to 351 Mt CO_2/year (Leskinen et al., 2020). Waste sector responsible for about 6% of Russian emissions is the only sector in the country where emissions now are higher than in 1990 that makes it a low-hanging fruit in terms of emissions reduction potential. The significant opportunities are related to energy efficiency improvement in housing and construction (Denisova, 2019; McKinsey & Company, 2009; Pao et al., 2011). Offsets may also link carbon regulation with renewable energy support: for instance, large companies may fulfil their emissions reduction commitment through building renewables energy capacities even if energy generated by these capacities is not consumed by these companies directly.

Conclusion

This paper contributes to the existing literature with the analysis of opportunities and options of carbon pricing in fossil fuel exporting countries with a special focus on Russia. In fossil fuel abundant and exporting countries, carbon pricing naturally faces constrains of falling corporate and state revenues coming from fossil fuel industries. Russia, as an energy exporting economy, has a different system of incentives underling climate policies compared to energy-importing economies where most of the existing carbon pricing initiatives have been launched. The opposition of business against carbon price and concerns of government agencies is much stronger in Russia due to the central role fossil fuels in the economy. The high role of fossil fuels in the economy combined with the lack of efficient economic and political institutions underlie the weakness of the climate policy in the country.

Although the political economy analysis of carbon pricing stays outside the scope of this research, one can notice strong resemblance of the Russia's and the Kazakhstan's climate policies stemming from similar historical patterns of economic and political development. Russia has not carbon price in place. Even though Kazakhstan managed to implement ETS in 2013, after eight years, the carbon price still takes value of 1 dollar per CO_2-eq. which is far from creating sufficient incentives for low-carbon transition (Howie et al., 2020). It contrasts to the level of carbon price in other developing economies (South Africa and Columbia) exporting fossil-fuels let alone the developed ones (Norway, Canada, and Australia). For example, South Africa puts the price on carbon at the level of seven dollars per CO_2-eq., while the carbon tax was introduced just in 2019 and covers 80% of emissions in the country. Starting from 2017, Columbia puts the price on carbon which currently takes the value of 21 dollar per CO_2-eq. and covers 24% of emissions.

Based on previous studies, that paper distinguished main risks of energy transition for Russian economy and highlights a set of external incentives for Russia to shift to more ambitious climate policies in the future. Firstly, the international and global pressure from so-called external actors (e.g. international organisations), from international markets is growing: from investors, buyers of Russian goods and foreign regulators (for instance, in the form of carbon border adjustment mechanism in the EU).

The role of external actors and membership in international organisations can either encourage incentives for more efficient socio-economic development through climate change mitigation policies or, on the contrary, sustain the lack of such an incentive. A few studies on the role of state's membership in such regional international organisations as the EU already demonstrated the impact of such a membership on diffusion of values and standards (e.g. see L.B. Andonova, 2003; Pevehouse, 2005; Arpino and Obydenkova 2019; Lankina et al., 2016a). Another set of studies demonstrated that membership can be associated not only with promotion of good governance and sustainable development (as it the case with the EU, the European Bank for Reconstruction and Development, the democracies-led Regional development banks, see Ben-Artzi 2016; Obydenkova & Vieira, 2020), but also with pragmatic economic benefits and economic development at any cost justified by such values as stability (e.g. the case of China-led international organisations, see Ambrosio 2008; Libman & Obydenkova, 2013, 2018a, 2018b; Kneuer and Demmelhuber eds. 2020; Izotov & Obydenkova, 2021).[12] Therefore, it is important to consider this ambiguity of international influence in terms of promotion and diffusion of values and practices across its member-states of different international organisations. Considering the importance of these issues for the understanding the diffusion of environmental policies and values, it must stay on the agenda for further studies.

Secondly, global green transition and related reduction of the demand for fossil fuels would push Russia to search for other sources of economic growth and diversify its economy. The climate policy, with a carbon price being a part of it, may be the one of the tools of such diversification.

The analysis of carbon pricing in energy-exporting economies shows that its feasibility depends on the regulatory design capable to carefully consider the specifics of socio-economic dynamics of a country or region where the regulation is introduced. Based on the investigation of cases of carbon regulation in other energy exporting countries (Canada, Norway, South Africa, Australia, and Kazakhstan) and the specifics of Russian emissions structure and energy-related taxation, we revealed four principles of emissions regulation which may alleviate the risks attributed to the carbon pricing in Russia.

Firstly, carbon regulation scheme should have balanced emission coverage, supplemented by various exemptions and supportive measures for vulnerable industries and social groups related to them. Secondly, carbon price should not be introduced in addition to the existing fiscal system in energy sector but rather should be integrated into it. Carbon regulation should be fiscal neutral, its introduction should be compensated by the proportional reduction of other taxes, first of all those that are related to energy use. Thirdly, regulation should be introduced and tightened gradually, giving the time to the economy to adjust, and to regulators to correct possible mistakes and disproportions. Fourthly, carbon offsets should be used in order to minimise costs of emissions reductions and open opportunities for cheap emissions reduction outside the regulated sectors and outside large business's activities. We consider these principles as necessary conditions of making carbon pricing in Russia cost-efficient, inclusive, compatible with the objective of economic growth in the country and, therefore, politically feasible.

There are two important limitations of the study. Firstly, we do not fully touch upon institutional and political economy constraints of carbon pricing in Russia as an economy in transition focusing solely on its economic regulatory design capable to smooth adverse effects for vulnerable social and business groups. Secondly, the paper does not consider the differences of multiple Russian regions which potentially may introduce carbon price independently from federal climate policy. The analysis of climate policy action at the level of Russian subnational entities – both fossil-fuel abundant ones and not – represents a promising area for further research.

Notes

1. Calculated by authors based on World Bank Open Data. Retrieved 7 April 2021, from https://data.worldbank.org/
2. Based on World Resource Institute, CAIT Climate Data Explorer, Historical GHG Emissions. Retrieved 7 April 2021, from https://www.climatewatchdata.org/
3. Ibid.
4. Ibid.
5. According to UNFCCC. *NDC registry*. Retrieved 7 April 2021 https://www4.unfccc.int/sites/ndcstaging/PublishedDocuments/Russia%20First/NDC_RF_ru.pdf
6. According to the draft of the Federal Law on Limiting GHG Emissions. Retrieved 25 April https://sozd.duma.gov.ru/bill/1116605-7
7. Calculated by authors based on UNFCCC emissions inventory data
8. Authors' calculation based on IEA World Energy Balances and the data provided by the subnational authorities
9. Based on IEA. *World Energy Statistics and Balances*. Retrieved 11 October 2020 from https://www.iea.org/subscribe-to-data-services/world-energy-balances-and-statistics
10. Excluding emissions from LULUCF.
11. Based on the ratio of MET taxes to total CO_2 emissions from the burning of fossil fuels
12. There is also a different issue of diffusion of values across the international organisations. Recent studies looked into how international organisations in post-Communist Eurasia (especially those led by China and Russia) interact with other IOs in the region and in global economic system (for summary, see Libman & Obydenkova, 2021a, p. 2021b).

Acknowledgments

This work is an output of a research project implemented as part of the Basic Research Program at the National Research University Higher School of Economics (HSE University). Support from the Individual Research Program of the Faculty of World Economy and International Affairs at National

Research University Higher School of Economics is gratefully acknowledged.

Disclosure statement

Authors declare no competing interests.

References

Ambrosio, T. (2008). Catching the 'Shanghai spirit': how the Shanghai Cooperation Organization promotes authoritarian norms in Central Asia. *Europe-Asia Studies,60*(8), 1321–1344.

Andonova, L. B. (2003). *Transnational politics of the environment: The European Union and Environmental Policy in Central and Eastern Europe.* MIT Press.

Andonova, L. B. (2008). The climate regime and domestic politics: The case of Russia. *Cambridge Review of International Affairs, 21*(4), 483–504. https://doi.org/10.1080/09557570802452789

Andonova, L. B., & Alexieva, A. (2012). Continuity and change in Russia's climate negotiations position and strategy. *Climate Policy, 12*(5), 614–629. https://doi.org/10.1080/14693062.2012.691227

Arabella Advisors. (2018). *The global fossil fuel divestment and clean energy investment movement.* https://www.arabellaadvisors.com/wp-content/uploads/2018/09/Global-Divestment-Report-2018.pdf

Arlinghaus, J. (2015). Impacts of carbon prices on indicators of competitiveness: A review of empirical findings. *OECD Environment Working Papers No. 87*, OECD. https://doi.org/10.1787/5js37p21grzq-en

Arpino, B., & Obydenkova, A. V. (2019). Democracy and political trust before and after the great recession 2008: The European Union and the United Nations. *Social Indicators Research*, 1–21.

BCG. (2020, July 29). *Uglerodnyj vyzov rossijskim eksporteram [Carbon challenge for Russian exporters].* https://www.bcg.com/ru-ru/press/29july2020-carbon-challenge-to-russian-exporters

Ben-Artzi, R. (2016). *Regional development banks in comparison:Banking strategies versus development goals.* Cambridge University Press.

BP. (2019). *BP energy outlook 2019.* https://www.bp.com/en/global/corporate/news-and-insights/press-releases/bp-energy-outlook-2019.html

Brink, C., Vollebergh, H. R., & Van Der Werf, E. (2016). Carbon pricing in the EU: Evaluation of different EU ETS reform options. *Energy Policy, 97*, 603–617. https://doi.org/10.1016/j.enpol.2016.07.023

Carbon Pulse. (2016). *Kazakhstan suspends ETS until 2018 – Minister*, Retrieved April 7, 2021, from https://carbon-pulse.com/16179/

Carl, J., & Fedor, D. (2016). Tracking global carbon revenues: A survey of carbon taxes versus cap-and-trade in the real world. *Energy Policy, 96*, 50–77. https://doi.org/10.1016/j.enpol.2016.05.023

Climate Doctrine of the Russian Federation. 2009. *Retrieved April 7, 2021, from* http://kremlin.ru/events/president/news/6365

Davydova, A. (2020, July 31). *Debaty o klimate stanovyatsya zharche [Climate debates are getting hotter].* Kommersant. https://www.kommersant.ru/doc/4435261l 11, 2021

Denisova, V. (2019). Energy efficiency as a way to ecological safety: Evidence from Russia. *International Journal of Energy Economics and Policy, 9*(5), 32–37. https://doi.org/10.32479/ijeep.7903

Edelgeriev, R. (2020, June 11). *"Cena na uglerod" kak instrument ekonomicheskoj i ekologicheskoj politiki ["Carbon Price" as a tool of economic and environmental policy].* Kommersant. https://www.kommersant.ru/doc/4377361

EU Parliament.*Towards a WTO-compatible EU carbon border adjustment mechanism.* 2020/2043(INI). Retrieved April 11, 2021, from https://oeil.secure.europarl.europa.eu/oeil/popups/ficheproce dure.do?lang=en&reference=2020/2043(INI)

European Commission. (n.d.). *Climate strategies & targets*. Retrieved December 29, 2020 from https://ec.europa.eu/clima/policies/strategies_en

Fan, Y., Jia, J. J., Wang, X., & Xu, J. H. (2017). What policy adjustments in the EU ETS truly affected the carbon prices? *Energy Policy, 103*, 145–164. https://doi.org/10.1016/j.enpol.2017.01.008

Finon, D. (2019). Carbon policy in developing countries: Giving priority to non-price instruments. *Energy Policy, 132*, 38–43. https://doi.org/10.1016/j.enpol.2019.04.046

Fredriksson, P. G., & Neumayer, E. (2013). Democracy and climate change policies: Is history important? *Ecological Economics, 95*(C), 11–19. https://doi.org/10.1016/j.ecolecon.2013.08.002

Goulder, L. H., & Parry, I. W. (2008). Instrument choice in environmental policy. *Review of Environmental Economics and Policy, 2*(2), 152–174. https://doi.org/10.1093/reep/ren005

Grainger, C. A., & Kolstad, C. D. (2010). Who pays a price on carbon? *Environmental and Resource Economics, 46*(3), 359–376. https://doi.org/10.1007/s10640-010-9345-x

Green, J. F. (2021). Does carbon pricing reduce emissions? A review of ex-post analyses. *Environmental Research Letters, 4*(16), 043004. https://doi.org/10.1088/1748-9326/abdae9

Grigoriev, L. M., Makarov, I. A., Sokolova, A. K., Pavlyushina, V. A., & Stepanov, I. A. (2020). Climate change and inequality: How to solve these problems jointly? *International Organisation Research Journal, 15*(1). https://iorj.hse.ru/data/2020/02/14/1576410997/Climate%20Change%20and%20Inequality.pdf

Hájek, M., Zimmermannová, J., Helman, K., & Rozenský, L. (2019). Energy policy. *Analysis of Carbon Tax Efficiency in Energy Industries of Selected EU Countries, 134*(C), 110955. https://doi.org/10.1016/j.enpol.2019.110955

Hoel, M., & Karp, L. (2001). Taxes and quotas for a stock pollutant with multiplicative uncertainty. *Journal of Public Economics, 82*(1), 91–114. https://doi.org/10.1016/S0047-2727(00)00136-5

Howie, P., Gupta, S., Park, H., & Akmetov, D. (2020). Evaluating policy success of emissions trading schemes in emerging economies: Comparing the experiences of Korea and Kazakhstan. *Climate Policy, 20*(5), 577–592. https://doi.org/10.1080/14693062.2020.1751030

IDDRI. (2015). *Deep decarbonization pathways project (2015)*. Pathways to deep decarbonization 2015 report, SDSN - IDDRI.

Ide, T. (2020). Recession and fossil fuel dependence undermine climate policy commitments. *Environmental Research Communications, 2*(10), 101002. https://doi.org/10.1088/2515-7620/abbb27

IEA (2019). *CO2 emissions from fuel combustion*. Retrieved September 19, 2020 from https://www.iea.org/subscribe-to-data-services/co2-emissions-statistics

IEA. (2020a). *World energy outlook 2020*. IEA, Paris. https://www.iea.org/reports/world-energy-outlook-2020

IEA. (2020b). *World energy statistics and balances*. Retrieved October 11, 2020, from https://www.iea.org/subscribe-to-data-services/world-energy-balances-and-statistics

IETA. (2018). *Colombia: An emissions trading case study*. https://www.ieta.org/resources/Resources/Case_Studies_Worlds_Carbon_Markets/2018/Colombia-Case-Study-2018.pdf

Izotov, V. S., & Obydenkova, A. V. (2021). Geopolitical games in Eurasian regionalism: Ideational interactions and regional international organisations. *Post-Communist Economies, 33*(2–3), 150–174. https://doi.org/10.1080/14631377.2020.1793584

Johnsson, F., Kjärstad, J., & Rootzén, J. (2019). The threat to climate change mitigation posed by the abundance of fossil fuels. *Climate Policy, 19*(2), 258–274. https://doi.org/10.1080/14693062.2018.1483885

Khokhlov, A., & Melnikov, Y. (2019). *Ugolnaya generaciya: Novye vyzovy i vozmozhnosti [Coal generation: New challenges and opportunities]*. Moskovskaya shkola upravleniya Skolkovo. https://energy.skolkovo.ru/downloads/documents/SEneC/Research/SKOLKOVO_EneC_Coal_generation_2019.01.01_Rus.pdf

Kneuer, M., & Demmelhuber, T. (2020). Conceptualizing Authoritarian Gravity Centers: Sources and Addressees, Mechanisms and Motives of Authoritarian Pressure and Attraction 1. In *Authoritarian Gravity Centers* (pp. 26–52). Routledge.

Kokorin, A. O., & Korppoo, A. (2014). *Russia's greenhouse gas target 2020: Projections, trends, and risks*. Friedrich-Ebert-Stiftung. Department of Central and Eastern Europe. https://doi.org/10.13140/2.1.3092.8005

Kozlova, M., Makarov, I., & Lanshina, T. (in press). Opposition to renewable energy development: Case of Russia. *Renewable Energy*.

KPMG. (2020, October 14). *The Assessment of impact of the carbon border adjustment (CBA) introduction on the Russian industry*.

Lankina, T., Libman, A., & Obydenkova, A. (2016a). Authoritarian and democratic diffusion in post-communist regions. *Comparative Political Studies*, 49(12), 1599–1629. https://doi.org/10.1177/0010414016628270

Lankina, T., Libman, A., & Obydenkova, A. (2016b). Appropriation and subversion: Pre-communist literacy, communist party saturation, post-Soviet democratic outcomes. *World Politics*, 68(2), 229–274. https://doi.org/10.1017/S0043887115000428

Leskinen, P., Lindner, M., Verkerk, P. J., Nabuurs, G. J., Van Brusselen, J., Kulikova, E., Hassegawa, M., & Lerink, B. Eds. (2020). *Russian forests and climate change: What science can tell us 11*. European Forest Institute.https://doi.org/10.36333/wsctu11

Libman, A., & Obydenkova, A. (2013). Informal governance and participation in non-democratic international organizations. *The Review of International Organizations*, 8(2), 221–245. https://link.springer.com/article/10.1007/s11558-012-9160-y

Libman, A., & Obydenkova, A. (2014). The governance of commons in a large nondemocratic state: The case of forestry in the Russian federation. *Publius: The Journal of Federalism*, 44(2), 298–323. https://doi.org/10.1093/publius/pjt065

Libman, A., & Obydenkova, A. (2019). Inequality and historical legacies: Evidence from post-communist regions. *Post-Communist Economies*, 31(6), 699–724. https://doi.org/10.1080/14631377.2019.1607440

Libman, A., & Obydenkova, A. (2021a). Global governance and interaction between international institutions: The challenge of the Eurasian international organizations. *Post-CommunistEconomies*, 33(2–3), 147–149. https://doi.org/10.1080/14631377.2020.1793585

Libman, A., & Obydenkova, A. (2021b). Global governance and Eurasian international organisations: Lessons learned and future agenda. *Post-Communist Economies*, 33(2–3), 359–377. https://doi.org/10.1080/14631377.2020.1793587

Libman, A., & Obydenkova, A. V. (2018a). Understanding authoritarian regionalism. *Journal of Democracy*, 29(4), 151–165. https://doi.org/10.1353/jod.2018.0070

Libman, A., & Obydenkova, A. V. (2018b). Regional international organizations as a strategy of autocracy: The Eurasian Economic Union and Russian foreign policy. *International Affairs*, 94(5), 1037–1058. https://doi.org/10.1093/ia/iiy147

Makarov, A. A., Mitrova, T. A., & Kulagin, V. A. (2019). *Global and Russian energy outlook 2019*. The Energy Research Institute of the Russian Academy of Sciences, Moscow School of Management SKOLKOVO. https://www.eriras.ru/files/forecast_2019_en.pdf

Makarov, I. A. (2016). Russia's participation in international environmental cooperation. *Strategic Analysis*, 40(6), 536–546. https://doi.org/10.1080/09700161.2016.1224062

Makarov, I. A., Chen, H., & Paltsev, S. (2020). Impacts of climate change policies worldwide on the Russian economy. *Climate Policy*, 20(10), 1242–1256. https://doi.org/10.1080/14693062.2020.1781047

Makarov, I. A., & Sokolova, A. K. (2017). Carbon emissions embodied in Russia's trade: Implications for climate policy. *Review of European and Russian Affairs*, 11(2), 1–20. https://doi.org/10.22215/rera.v11i2.1192

Makarov, I. A., & Stepanov, I. A. (2017). Uglerodnoye regulirovanie: Varianty i vysovy dlya Rossii. Углеродное регулирование: варианты и вызовы для России [Carbon regulation: Options and challenges for Russia]. *Moscow State University Bulletin*, 6(6), 3–22. ISSN 0130–0105.

Marcu, A. (2021). *European CBAM: Consequences for Russia's economy. Presentation at the Online seminar HSE University*. Retrieved April 7, 2021, from https://we.hse.ru/mirror/pubs/share/438765735.pdf

Manley, D., Cust, J. F., & Cecchinato, G. (2017). Stranded nations? The climate policy implications for fossil fuel-rich developing countries.*IRPN: Innovation Strategy (Topic)*.

Mascher, S. (2018). Striving for equivalency across the Alberta, British Columbia, Ontario and Québec carbon pricing systems: The Pan-Canadian carbon pricing benchmark. *Climate Policy, 18*(8), 1012–1027. https://doi.org/10.1080/14693062.2018.1470489

McKinsey & Company. (2009). *Pathways to an energy and carbon efficient Russia*. Retrieved April 7, 2021, from https://www.mckinsey.com/~/media/mckinsey/dotcom/client_service/sustainability/cost%20curve%20pdfs/russian_cost_curve_summary_english.ashx

Meckling, J., Sterner, T., & Sterner, T. (2017). Policy sequencing toward decarbonization. *Nature Energy, 2*(12), 12. https://doi.org/10.1038/s41560-017-0025-8

Ministry of Energy. (2019). *Alexander Novak: «к 2024 godu my mozhem uvelichit investitsii b TAK na 50%» [Alexander Novak: 'By 2024, we can increase investment in energy complex by 50%]* Ministry of Energy. (n.d.). Minenergo. Retrieved April 7, 2021, from https://minenergo.gov.ru

Ministry of Finance. (2020). *Kratkaya informatsiya ob ispolnenii federalnogo budgeta [Brief information about the execution of the Federal budget]*. Retrieved April 7, 2021, from https://www.minfin.ru/ru/statistics/fedbud/execute/?id_65=80041-yezhegodnaya_informatsiya_ob_ispolnenii_federalnogo_byudzhetadannye_s_1_yanvarya_2006_g.#

Mitrova, T., & Melnikov, Y. (2019). Energy transition in Russia. *Energy Transitions, 3*(1–2), 73–80. https://doi.org/10.1007/s41825-019-00016-8

Narassimhan, E., Gallagher, K. S., Koester, S., & Alejo, J. R. (2018). Carbon pricing in practice: A review of existing emissions trading systems. *Climate Policy,18*(8), 967–991.

Nazarov, Z., & Obydenkova, A. V. (2020). Democratization and firm innovation: Evidence from European and Central Asian post-communist states. *Post-Communist Economies, 32*(7), 833–859. https://doi.org/10.1080/14631377.2020.1745565

Obydenkova, A., & Bruno, A. (2018). Corruption and Trust in the European Union and National Institutions: Changes over the great recession across European states. *Journal of Common Market Studies, 56*(3), 594–611. https://doi.org/10.1111/jcms.12646

Obydenkova, A., Nazarov, Z., & Salahodjaev, R. (2016). The process of deforestation in the weak democracies and the role of intelligence. *Environmental Research, 148*, 484–490. https://doi.org/10.1016/j.envres.2016.03.039

Obydenkova, A. V., & Salahodjaev, R. (2016). Intelligence, democracy, and international environmental commitment. *Environmental Research, 147*, 82–88. https://doi.org/10.1016/j.envres.2016.01.042

Obydenkova, A. V., & Salahodjaev, R. (2017). *Climate change policies: The role of democracy and social cognitive capital. Environmental research, 157*, 182–189. http://dx.doi.org/10.1016/j.envres.2017.05.009.

Obydenkova, A. V., & Vieira, V. G. R. (2020). The limits of collective financial statecraft: Regional development banks and voting alignment with the United States at the United Nations General Assembly. *International Studies Quarterly, 64*(1), 13–25. https://doi.org/10.1093/isq/sqz080

OECD. (2020). *Air and climate: Air emissions by source*. Environment Statistics. https://doi.org/10.1787/env-data-en.

Pao, H.-T., Yu, H.-C., & Yang, Y.-H. (2011). Modeling the CO2 emissions, energy use, and economic growth in Russia. *Energy, 36*(8), 5094–5100. https://doi.org/10.1016/j.energy.2011.06.004

Payne, R. A. (1995). Freedom and the Environment. *Journal of Democracy, 6*(3), 41–55. https://doi.org/10.1353/jod.1995.0053

Peszko, G., Van Der Mensbrugghe, D., Golub, A., Ward, J., Zenghelis, D., Marijs, C., ... Midgley, A. 2020). *Diversification and cooperation in a decarbonizing World: Climate strategies for fossil fuel-dependent countries*. The World Bank. Retrieved April 7, 2021, from https://openknowledge.worldbank.org/handle/10986/34011

Pevehouse, J. C. (2005). *Democracy from above? Regional organizations and democratization*. Cambridge University Press.

Pizer, W. A. (2002). Combining price and quantity controls to mitigate global climate change. *Journal of Public Economics, 85*(3), 409–434. https://doi.org/10.1016/S0047-2727(01)00118-9

Pop-Eleches, G. & Tucker, J. (2017). *Communism's Shadow*. Princeton: Princeton University Press. https://doi.org/10.1515/9781400887828

Presidential Decree on GHG Emissions Reduction. 2020. Administration of President of Russian Federation. Retrieved April 7, http://www.kremlin.ru/acts/bank/45990

Schmitz, H. (2017). Who drives climate-relevant policies in the rising powers? *New Political Economy*, *22*(5), 521–540. https://doi.org/10.1080/13563467.2017.1257597

Shirov, A. (2021). *Stsenarii vsyo eschyo ostayuttsya nedostatochno prozrachnymi [The scenarios remain insufficiently clear]*, Kommersant. Retrieved January 19, 2021, from https://www.kommersant.ru/doc/4653101.

The project of the strategy of the long-term development of Russia with low greenhouse gas emissions 2050. (2020) Retrieved April 7, 2021, from https://economy.gov.ru/material/news/minekonomrazvitiya_rossii_podgotovilo_proekt_strategii_dolgosrochnogo_razvitiya_rossii_s_nizkim_urovnem_vybrosov_parnikovyh_gazov_do_2050_goda_.html

Tørstad, V., Sælen, H., & Bøyum, L. S. (2020). The domestic politics of international climate commitments: Which factors explain cross-country variation in NDC ambition? *Environmental Research Letters*, *15*(2), 024021. https://doi.org/10.1088/1748-9326/ab63e0

Weisbach, D. A., & Metcalf, G. E. (2009). The design of a carbon tax. *SSRN Electronic Journal*, *33*(2), 499–506. https://doi.org/10.2139/ssrn.1327260

World Bank. (2020). *State and trends of carbon pricing*. Retrieved April 7, 2021, from https://openknowledge.worldbank.org/handle/10986/33809

Post-Soviet states and CO_2 emissions: the role of foreign direct investment

Raufhon Salahodjaev and Arletta Isaeva

ABSTRACT
Natural resource abundance, growth-oriented strategies and low environmental concern of post-Soviet states may exacerbate the consequences of climate change significantly. This study considers the relationship between CO_2 emissions, economic development, foreign investment inflows, trade and energy use in 20 post-Soviet states between 1995 and 2017. A panel cointegration test reveals the long-term cointegrating relationship between the variables. Long-term elasticities are reported using Dynamic Ordinary Least Squares and Fully Modified Ordinary Least Squares regressions, which yield quite similar results: GDP per capita, foreign direct investment (FDI) inflows, trade and energy use positively related to CO_2 emissions per capita in the long term. A panel causality test, however, identifies unidirectional causality running from CO_2 emissions to energy use at $p<0.01$. In other words, greater economic activity in terms of foreign capital inflows, larger trade shares, extensive energy use and economic development, harm the environment through increasing CO_2 emissions and strengthen the need for greater environmental and climate change concerns. The study aims to contribute to this Special Issue through accounting for the role of foreign direct investment and foreign trade in the sustainable development of post-Soviet states.

1. Introduction

Global climate change and its warming trend is a dismal consequence of human activity and it is believed that global temperatures will continue to demonstrate a significant increase along with growing greenhouse gases. According to NASA, global surface temperatures in 2020 and 2016 were the hottest on record. Moreover, the past 7 years have been the warmest 7 years in NASA's observation history.[1] One of the crucial drivers of climate change is the rise in the levels of CO_2 emissions in the atmosphere. Compared to other reactive gases, such as nitrous oxide, ozone and other ozone-forming chemicals, CO_2 is relatively long-lived and can stay in the atmosphere for between 300 and 1000 years, thereby creating long-lasting consequences for humanity. Since the beginning of the industrial era, concentrations of CO_2 emissions have increased by 47% (Buis, 2019) and at the same time global temperature has increased by 2°C since 1880–1900 (Lindsey & Dahlman, 2021) which have jointly led to an increase in accumulated heat and thus, to temperature extremes and seasonal shifts. According to Dellink et al. (2019), it is projected that by 2060 global economy losses will constitute 1.0–3.3% and labour productivity and agriculture will suffer the most.

The socioeconomic consequences of growing CO_2 emissions and climate change provide a significant threat for development and livelihoods by altering physical geography, impairing the environmental situation, undermining food security and destroying livelihoods. Underdeveloped and developing economies, which rely heavily on agriculture, are at greater risk from the negative impact of climate change and stagnation. Human wellbeing is impacted indirectly through loss of biodiversity, environmental deterioration, increased risk of extreme weather events (e.g. drought, floods), health risks, greater exposure to hunger and water crises and finally, the need for continuous adaptation of daily activities in all areas including agriculture, forestry, tourism and infrastructure. Therefore, the causes and correlates of CO_2 emissions across developing and developed countries have been intensively investigated in the empirical literature (Udara Willhelm Abeydeera et al., 2019).

Sample cross-national studies show that energy consumption and economic growth are among the drivers of carbon emissions across countries (Chen et al., 2012; Menegaki, 2014). The logic behind the growth–energy–emissions nexus is twofold. First, it is explained and suggested by the Environmental Kuznets Curve (EKC) that a parabolic relationship exists between economic growth and CO_2 emissions (Grossman & Krueger, 1991; Iwata et al., 2012; Leal & Marques, 2020). Second, there is a causal relationship between energy consumption and economic growth and four underlying hypotheses – growth, conservation, feedback and neutrality. Resource abundant economies often focus their attention on resource mining and exports to satisfy their growth-related intentions, underestimating the importance of environmental policies. At the same time, higher consumption of conventional energy sources is associated with burning coal, oil and gas, which in turn leads to greater carbon dioxide emissions (Sadikov et al., 2020; Salahuddin & Gow, 2014; Soytas et al., 2007).

On the other hand, a separate strand of empirical literature shows that drivers of CO_2 emissions and energy use, such as Foreign Direct Investment (FDI), tourism, trade and financial development, among others, may also have both direct and indirect effects on carbon emissions (Gökmenoğlu & Taspinar, 2016; Jebli et al., 2019). FDI may influence environmental degradation through two conflicting channels: the 'pollution haven' hypothesis and the 'halo effect' hypothesis. The pollution haven hypothesis suggests that the relocation of 'dirty' industries from high-income countries to less economically developed countries leads to the rise in CO_2 emissions in the host countries. FDI increases energy consumption and financial development which, as suggested above, are among the main drivers of air pollution. In addition, less stringent environmental standards in developing countries attract foreign companies driven by the goal of production cost minimisation, again increasing carbon emissions. In contrast, the pollution halo hypothesis implies that there is a negative link between FDI and environmental degradation (Balsalobre-Lorente et al., 2019). These studies suggest that FDI brings innovations and energy efficient and environmentally friendly technologies that permit nations to decrease carbon emissions.

Similar arguments are put forward by research investigating the roles that trade expansion and policies play in explaining carbon emissions. For example, trade openness may reduce market failures, improve the strategy of resource distribution by the economic system and speed up the adoption of international environmental standards (Shahbaz et al., 2017). In contrast, opponents of trade openness refer to the neoclassical model which postulates that international economic division would result in an increase in air pollution with the expansion of trade in less developed nations (Copeland & Taylor, 1995). Financial development may either bring environmentally friendly technologies and reduce CO_2 emissions (Shahbaz et al., 2013) or it may nourish already well-established sectors, which are based on fossil fuels, and thus increase the amounts of CO_2 emitted (Abbasi & Riaz, 2016). Such a negative relationship is particularly true for developing and emerging economies, whose main goal is to increase income. Improved financial systems, however, may reduce the carbon footprint later when the financial sector is liberalised greatly.

In light of the significant socioeconomic impact of carbon emissions, the aim of this research is to explore the long-term and causal relationship between CO_2 emissions, economic growth, foreign direct investment (FDI hereafter), energy consumption and trade in a sample of 20 post-Soviet countries: Armenia, Azerbaijan, Belarus, Bulgaria, Croatia, Czech Republic, Estonia, Hungary, Kazakhstan, Kyrgyz Republic, Latvia, Lithuania, Moldova, Poland, Romania, Russian Federation, Slovak Republic, Slovenia, Turkmenistan and Ukraine, between 1995 and 2017. Countries of the post-Soviet bloc represent a curious sample in this sense because of resource abundance, great aspirations for achieving high growth rates, extensive energy use and above-average carbon emissions. Moreover, the political background of the post-Soviet economies has imposed certain attitudes, such as low environmental concern. With the exception of Russia and some other former Soviet states, the Central European post-Soviet economies mostly became members of the EU. EU membership was transformative for the new post-Soviet EU members not only in strengthening democracy, human rights and a market economy, but also in affecting public resources management – this trend remained even despite the financial crisis in 2008 (Armingeon & Ceka, 2014; Armingeon & Guthmann, 2014; Arpino & Obydenkova, 2020; Obydenkova, 2012; Obydenkova & Arpino, 2018). EU membership is associated with certain expectations to promote a green agenda or at least to consider the goals and values of sustainable development, unlike the path of their non-EU counterparts. Finally, climate change issues hit the post-Soviet bloc harshly. For example, the climate change performance index for 2021 ranks Kazakhstan 55th, Russia 52nd, Slovenia 51st, Hungary 50th, Poland 48th and Czech Republic 47th of 61 nations.[2] These features of the post-Soviet states make them an interesting object of research in order to explore the interrelationship between economic growth, energy consumption, FDI and carbon emissions.

The rest of the study is developed as follows. Section 2 provides a brief overview of the related literature. Section 3 presents the data and empirical methodology, while Section 4 offers the main results. Finally, Section 5 concludes the study and provides policy recommendations.

2. Literature review

2.1. Economic growth, energy and CO_2 emissions

The literature on the CO_2–energy–growth nexus has been growing quickly over the last two decades. For example, Ang (2007) uses French data between 1960 and 2000 to explore the dynamic causal relationship between carbon dioxide emissions, energy consumption and economic development by applying the cointegration approach and vector error-correction model. Ang's findings suggest that economic development enhances both energy consumption and pollution in the long term. Similar results are obtained by Acaravci and Ozturk (2010), who find that economic growth caused energy consumption and energy consumption caused CO_2 emissions by employing an autoregressive distributed lag (ARDL) bound testing approach for 19 European countries. Their findings suggest a long-term cointegrating relationship between CO_2 emissions, energy consumption and GDP per capita in seven economies in their sample. Positive long-term elasticities were observed between emissions and energy consumption and GDP per capita. Granger causality models reveal short-term bidirectional causality running from GDP per capita to energy consumption for some countries. For Denmark and Italy, a causal relationship between GDP per capita and carbon emissions is observed. Al-mulali and Normee Che Sab (2013) explore the link between the variables in 16 emerging countries including Brazil, Chile, China, Egypt, India, Indonesia, Jordan, Malaysia, Mauritius, Mexico, Morocco, Pakistan, Peru, Philippines, South Africa and Thailand during 1980–2008. The Pedroni panel cointegration reveals the long-term relationship between energy consumption, carbon emissions and economic development. Based on Granger-causality test results, energy consumption enhances both economic development and carbon emissions. All in all, previous studies support a long-term relationship between the variables as well as a causal relationship in different groups of countries and timeframes.

Apart from cross-country analysis, the relationship has been widely studied in single-country research. Zhang and Cheng (2009) explore the relationship in China between 1960 and 2007 by employing Granger's approach. They conclude that the Chinese government may adopt energy conservative policies to reduce carbon emissions without any negative impact on economic growth as their empirical analyses demonstrate no causality running from energy and emissions to economic growth. Using data on Russia during 1990–2007, Pao et al. (2011) conclude that emissions are elastic with respect to energy use and inelastic with respect to economic development. Causality analysis indicates significant bidirectional causal relationships between the variables. In other words, change in the amount of carbon emissions is more responsive to changes in the amounts of energy consumed, rather than to changes in GDP.

Bastola and Sapkota (2015) investigate the relationship between economic growth, energy and CO_2 emissions in Nepal. The Granger causality test reveals a causal bidirectional relationship between energy and carbon emissions, and unidirectional causality running from economic growth to carbon emissions and energy consumption. In other words, more extensive energy consumption directly leads to greater carbon emissions, while rapid economic development enhances carbon emissions and energy consumption. Similarly, Rahman and Kashem (2017) employ the cointegration approach and causality analysis to investigate the relationship between emissions, energy use, and economic and industrial development in Bangladesh between 1972 and 2011. Their findings imply that industrial development and economic growth both cause carbon emissions. Environmental policies thus will impact economic development negatively, exacerbating poverty and unemployment, which in turn may be responsible for tensions.

Such interrelations increase concerns about the adoption of renewable energy sources. For example, Saidi and Omri (2020) conclude that the promotion of renewable energy technologies should have beneficial effects for economic growth and the quality of the environment. Their study is based on 15 major renewable energy-consuming countries between 1990 and 2014. The authors adopt the vector error-correction model and Pedroni cointegration test to assess this relationship. The study finds that there is bidirectional causality between energy consumption and economic growth. In the short run, energy consumption is also bidirectionally related to carbon emissions. Economic growth and carbon emissions have a bidirectional causal relationship both in the short- and long-run.

Natural resources are often a major source of growth and a buffer to various economic shocks, although at the expense of the environment. Hussain et al. (2020) explore the link between natural resource extraction, energy use and CO_2 emissions in a sample of Belt and Road Initiative countries over the period 1990–2014 and suggest that a 10% increase in natural resource dependence leads to nearly a 0.3% rise in carbon emissions. The research by Nathaniel et al. (2020) is driven by the fact that African countries are heavily dependent on energy consumption and, similar to Saidi and Omri (2020), it suggests fostering the development of a financial and renewable energy sector. Using data for selected African economies from 1990 to 2014, the authors explore the relationship between economic growth and CO_2 emissions under both static and dynamic econometric frameworks. The study finds that firstly, trade openness improves economic growth but also leads to a deterioration in environmental quality in the regions. Apart from that, non-renewable energy consumption is causal to economic growth and harmful for air quality. Moreover, resource abundance allows energy exports, industry development and brings foreign investments, yet usually in so-called 'dirty' sectors of the economy. Petrović-Ranđelović et al. (2020) explore the drivers of carbon emissions in CIVETS (Colombia, Indonesia, Viet Nam, Egypt, Turkey and South Africa) countries for the period 1989–2016. The study adopts unit root tests, panel cointegration tests and panel causality tests to achieve this aim. The study finds that GDP and per capita energy use have a causal effect on CO_2 emissions. Apart from that, economic development increases the demand for energy use, and energy use leads to an increase in FDI.

Sadikov et al. (2020) employ data on post-Soviet states between 1990 and 2018 to study the long-term relationship between the variables. Empirical estimates are based on Pedroni's panel cointegration technique and Pesaran's Pooled Mean Group estimator (PMG), which confirm the cointegrating short and long-term relationship between CO_2 emissions, economic growth and use of energy. At the same time, Umurzakov et al. (2020) confirm that economic growth increases energy consumption in post-Soviet states, which means that greater aspirations for development of post-Soviet economies will be followed by increasing energy usage. In other words, economic growth, energy use and carbon emissions are significantly interrelated in a sample of post-Soviet economies. Indeed, the economic development of many post-Soviet states, such as the Russian

Federation, Azerbaijan, Turkmenistan, Kazakhstan, Tajikistan, Kyrgyzstan, Uzbekistan and others, has been built on extracting and exporting natural resources including energy, which is a major road to capitalism (Bolesta, 2019).

Speaking of post-Soviet states, one can note that discussing the so-called Dutch disease is rather relevant. The Soviet economy can be characterised by over-industrialisation and centralised price-setting, yet newly independent states have proceeded with harsh market-oriented reforms. At the same time, the Soviet bloc was abundant with natural resources which made the country one of the world's largest energy suppliers. Soviet dissolution has facilitated the establishment of several major oil and gas producers, who in turn made up the Caspian Basin – the Russian Federation, Azerbaijan, Kazakhstan, Turkmenistan and Uzbekistan.

There is a common communist past mirrored in many social, political and economic legacies, including administrative and territorial division, centralised planning and policy making, and emerging civil society. The Soviet heritage is evident in the current political and institutional structure of natural resource management and characterised by large state shares in the mining and energy sector. In this sense, post-Soviet leaders have adopted strategies which will ensure their continued political rule, with natural resources providing them with enough power to gain political support and to confront rivals (Luong & Weinthal, 2001). In other words, post-Soviet politicians employ energy sector development strategies which bring political benefits, rather than taking economically optimal decisions.

Horvath and Zeynalov (2016) state that the presence of a natural resource curse in post-Soviet states depends on institutional quality. Specifically, in those post-Soviet republics where institutional development is comparatively higher (e.g. Baltic countries), natural resource exports do not crowd out the manufacturing sector, while countries with poor institutions (e.g. Azerbaijan, Kazakhstan, Russian Federation) suffer from natural resource abundance. Azerbaijan and Kazakhstan, in this sense, are representative examples of post-Soviet autocracies characterised by neopatrimonial regimes and high natural resource revenues, which consequently nourish autocratic powers (Franke et al., 2009). Azerbaijan, Kazakhstan and Turkmenistan, for instance, export hydrocarbons extensively and use these proceeds to '… sustain the high rate of capital formation …', yet issues such as human capital, capital stock diversification and natural resource exploitation also require investments (Kalyuzhnova & Kaser, 2006). Moreover, Cieślik and Goczek (2018) explain that the resource curse in the post-Soviet states is associated with an increase in corruption. An abundance of resources and minerals, including gas, oil and metals, enrich officials who distribute the rights for resource exploitation.

To sum up, previous studies suggest that economic growth and energy use are related to CO_2 emissions. The relationship is more evident in resource abundant economies since their economic activity deals with fossil fuels when producing, trading and exporting. At the same time, in transition economies, environmental requirements are often neglected as countries aspire to achieve higher growth rates. This in turn exacerbates the consequences of climate change and may lead to negative socioeconomic issues. In some post-Soviet states where there is Dutch disease, the risk of being trapped in serious environmental issues such as drought and weather-shocks are especially high.

2.2. FDI, trade and CO_2 emissions

Apart from the CO_2–energy–growth interrelation, in recent years there has been growing interest in the contribution of FDI and international trade to pollution and climate change. For FDI, results are at best mixed, with some studies confirming pollution-reducing effects, others showing it to be pollution-enhancing and some studies stating no significant relationship. For example, Hao and Liu (2015) investigate the relationship in China – the biggest CO_2 emitter. In general, FDI negatively impacts carbon emissions through GDP per capita. It means that within economic development, foreign capital inflows may finance more environmentally friendly technologies or contribute to the adoption of renewable energy sources. Trade, however, has no effect on carbon emissions. Haug and Ucal (2019) apply the nonlinear asymmetric ARDL model to explore the effect of FDI and trade on carbon emissions in Turkey. The authors employ three different measures of CO_2 emissions which are CO_2 emissions per capita, CO_2 intensity and CO_2 sectoral emissions. They derive several interesting conclusions regarding FDI, exports and imports. When using emissions per capita as the dependent variable, FDI is insignificant. In the short term, exports reduce CO_2 emissions, yet in the long term their impact is insignificant. Similarly, imports are insignificant in the long term, while in the short term they enhance CO_2 emissions. In contrast, when modelling CO_2 intensity, neither FDI nor imports/exports are significant. Furthermore, the relationship between CO_2 emissions and international trade is asymmetric for two sectors. He et al. (2020) examine the emissions–trade–FDI relationship in BRICS countries employing the Bootstrap Autoregressive Distributed Lagged Model (ARDL) method. Their findings reveal a cointegrating relationship between the variables in some countries. There is no causal relationship between FDI and CO_2, yet there is a causal relationship between CO_2 and trade. Moreover, trade and FDI also exhibit a positive causal relationship. In general, time-series analyses confirm the relationship between carbon emissions, FDI and trade.

In fact, one should recognise that foreign capital inflows are often attributed to already established, income-bearing sectors of the economy, which in turn exacerbates environmental pollution. For example, Blanco et al. (2013) explore the relationship between sector-specific FDI and carbon emissions. Their findings suggest that in 18 Latin American countries, foreign capital inflows in the pollution-intensive sector cause CO_2 emissions. Similarly, Hakimi and Hamdi (2016) study the effects of trade liberalisation and FDI inflows on environmental degradation in Morocco and Tunisia using various econometric approaches. Their findings suggest that FDI inflows are usually invested in pollution-intensive sectors, thereby degrading environments. For members of the Eurasian Economic Union (EEU), whose members are Armenia, Belarus, Kazakhstan, Kyrgyzstan and Russia, natural resources attract FDI but mostly in extractive industries (Hartwell, 2016). In post-Soviet Kazakhstan, for example, more than half of the FDI inflows since 1991 were attracted to the mining sector and extractive industries (Sadik-Zada, 2020). Thus, foreign capital inflows may destroy the environment by being invested in 'dirty' sectors.

Trade liberalisation assumes greater economic activity, with industry, transport and energy sector development, again enhancing carbon dioxide emissions. Khan et al. (2020, p. 10) explore the effect of international trade on carbon emissions for the period 1990–2018. Their study finds that export expansions have a negative effect on carbon emissions, while GDP and imports have a positive impact on CO_2 emissions. The authors suggest that 'in order to reduce the effect of economic growth and imports on consumption-based carbon emissions, domestic consumption level should be targeted, especially those sectors which are more energy intensive and causing to increase carbon emissions'. Similarly, Hotak et al. (2020) use data for 58 countries during the period 1990–2014 to explore the relationship between international trade and carbon emissions. The study finds that trade has a positive effect on carbon emissions in high-income countries, while there is no statistically significant relationship in a sample of low-income countries. The study suggests that high-income countries should promote energy saving and less emission-intensive technologies. Moreover, developed economies take advantage of developing countries by transferring 'dirty' manufacturing industries to them, which will lead to environmental improvement in the former and degradation in the latter. As evidenced by Essandoh et al. (2020), there is a negative long-term relationship between trade and CO_2 emissions in developed economies, yet the opposite is true for developing countries.

FDI is a crucial ingredient of economic growth in post-Soviet countries as they struggle with the historical legacies of Communism (e.g. inherited trade ties with former Soviet partners and newly opened opportunities of FDI); on the one hand, they must undergo reforms which require an influx of substantial capital to generate employment, while on the other hand promoting structural transformation and firm innovation (Beissinger, 2002; Beissinger & Kotkin, 2014; Izotov & Obydenkova, 2020; Lankina et al., 2016a, 2016b; Libman & Obydenkova, 2014a, 2019, 2020; Nazarov & Obydenkova, 2020; Pop-Eleches & Tucker, 2017). For example, Popescu (2014, p. 8153) argues that 'transition countries ... are well positioned to gain from the technology and knowledge shift related to FDI. Attracting FDI is an important matter in the policy program in transition countries'. Apart from that, FDI increases entrepreneurship rates, promotes exports and improves human capital which in turn enhances economic growth (Zhang, 2001). Moreover, increasing shares of trade turnover in post-Soviet economies, especially in those which are largely dependent on natural resource extraction, demonstrate high volatility of prices of minerals and negative expectations on future mineral processes (Kalyuzhnova & Kaser, 2006). This puts post-Soviet states in danger of mineral price fluctuations and climate change issues at the same time.

Previous studies have demonstrated that FDI may either positively or negatively impact CO_2 emissions, while trade usually contributes to atmospheric pollution. FDI and trade are significant factors for economic development of transition economies, which may provide a great push towards capitalism, bring prosperity and improve livelihoods. However, if taken together with low environmental concern and poor climate change awareness, it may also exacerbate existing environmental problems.

3. Data and methods

3.1. Data and sample

The current study explores long-term determinants of carbon dioxide emissions as well as their causal interlinkages, employing a sample of secondary data on 20 post-Soviet economies between 1995 and 2017. To satisfy the criteria of some empirical tests, we work with a strongly balanced panel sample including Armenia, Azerbaijan, Belarus,

Bulgaria, Croatia, Czech Republic, Estonia, Hungary, Kazakhstan, Kyrgyz Republic, Latvia, Lithuania, Moldova, Poland, Romania, Russian Federation, Slovak Republic, Slovenia, Turkmenistan and Ukraine. Unavailability of data on some countries forced their exclusion from the analyses. The total number of observations is 480. Table 1 provides summary statistics.

3.1.1. Dependent variable: CO_2 emissions per capita

Average CO_2 emissions rate in our sample is 6.6 metric tons per capita. Between 1995 and 2017 average CO_2 emissions demonstrated an increasing, yet significantly fluctuating, trend (see Figure 1). A dramatic decline in emissions between 1995 and 1999 was due to a significant economic slowdown and economic restructuring as a result of the dissolution of the Soviet Union. That period was followed by an uprise in carbon emissions, accompanied by gradual economic recovery. The second most dramatic decline can be observed in 2008–2009 during the global financial crisis of 2008 and the fall in oil price. Thereafter, carbon dioxide emissions have never been higher than the peak in 2007, of 7.1 metric tons per capita. In 2017 the largest CO_2 emissions were observed in Kazakhstan,

Table 1. Summary statistics.

Variable	Indicator	Source	Mean	Std. Dev.	Min	Max
CO_2	CO_2 emissions per capita (metric tons)	Global Carbon Atlas	6.6	3.7	0.8	17.6
Y	GDP per capita (constant 2010 US$)	World Development Indicators (WDI)	8870.5	6071.5	521.7	26,190.5
FDI	Foreign direct investment, net inflows (% of GDP)	World Development Indicators (WDI)	5.3	7.1	−41.5	55.1
T	Trade (% of GDP)	World Development Indicators (WDI)	102.0	32.6	35.2	190.4
EN	Energy use (kg of oil equivalent) per $1,000 GDP (constant 2017 PPP)	World Development Indicators (WDI)	184.4	126.2	69.4	816.0

Note: Based on authors' calculations.

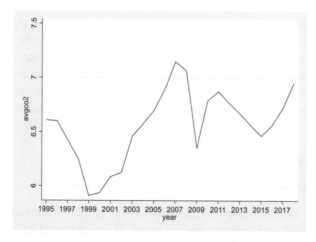

Figure 1. Trend in per capita CO_2 emissions between 1995 and 2017. This figure is created by the authors based on sample post-Soviet states.

Estonia and Turkmenistan (see Figure 2). Relatively high pollution levels in Kazakhstan, Turkmenistan and Russian Federation may be due to significant dependence on fossil fuels and comparatively low environmental concern that arguably is not advocated by so-called non-democratic regional international organisations also known as authoritarian regionalism (Libman & Obydenkova, 2018a, 2018b). On the other hand, Estonia also demonstrates relatively large amounts of carbon dioxide emissions compared to the rest of the EU members. Countries with the lowest emissions shares in our sample are pre-industrialised economies – Armenia, Kyrgyz Republic and Moldova.

3.1.2. Independent variables

Following previous studies (Li et al., 2020), we describe CO_2 emissions by GDP per capita, foreign direct investment, trade and energy use. Average GDP per capita is about 9000 USD per person. Mean foreign capital inflow is 5% of GDP, which is greater than the global average. Post-Soviet states are quite open in terms of trade: average GDP share of exports and imports of goods and services is 102%. Average energy use is 184 kg of oil equivalent per 1000 USD GDP.

3.2. Methodology

3.2.1. Model

Following Li et al. (2020) and Sadikov et al. (2020), CO_2 emissions can be described as follows:

$$CO2_{i,t} = f\left(Y_{i,t}, FDI_{i,t}, T_{i,t}, EN_{i,t}\right) \quad (1)$$

where CO_2 is carbon dioxide emissions per capita, Y is GDP per capita, FDI is foreign direct investment as a share of GDP, T trade as a share of GDP and EN energy use. Here i and t represent individual and temporal dimensions.

All variables are expressed in different measurement units. It is therefore suggested that Eq. (1) be transformed into logarithmic form as it decreases data sharpness and improves the distributional properties of the data (Paramati et al., 2017; Zafar et al., 2020). Thus, we transform Eq. (1) as follows:

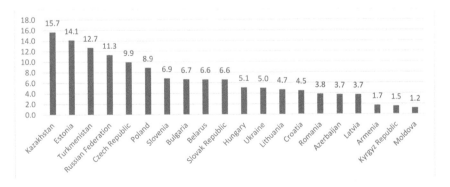

Figure 2. CO_2 emissions per capita in 2017. This figure is created by the authors based on sample post-Soviet states.

$$\ln CO2_{i,t} = \beta_0 + \beta_1 \ln Y_{i,t} + \beta_2 \ln FDI_{i,t} + \beta_3 \ln T_{i,t} + \beta_4 \ln EN_{i,t} \qquad (2)$$

where all above-mentioned variables are expressed in natural logarithms; i and t represent individual and temporal dimensions.

3.2.2. Panel unit-root test

We first investigate the order of integration employing five panel unit root tests – an LLC test by Levin et al. (2002), Breitung's test by Breitung (2002), an IPS test by Im et al. (2003) and two Fisher-type tests by Maddala and Wu (1999). If all variables are stationary at the level form, we continue our analyses with Ordinary Least Squares (OLS), otherwise we adopt a cointegration approach. As Pedroni (1999) states, stationarity testing is imperative for the cointegration approach since a cointegrating relationship arises in a set of variables, which are individually integrated of order one and stationary.

3.2.3. Pedroni's cointegration

Once stationarity is approved, we employ Pedroni's (Pedroni, 1999) panel cointegration test. Using seven parametric and non-parametric test statistics, Pedroni's approach tests the null hypothesis of no cointegration, in a one-tailed test and follows a normal distribution. Test statistics represent either group-mean average or panel estimates (Neal, 2014). A cointegrating relationship is confirmed if the majority of test statistics reject the null.

Previous research provides plenty of econometric techniques to obtain long-term coefficients of cointegrating variables in time-series and panel data. Fully Modified Ordinary Least Squares (FMOLS) is typically applied when all variables exhibit a cointegrating relationship (Pedroni, 2001). It provides more robust estimates compared to Dynamic Ordinary Least Squares (DOLS) (Gozgor et al., 2020) and avoids the loss of degrees of freedoms, which is common when applying the latter. Long-term elasticities are reported using time-series cointegrated regression estimators – DOLS and FMOLS.

3.2.4. Dumitrescu and Hurlin's causality test

To investigate the causal relationship, we employ the panel non-causality test for heterogeneous panels developed by Dumitrescu and Hurlin (2012), which is modelled as follows:

$$y_{i,t} = a_i + \sum_{k=1}^{K} \gamma_{ik} y_{i,t-k} + \sum_{k=1}^{K} \beta_{ik} x_{i,t-k} + \varepsilon_{i,t} \qquad (3)$$

where $x_{i,t}$ and $y_{i,t}$ are observations of two stationary variables in a strongly balanced panel dataset for individual i in period t.

By running individual regressions, the test produces individual Wald statistics, which are averaged across panels. The test reports underlying z-bar and z-tilde statistics to reject or accept the null hypothesis of a non-causal relationship. As Lopez and Weber (2017) suggest, z-bar tilde is preferable for samples with a relatively small number of observations (N) and time periods (T).

4. Results and discussion

The following section provides the results of empirical testing and a results discussion. We first report the results of panel unit root tests in Table 2. Most of the variables included in our model are non-stationary at the level form. We therefore take the first differences between the variables. At a 1% significance level our variables are stationary at I(1). These results indicate that OLS results will be biased and the use of more sophisticated techniques is required.

Once we have confirmed integration order, we obtain Pedroni's cointegration test results (Table 3). Six out of seven test statistics support the alternative hypothesis at $p<0.01$, thereby confirming a cointegrating relationship between the variables. Additionally, Kao's (1999) panel cointegration test is performed to verify results and also

Table 2. Panel unit-root test results.

Form	Variable	LLC	Breitung	IPS	ADF Fisher	PP Fisher
Level	ln CO_2	−3.2710***	−0.4744	−0.3052	74.7495***	53.3027*
		(0.0005)	(0.3176)	(0.3801)	(0.0000)	(0.0776)
First-difference	Δ ln CO_2	−9.5920***	−9.4082***	−10.8193***	240.4670***	418.3082***
		(0.0000)	(0.0000)	(0.0000)	(0.0000)	(0.0000)
Level	ln Y	−3.7591***	9.3206	2.2484	24.9976	21.8357
		(0.0001)	(1.0000)	(0.9877)	(0.9694)	(0.9914)
First-difference	Δ ln Y	−7.3121***	−9.0457***	−8.8130***	158.4345***	266.3468***
		(0.0000)	(0.0000)	(0.0000)	(0.0000)	(0.0000)
Level	ln Tr	−3.0666***	1.7457	−0.1807	60.1867**	42.8248
		(0.0011)	(0.9596)	(0.4283)	(0.0211)	(0.3509)
First-difference	Δ ln Tr	−10.7482***	−8.2531***	−10.1005***	250.9916***	346.0489***
		(0.0000)	(0.0000)	(0.0000)	(0.0000)	(0.0000)
Level	ln FDI	−3.8447***	−6.6865***	−4.5754***	82.7063***	122.9000***
		(0.0001)	(0.0000)	(0.0000)	(0.0001)	(0.0000)
First-difference	Δ ln FDI	−10.3885***	−12.2824***	−10.7696***	282.3448***	624.4000***
		(0.0000)	(0.0000)	(0.0000)	(0.0000)	(0.0000)
Level	ln EN	−6.5048***	8.0202	−0.0346	64.0637***	43.7908
		(0.0000)	(1.0000)	(0.4862)	(0.0092)	(0.3138)
First-difference	Δ ln EN	−6.7307***	−8.9911***	−10.2674***	150.7069***	346.1068***
		(0.0000)	(0.0000)	(0.0000)	(0.0000)	(0.0000)

Note: ***, ** and * indicate significance at 1%, 5% and 10% levels, respectively. Figures in parentheses are *p*-values.

Table 3. Pedroni's panel cointegration.

Test statistic	Score
V-stat	−1.22
Panel rho-stat	−3.93***
Panel PP-stat	−15.57***
Panel ADF-stat	−8.83***
Group rho stat	−2.712***
Group PP stat	−19.74***
Group ADF stat	−9.13***
Kao's ADF	−11.91***

Note: ***, ** and * indicate significance at 1%, 5% and 10% levels, respectively.

supports cointegration between variables. Since a cointegrating relationship is confirmed, we re-estimate Eq. (2) to obtain coefficients of regression. All variables are represented in natural logs, so the coefficients are long-term elasticities.

Table 4 provides long-term elasticities by estimating Eq. (2) with both FMOLS and DOLS. Both estimators provide similar results. GDP per capita positively related to CO_2 emissions in the long term. According to the FMOLS estimator, the 1% increase in GDP per capita is associated with a 0.83% increase in CO_2 emissions ($p<0.01$), which supports the growth–pollution nexus and findings of Sadikov et al. (2020). Energy consumption also enhances CO_2 emissions in the long term. On average, a 1% increase in energy use is associated with a 0.1% increase in CO_2 emissions, ceteris paribus.

Higher trade shares increase CO_2 emissions as FMOLS suggest: a 1% increase in trade share related to a 0.09% increase in CO_2 emissions and was significant at $p<0.01$. The coefficient of trade is insignificant in the DOLS estimator. Foreign direct inflows are positively associated with CO_2 emissions in the long term and the result is significant in both DOLS and FMOLS regressions.

Furthermore, we report causality test results in Table 5. We tested eight non-causality hypotheses to reveal causal interlinkages among emissions, GDP per capita, trade, FDI and energy use. Our analyses reveal unidirectional causality running from CO_2 emissions to energy use, at $p<0.01$. Unfortunately, we fail to reveal a causal relationship among other variables, yet we are still able to derive some policy implications.

Economic development is related to growing industry, production, trade and tourism, which in turn leads to higher pollution levels. In the case of post-Soviet economies, environmental concern is of lower importance, compared to growth. Moreover, as some post-Soviet economies are abundant with conventional natural resources such as oil and gas their use is quite extensive. In fact, the Soviet Union was the largest oil producer and second-largest producer of natural gas (Nicholls & Potter, 1994). In 1978, 64% of Soviet hard-currency earnings came from energy exports (Gustafson, 1981). The USSR's share of natural resources in total mining output constituted 25% in 1989. During that time, mining operations by the Soviet bloc had been increasing twice every 8–10 years whilst the world's mining operations doubled every 15 years. Along with extensive energy use, environmental issues which academia raised were, however, of secondary importance (Wolfson, 1989). After the dissolution of the Soviet Union, environmental issues were still neglected. In post-Soviet Russia for example, a general determinant of economic

Table 4. Long-term elasticities.

	DOLS	FMOLS
Δ ln Y	0.89***	0.83***
	(11.95)	(44.98)
Δ ln Tr	0.00	0.09***
	(0.91)	(7.89)
Δ ln FDI	0.01***	0.05***
	(4.67)	(5.13)
Δ ln EN	0.12***	0.80***
	(6.49)	(54.17)

Note: ***, ** and * indicate significance at 1%, 5% and 10% levels, respectively. Figures in parentheses are *t*-statistic.

Table 5. Dumitrescu and Hurlin's non-causality test.

Hypothesis	Test statistic (z-bar tilde)	Optimal number of lags (AIC)
CO_2 does not cause Y	0.8386	1
	(0.4017)	
Y does not cause CO_2	1.0637	1
	(0.2875)	
CO_2 does not cause Tr	0.2141	5
	(0.8305)	
Tr does not cause CO_2	−0.6718	1
	(0.5017)	
CO_2 does not cause FDI	0.1048	5
	(0.9166))	
FDI does not cause CO_2	−1.2476	1
	(0.2122)	
CO_2 does not cause EN	8.2532***	1
	(0.0000)	
EN does not cause CO_2	−0.4779	1
	(0.6327)	

Note: ***, ** and * indicate significance at 1%, 5% and 10% levels, respectively. Figures in parentheses are *p*-values.

growth is the availability of natural resources (Mau & Yanovskiy, 2002). For modern Kazakhstan, natural resources are important in defending state interests, assuring a strong geopolitical position (Karatabanov & Dzhanalieva, 2019).

As for causal links, our analyses show that CO_2 emissions create additional pressure on energy use and therefore a demand for energy is present. Although a product of energy use, CO_2 emissions indirectly require more energy through energy-intensive and large industries. Several possible channels through which CO_2 causes extra energy use is the manufacturing sector and energy-intensive industry development, which require ever-increasing amounts of energy as they expand.

Our study suggests that international trade is positively related to CO_2 emissions. Most post-Soviet countries are developing economies, where environmental policies are less stringent in order to achieve comparative advantages in their production (Yasmeen et al., 2019). International trade based on traditional production methods and low environmental concerns are therefore deteriorating the environment.

Furthermore, we confirm a positive long-term relationship between FDI and CO_2 emissions in our sample. Indeed, some studies state that FDI inflows may attract investment into the most polluting industries (Iwasaki & Suganuma, 2005; Lee, 2009); especially when economic growth is prioritised over environmental protection, FDI is likely to be attracted to the most profitable industries. For example, between 1990 and 2003, natural resource endowments were among the most critical factors for allocation of foreign investments in Russia and the lion's share of foreign capital flows were in energy-intensive sectors of the economy (Iwasaki & Suganuma, 2005). In Central Asian and Eastern European economies, natural resource endowments stimulate FDI in agriculture and manufacturing sectors (Doytch & Eren, 2012).

All in all, FDI, trade and economic growth are positively related to CO_2 emissions in post-Soviet economies, while the relationship between energy and CO_2 emissions is causal. Our results strengthen the need for intervention, requiring policymakers to adopt more environmentally friendly strategies to achieve long-term national development goals.

5. Conclusion

This study explores and tests the links between economic growth, energy consumption, trade openness, FDI and carbon emissions, by using a sample of 20 post-Soviet countries. This paper covers the period 1995–2017. For the econometric analysis we have relied on Pedroni's cointegration test, FMOLS and DOLS regression panels, and Dumirescu and Hurlin's panel Granger non-causality test. The findings from the panel cointegration test reveal long-term cointegrating relationships between the variables. Long-term elasticities are reported with DOLS and FMOLS regressions, which yield quite similar results: GDP per capita, FDI inflows, trade and energy use are positively related to CO_2 emissions per capita in the long term. The panel causality test, however, identifies unidirectional causality running from CO_2 emissions to energy use.

There are several principal points of interest in this research. First, we find that a 1% increase in GDP per capita is associated with a 0.83% increase in CO_2 emissions. This implies that economic growth in transition countries leads to greater carbon emissions. Therefore, policymakers should foster the rapid adoption of innovative, efficient technologies that would promote economic growth with a lower carbon footprint. In addition, these countries should actualise novel environmental policies to decrease carbon emissions.

Second, we document that both FDI and trade openness have a positive impact on CO_2 emissions in our sample. Thus, our study confirms the 'pollution haven' hypothesis for post-Soviet countries (Balsalobre-Lorente et al., 2019). One potential solution to this dilemma is to create tax and other incentives for foreign companies to channel their FDI in low-carbon economic sectors such as high-tech, for example. This is especially relevant for the post-Soviet EU-member countries, where aggressive tax planning is significantly related to FDI allocation (Pavel et al., 2020).

Apart from that, carbon emissions may be reduced if polluting industries undergo technological upgrading and adopt energy-efficient technologies (Zhang & Zhang, 2018). In post-Soviet states, at the micro-level, firms' innovation may be enhanced through democratisation. Innovative investments are lower in authoritarian economies and they increase with democratisation, influencing public policies related to environmental challenges, such as deforestation for example (Libman & Obydenkova, 2014b; Nazarov & Obydenkova, 2020; Obydenkova et al., 2016; Obydenkova & Salahodjaev, 2016, 2017). On the other hand, Bae et al. (2017) discuss the role of corruption, democracy and economic freedom and their links with the growth–emissions nexus in post-Soviet economies. Economic growth is associated with greater economic activity and thus larger amounts of carbon dioxide emissions. Moreover, some international organisations, such as the United Nations (UN), can arguably increase environmental accountability and awareness of national governments or at least help to raise environmental and other global issues on a national agenda (e.g. Ciplet, 2014; Conca et al., 2017; Kuyper & Bäckstrand, 2016; Obydenkova & Vieira, 2020). Increased transparency, democratisation and economic freedom enhances economic growth, but forces the government to have environmental accountability and audits, thus, arguably, grasping better control over such increases in CO_2 emissions. Therefore, the effect of economic freedom on CO_2 emissions may vary depending on political regime and government size and structure in particular (Bjørnskov, 2018). In this regard, policies aimed at CO_2 emissions' control by providing entities with permission or rights for emissions for a certain period would be relevant.

Finally, the findings of this research highlight that transition countries need to integrate climate change considerations in long-term development strategies more profoundly to decrease carbon emissions and maintain sustainable economic development. In this sense, post-Soviet economies, such as the Russian Federation, Central Asian and Caucasian economies may adopt the experience of other post-Soviet Central and Eastern European republics – current EU members. Substantial decline in CO_2 emissions in those countries was not only due to the end of the Soviet era and deindustrialisation, but also due to more stringent environmental policies and, as a consequence, the entry of less polluting firms. In the Czech Republic, in particular, environmental policies were mainly associated with air protection policies through increased emission charges, which became crucial in order for emissions to decline during the 1990s (Earnhart & Lizal, 2008). Moreover, environmental protection policies may be implemented in a safe manner, without affecting economic development. For instance, CO_2 reduction may be promoted by creating incentives to switch to clean energy sources (Sineviciene et al., 2019). Such measures may include preferences or tax relief for entities which invest in renewable energy facilities and green technologies – issues that are all considered in this Special Issue. This would also help to rationalise the usage of energy sources between fossil fuels and renewables taking into account the 'externalities', such as the effects of international organisations (e.g. the UN versus the EU) and the specificity of the most crucial trading partners and investors (e.g. such as China or Russia). Lastly, the CO_2 emissions may be affected in the long run by integration and democratisation in the region. Nascent research suggests that these processes have numerous important implications for the socioeconomic outcomes in the post-Soviet space as different contributions to this Special Issue demonstrate in detail.

Notes

1. https://climate.nasa.gov/news/3061/2020-tied-for-warmest-year-on-record-nasa-analysis-shows/.
2. The Climate Change Performance Index 2021,https://newclimate.org/2020/12/07/the-climate-change-performance-index-2021/.

Disclosure statement

No potential conflict of interest was reported by the authors.

ORCID

Raufhon Salahodjaev http://orcid.org/0000-0002-5578-811X
Arletta Isaeva http://orcid.org/0000-0002-7577-7100

References

Abbasi, F., & Riaz, K. (2016). CO2 emissions and financial development in an emerging economy: An augmented VAR approach. *Energy Policy, 90*, 102–114. https://doi.org/10.1016/j.enpol.2015.12.017

Acaravci, A., & Ozturk, I. (2010). On the relationship between energy consumption, CO2 emissions and economic growth in Europe. *Energy, 35*(12), 5412–5420. https://doi.org/10.1016/j.energy.2010.07.009

Al-mulali, U., & Normee Che Sab, C. (2013). Energy consumption, pollution and economic development in 16 emerging countries. *Journal of Economic Studies, 40*(5), 686–698. https://doi.org/10.1108/JES-05-2012-0055

Ang, J. B. (2007). CO2 emissions, energy consumption, and output in France. *Energy Policy, 35*(10), 4772–4778. https://doi.org/10.1016/j.enpol.2007.03.032

Armingeon, K., & Ceka, B. (2014). The loss of trust in the European Union during the great recession since 2007: The role of heuristics from the national political system. *European Union Politics, 15*(1), 82–107. https://doi.org/10.1177/1465116513495595

Armingeon, K., & Guthmann, K. (2014). Democracy in crisis? The declining support for national democracy in European countries, 2007–2011. *European Journal of Political Research, 53*(3), 423–442. https://doi.org/10.1111/1475-6765.12046

Arpino, B., & Obydenkova, A. (2020). Democracy and political trust before and after the great recession 2008: The European Union and the United Nations. *Social Indicators Research, 148*(2), 395–415. https://doi.org/10.1007/s11205-019-02204-x

Bae, J. H., Li, D. D., & Rishi, M. (2017). Determinants of CO2 emission for post-Soviet Union independent countries. *Climate Policy, 17*(5), 591–615. https://doi.org/10.1080/14693062.2015.1124751

Balsalobre-Lorente, D., Gokmenoglu, K. K., Taspinar, N., & Cantos-Cantos, J. M. (2019). An approach to the pollution haven and pollution halo hypotheses in MINT countries. *Environmental Science and Pollution Research, 26*(22), 23010–23026. https://doi.org/10.1007/s11356-019-05446-x

Bastola, U., & Sapkota, P. (2015). Relationships among energy consumption, pollution emission, and economic growth in Nepal. *Energy, 80*, 254–262. https://doi.org/10.1016/j.energy.2014.11.068

Beissinger, M., & Kotkin, S. (Eds.). (2014). *Historical legacies of communism in Russia and Eastern Europe*. Cambridge University Press. https://scholar.princeton.edu/mbeissinger/publications/historical-legacies-communism-russia-and-eastern-europe

Beissinger, M. R. (2002). *Nationalist mobilization and the collapse of the Soviet state*. Cambridge University Press; https://scholar.princeton.edu/mbeissinger/publications/nationalist-mobilization-and-collapse-soviet-state

Bjørnskov, C. (2018). Do liberalising reforms harm the environment? Evidence from the post-communist transition. *Economic Affairs, 38*(1), 22–37. https://doi.org/10.1111/ecaf.12277

Blanco, L., Gonzalez, F., & Ruiz, I. (2013). The impact of FDI on CO2 emissions in Latin America. *Oxford Development Studies, 41*(1), 104–121. https://doi.org/10.1080/13600818.2012.732055

Bolesta, A. (2019). From socialism to capitalism with communist characteristics: The building of a post-socialist developmental state in Central Asia. *Post-Communist Economies*, 1–28. https://doi.org/10.1080/14631377.2019.1694350

Breitung, J. (2002). Nonparametric tests for unit roots and cointegration. *Journal of Econometrics, 108*(2), 343–363. https://doi.org/10.1016/S0304-4076(01)00139-7

Buis, A. (2019, October 9). The atmosphere: getting a handle on carbon dioxide. *NASA. Global Climate Change*. https://climate.nasa.gov/news/2915/the-atmosphere-getting-a-handle-on-carbon-dioxide/

Chen, P. Y., Chen, S. T., & Chen, C. C. (2012). Energy consumption and economic growth – new evidence from meta-analysis. *Energy Policy, 44*, 245–255. https://doi.org/10.1016/j.enpol.2012.01.048

Cieślik, A., & Goczek, Ł. (2018). Initial conditions and privatisation as causes of post-communist corruption. *Post-Communist Economies, 30*(1), 36–55. https://doi.org/10.1080/14631377.2017.1361693

Ciplet, D. (2014). Contesting climate injustice: Transnational advocacy network struggles for rights in UN climate politics. *Global Environmental Politics*, 1 November 2014. *14*(4), 75–96. https://doi.org/10.1162/GLEP_a_00258.

Conca, K., Thwaites, J., & Lee, G. (2017). Climate change and the un security council: Bully Pulpit or Bull in a China Shop? *Global Environmental Politics*, 1 May 2017. *17*(2), 1–20. https://doi.org/10.1162/GLEP_a_00398.

Copeland, B. R., & Taylor, M. S. (1995). Trade and transboundary pollution. *The American Economic Review*, *85*(4), 716–737. http://www.jstor.org/stable/2118228

Dellink, R., Lanzi, E., & Chateau, J. (2019). The sectoral and regional economic consequences of climate change to 2060. *Environmental and Resource Economics*, *72*(2), 309–363. https://doi.org/10.1007/s10640-017-0197-5

Doytch, N., & Eren, M. (2012). Institutional determinants of sectoral FDI in Eastern European and Central Asian countries: The role of investment climate and democracy. *Emerging Markets Finance and Trade*, *48*(sup4), 14–32. https://doi.org/10.2753/REE1540-496X4806S402

Dumitrescu, E.-I., & Hurlin, C. (2012). Testing for Granger non-causality in heterogeneous panels. *Economic Modelling*, *29*(4), 1450–1460. https://doi.org/10.1016/j.econmod.2012.02.014

Earnhart, D., & Lizal, L. (2008). Pollution reductions in the Czech Republic. *Post-Communist Economies*, *20*(2), 231–252. https://doi.org/10.1080/14631370802018999

Essandoh, O. K., Islam, M., & Kakinaka, M. (2020). Linking international trade and foreign direct investment to CO2 emissions: Any differences between developed and developing countries? *Science of the Total Environment*, *712*, 136437. https://doi.org/10.1016/j.scitotenv.2019.136437

Franke, A., Gawrich, A., & Alakbarov, G. (2009). Kazakhstan and Azerbaijan as post-Soviet rentier states: Resource incomes and autocracy as a double 'curse' in post-Soviet regimes. *Europe-Asia Studies*, *61*(1), 109–140. https://doi.org/10.1080/09668130802532977

Gökmenoğlu, K., & Taspinar, N. (2016). The relationship between CO2 emissions, energy consumption, economic growth and FDI: The case of Turkey. *The Journal of International Trade & Economic Development*, *25*(5), 706–723. https://doi.org/10.1080/09638199.2015.1119876

Gozgor, G., Mahalik, M. K., Demir, E., & Padhan, H. (2020). The impact of economic globalization on renewable energy in the OECD countries. *Energy Policy*, *139*, 111365. https://doi.org/10.1016/j.enpol.2020.111365

Grossman, G. M., & Krueger, A. B. (1991). *Environmental impacts of a North American free trade agreement, No. W3914*. National Bureau of Economic Research. https://doi.org/10.3386/w3914

Gustafson, T. (1981). Energy and the Soviet bloc. *International Security*, *6*(3), 65–89. https://doi.org/10.2307/2538607

Hakimi, A., & Hamdi, H. (2016). Trade liberalization, FDI inflows, environmental quality and economic growth: A comparative analysis between Tunisia and Morocco. *Renewable and Sustainable Energy Reviews*, *58*, 1445–1456. https://doi.org/10.1016/j.rser.2015.12.280

Hao, Y., & Liu, Y.-M. (2015). Has the development of FDI and foreign trade contributed to China's CO2 emissions? An empirical study with provincial panel data. *Natural Hazards*, *76*(2), 1079–1091. https://doi.org/10.1007/s11069-014-1534-4

Hartwell, C. A. (2016). Improving competitiveness in the member states of the Eurasian Economic Union: A blueprint for the next decade. *Post-Communist Economies*, *28*(1), 49–71. https://doi.org/10.1080/14631377.2015.1124554

Haug, A. A., & Ucal, M. (2019). The role of trade and FDI for CO2 emissions in Turkey: Nonlinear relationships. *Energy Economics*, *81*, 297–307. https://doi.org/10.1016/j.eneco.2019.04.006

He, F., Chang, K.-C., Li, M., Li, X., & Li, F. (2020). Bootstrap ARDL test on the relationship among trade, FDI, and CO2 emissions: Based on the experience of BRICS countries. *Sustainability*, *12*(3), 1060. https://doi.org/10.3390/su12031060

Horvath, R., & Zeynalov, A. (2016). Natural resources, manufacturing and institutions in post-Soviet countries. *Resources Policy*, *50*, 141–148. https://doi.org/10.1016/j.resourpol.2016.09.007

Hotak, S., Islam, M., Kakinaka, M., & Kotani, K. (2020). Carbon emissions and carbon trade balances: International evidence from panel ARDL analysis. *Environmental Science and Pollution Research*, *27*(19), 24115–24128. https://doi.org/10.1007/s11356-020-08478-w

Hussain, J., Khan, A., & Zhou, K. (2020). The impact of natural resource depletion on energy use and CO2 emission in belt & road initiative countries: A cross-country analysis. *Energy*, *199*, 117409. https://doi.org/10.1016/j.energy.2020.117409

Im, K. S., Pesaran, M. H., & Shin, Y. (2003). Testing for unit roots in heterogeneous panels. *Journal of Econometrics*, *115*(1), 53–74. https://doi.org/10.1016/S0304-4076(03)00092-7

Iwasaki, I., & Suganuma, K. (2005). Regional distribution of foreign direct investment in Russia. *Post-Communist Economies*, *17*(2), 153–172. https://doi.org/10.1080/14631370500104828

Iwata, H., Okada, K., & Samreth, S. (2012). Empirical study on the determinants of CO2 emissions: Evidence from OECD countries. *Applied Economics*, *44*(27), 3513–3519. https://doi.org/10.1080/00036846.2011.577023

Izotov, V., & Obydenkova, A. (2020) *Geopolitical games in Eurasian regionalism: Ideational interactions and regional international organisations*. Post-Communist Economies, *33*(2-3), 150-174.https://doi.org/10.1080/14631377.2020.1793584

Jebli, M. B., Youssef, S. B., & Apergis, N. (2019). The dynamic linkage between renewable energy, tourism, CO 2 emissions, economic growth, foreign direct investment, and trade. *Latin American Economic Review*, *28*(1), 1–19. https://doi.org/10.1186/s40503-019-0063-7

Kalyuzhnova, Y., & Kaser, M. (2006). Prudential management of hydrocarbon revenues in resource-rich transition economies. *Post-Communist Economies*, *18*(2), 167–187. https://doi.org/10.1080/14631370600619857

Kao, C. (1999). Spurious regression and residual-based tests for cointegration in panel data. *Journal of Econometrics*, *90*(1), 1–44. https://doi.org/10.1016/S0304-4076(98)00023-2

Karatabanov, R. A., & Dzhanalieva, K. M. (2019). Assessment of natural-resource factor of geopolitical security of the Republic of Kazakhstan. *ҚАЗАҚСТАН РЕСПУБЛИКАСЫ*, *4*(326), 89–93. https://doi.org/10.32014/2019.2518-1483.121

Khan, Z., Ali, M., Jinyu, L., Shahbaz, M., & Siqun, Y. (2020). Consumption-based carbon emissions and trade nexus: Evidence from nine oil exporting countries. *Energy Economics*, *89*, 104806. https://doi.org/10.1016/j.eneco.2020.104806

Kuyper, J. W., & Bäckstrand, K. (2016). Accountability and representation: Nonstate actors in UN climate diplomacy. *Global Environmental Politics*, 1 May 2016. *16*(2), 61–81. https://doi.org/10.1162/GLEP_a_00350.

Lankina, T., Libman, A., & Obydenkova, A. (2016a). Authoritarian and democratic diffusion in post-Soviet regions. *Comparative Political Studies*, *49*(12), 1599–1629. https://doi.org/10.1177/0010414016628270

Lankina, T., Libman, A., & Obydenkova, A. (2016b). Appropriation and subversion: Pre-communist literacy, communist party saturation, Post-Soviet democratic outcomes. *World Politics*, *68*(2), 229–274. https://doi.org/10.1017/S0043887115000428

Leal, P. H., & Marques, A. C. (2020). Rediscovering the EKC hypothesis for the 20 highest CO2 emitters among OECD countries by level of globalization. *International Economics*, *164*, 36–47. https://doi.org/10.1016/j.inteco.2020.07.001

Lee, C. G. (2009). Foreign direct investment, pollution and economic growth: Evidence from Malaysia. *Applied Economics*, *41*(13), 1709–1716. https://doi.org/10.1080/00036840701564376

Levin, A., Lin, C. F., & Chu, C. S. J. (2002). Unit root tests in panel data: Asymptotic and finite-sample properties. *Journal of Econometrics*, *108*(1), 1–24. https://doi.org/10.1016/S0304-4076(01)00098-7

Li, R., Jiang, H., Sotnyk, I., Kubatko, O., & Almashaqbeh, Y. A., . I. (2020). The CO2 emissions drivers of Post-Soviet economies in Eastern Europe and Central Asia. *Atmosphere*, *11*(9), 1019. https://doi.org/10.3390/atmos11091019

Libman, A., & Obydenkova, A. (2014a). International trade as a limiting factor in democratization: An analysis of subnational regions in Post-Soviet Russia. *Studies in Comparative International Development*, *49*(2), 168–196. https://doi.org/10.1007/s12116-013-9130-2

Libman, A., & Obydenkova, A. (2014b). The governance of commons in a large nondemocratic state: The case of forestry in the Russian Federation. *Publius: The Journal of Federalism*, *44*(2), 298–323. https://doi.org/10.1093/publius/pjt065;

Libman, A., & Obydenkova, A. (2019). Inequality and historical legacies: Evidence from post-communist regions. *Post-Communist Economies*, *31*(6), 699–724. https://doi.org/10.1080/14631377.2019.1607440

Libman, A., & Obydenkova, A. V. (2018a). Understanding authoritarian regionalism. *Journal of Democracy*, *29*(4), 151–165. https://doi.org/10.1353/jod.2018.0070

Libman, A., & Obydenkova, A. V. (2018b). Regional international organizations as a strategy of autocracy: The Eurasian Economic Union and Russian foreign policy. *International Affairs*, *94*(5), 1037–1058. https://doi.org/10.1093/ia/iiy147

Libman, A., & Obydenkova, A. V. (2020). Proletarian internationalism in action? communist legacies and attitudes towards migrants in Russia. *Problems of post-Communism*, *67*(4–5), 402–416. https://doi.org/10.1080/10758216.2019.1640068

Lindsey, R., & Dahlman, L. (2021, March 15). Climate change: Global temperature.Climate.gov. https://www.climate.gov/news-features/understanding-climate/climate-change-global-temperature

Lopez, L., & Weber, S. (2017). Testing for granger causality in panel data. *The Stata Journal*, *17*(4), 972–984. https://doi.org/10.1177/1536867X1801700412

Luong, P. J., & Weinthal, E. (2001). Prelude to the resource curse: Explaining oil and gas development strategies in the Soviet successor states and beyond. *Comparative Political Studies*, *34*(4), 367–399. https://doi.org/10.1177/0010414001034004002

Maddala, G. S., & Wu, S. (1999). A comparative study of unit root tests with panel data and a new simple test. *Oxford Bulletin of Economics and Statistics*, *61*(S1), 631–652. https://doi.org/10.1111/1468-0084.0610s1631

Mau, V., & Yanovskiy, K. (2002). Political and legal factors of economic growth in Russian regions. *Post-Communist Economies*, *14*(3), 321–339. https://doi.org/10.1080/1463137022000013403

Menegaki, A. N. (2014). On energy consumption and GDP studies; A meta-analysis of the last two decades. *Renewable and Sustainable Energy Reviews*, *29*, 31–36. https://doi.org/10.1016/j.rser.2013.08.081

Nathaniel, S., Barua, S., Hussain, H., & Adeleye, N. (2020). The determinants and interrelationship of carbon emissions and economic growth in African economies: Fresh insights from static and dynamic models. *Journal of Public Affairs*, *21* (1), e2141. DOI:10.1002/pa.2141

Nazarov, Z., & Obydenkova, A. V. (2020). Democratization and firm innovation: Evidence from European and Central Asian post-communist states. *Post-Communist Economies*, *32*(7), 833–859. https://doi.org/10.1080/14631377.2020.1745565

Neal, T. (2014). Panel Cointegration Analysis with Xtpedroni. *The Stata Journal*, *14*(3), 684–692. https://doi.org/10.1177/1536867X1401400312

Nicholls, M., & Potter, H. (1994). Regional initiatives in the former Soviet Bloc: A review of multi-country trade groups, environment initiatives and infrastructure projects. *Communist Economies and Economic Transformation*, *6*(3), 315–340. https://doi.org/10.1177/1536867X1401400312

Obydenkova, A. (2012). Democratization at the Grassroots: The European Union's external impact. *Democratization*, *19*(2), 230–257. DOI: abs/10.1080/13510347.2011.576851 https://www.tandfonline.com/doi/abs/10.1080/13510347.2011.576851

Obydenkova, A., & Arpino, B. (2018). Corruption and Trust in the European Union and National Institutions: Changes over the great recession across European States. *Journal of Common Market Studies*, *56*(3), 594–611. DOI: abs/10.1111/jcms.12646 https://onlinelibrary.wiley.com/doi/abs/10.1111/jcms.12646

Obydenkova, A., Nazarov, Z., & Salahodjaev, R. (2016). The process of deforestation in the weak democracies and the role of intelligence. *Environmental Research*, *148*, 484–490. https://doi.org/10.1016/j.envres.2016.03.039

Obydenkova, A. V., & Salahodjaev, R. (2016). Intelligence, democracy, and international environmental commitment. *Environmental Research*, *147*, 82–88. https://doi.org/10.1016/j.envres.2016.01.042

Obydenkova, A. V., & Salahodjaev, R. (2017). Climate change policies: The role of democracy and social cognitive capital. *Environmental Research*, *157*, 182–189. http://dx.doi.org/10.1016/j.envres.2017.05.009

Obydenkova, A. V., & Vieira, V. G. R. (2020). The limits of collective financial statecraft: Regional development banks and voting alignment with the United States at the United Nations General Assembly. *International Studies Quarterly, 64*(1), 13–25. https://doi.org/10.1093/isq/sqz080

Pao, H.-T., Yu, H.-C., & Yang, Y.-H. (2011). Modeling the CO2 emissions, energy use, and economic growth in Russia. *Energy, 36*(8), 5094–5100. https://doi.org/10.1016/j.energy.2011.06.004

Paramati, S. R., Shahbaz, M., & Alam, M. S. (2017). Does tourism degrade environmental quality? A comparative study of Eastern and Western European Union. *Transportation Research Part D: Transport and Environment, 50*, 1–13. https://doi.org/10.1016/j.trd.2016.10.034

Pavel, J., Tepperová, J., & Arltová, M. (2020). Tax factors affecting FDI allocation in the EU post-socialist states. *Post-Communist Economies,33*(6), 710-725. https://doi.org/10.1080/14631377.2020.1827198

Pedroni, P. (1999). Critical values for cointegration tests in heterogeneous panels with multiple regressors. *Oxford Bulletin of Economics and Statistics, 61*(S1), 653–670. https://doi.org/10.1111/1468-0084.61.s1.14

Pedroni, P. (2001), "Fully modified OLS for heterogeneous cointegrated panels". In B.H. Baltagi, T.B Fomby, & R. Carter Hill   (Eds.), *Nonstationary Panels, Panel Cointegration, and Dynamic Panels (Advances in Econometrics, Vol. 15),* Emerald Group Publishing Limited, Bingley, pp. 93-130. https://doi.org/10.1016/S0731-9053(00)15004-2

Petrović-Ranđelović, M., Mitić, P., Zdravković, A., Cvetanović, D., & Cvetanović, S. (2020). Economic growth and carbon emissions: Evidence from CIVETS countries. *Applied Economics, 52*(16), 1806–1815. https://doi.org/10.1080/00036846.2019.1679343

Pop-Eleches, G., & Tucker, J. A. (2017). *Communism's shadow: Historical legacies and contemporary political attitudes.* Princeton University Press; https://press.princeton.edu/books/hardcover/9780691175584/communisms-shadow

Popescu, G. H. (2014). FDI and economic growth in Central and Eastern Europe. *Sustainability, 6*(11), 8149–8163. https://doi.org/10.3390/su6118149

Rahman, M. M., & Kashem, M. A. (2017). Carbon emissions, energy consumption and industrial growth in Bangladesh: Empirical evidence from ARDL cointegration and granger causality analysis. *Energy Policy, 110*, 600–608. https://doi.org/10.1016/j.enpol.2017.09.006

Sadikov, A., Kasimova, N., Isaeva, A., Khachaturov, A., & Salahodjaev, R. (2020). Pollution, energy and growth: Evidence from post-Soviet countries. *International Journal of Energy Economics and Policy, 10*(6), 656–661. https://doi.org/10.32479/ijeep.9637

Sadik-Zada, E. R. (2020). Addressing the growth and employment effects of the extractive industries: White and black box illustrations from Kazakhstan. *Post-Communist Economies, 33*(4), 405–434. https://doi.org/10.1080/14631377.2020.1745557

Saidi, K., & Omri, A. (2020). The impact of renewable energy on carbon emissions and economic growth in 15 major renewable energy-consuming countries. *Environmental Research, 186*, 109567. https://doi.org/10.1016/j.envres.2020.109567

Salahuddin, M., & Gow, J. (2014). Economic growth, energy consumption and CO2 emissions in Gulf Cooperation Council countries. *Energy, 73*, 44–58. https://doi.org/10.1016/j.energy.2014.05.054

Shahbaz, M., Nasreen, S., Ahmed, K., & Hammoudeh, S. (2017). Trade openness–carbon emissions nexus: The importance of turning points of trade openness for country panels. *Energy Economics, 61*, 221–232. https://doi.org/10.1016/j.eneco.2016.11.008

Shahbaz, M., Solarin, S. A., Mahmood, H., & Arouri, M. (2013). Does financial development reduce CO2 emissions in Malaysian economy? A time series analysis. *Economic Modelling, 35*, 145–152. https://doi.org/10.1016/j.econmod.2013.06.037

Sineviciene L., Kubatko O.V., Sotnyk I.M., Lakstutiene A. (2019) Economic and Environmental Performance of Post-Communist Transition Economies. In: M. Bilgin, H. Danis , E. Demir & U. Can (Eds.) *Eurasian Economic Perspectives. (Eurasian Studies in Business and Economics, Vol. 11/1.)* Springer, Cham. https://doi.org/10.1007/978-3-030-18565-7_10

Soytas, U., Sari, R., & Ewing, B. T. (2007). Energy consumption, income, and carbon emissions in the United States. *Ecological Economics, 62*(3–4), 482–489. https://doi.org/10.1016/j.ecolecon.2006.07.009

Udara Willhelm Abeydeera, L. H., Wadu Mesthrige, J., & Samarasinghalage, T. I. (2019). Global research on carbon emissions: A scientometric review. *Sustainability*, *11*(14), 3972. https://doi.org/10.3390/su11143972

Umurzakov, U., Mirzaev, B., Salahodjaev, R., Isaeva, A., & Tosheva, S. (2020). Energy consumption and economic growth: Evidence from post-communist countries. *International Journal of Energy Economics and Policy*, *10*(6), 59. https://doi.org/10.32479/ijeep.10003

Wolfson, Z. (1989). Natural resources development: An economic and environmental problem in the USSR. *Communist Economies*, *1*(1), 79–88. https://doi.org/10.1080/14631378908427591

Yasmeen, R., Li, Y., & Hafeez, M. (2019). Tracing the trade–pollution nexus in global value chains: Evidence from air pollution indicators. *Environmental Science and Pollution Research*, *26*(5), 5221–5233. https://doi.org/10.1007/s11356-018-3956-0

Zafar, M. W., Shahbaz, M., Sinha, A., Sengupta, T., & Qin, Q. (2020). How renewable energy consumption contribute to environmental quality? The role of education in OECD countries. *Journal of Cleaner Production*, *268*, 122149. https://doi.org/10.1016/j.jclepro.2020.122149

Zhang, K. H. (2001). Does foreign direct investment promote economic growth? Evidence from East Asia and Latin America. *Contemporary Economic Policy*, *19*(2), 175–185. https://doi.org/10.1111/j.1465-7287.2001.tb00059.x

Zhang, X.-P., & Cheng, X.-M. (2009). Energy consumption, carbon emissions, and economic growth in China. *Ecological Economics*, *68*(10), 2706–2712. https://doi.org/10.1016/j.ecolecon.2009.05.011

Zhang, Y., & Zhang, S. (2018). The impacts of GDP, trade structure, exchange rate and FDI inflows on China's carbon emissions. *Energy Policy*, *120*, 347–353. https://doi.org/10.1016/j.enpol.2018.05.056

Nuclear supply chain and environmental justice struggles in Soviet and Post-Soviet countries

Ksenija Hanaček and Joan Martinez-Alier

ABSTRACT
This article addresses and contributes to the discussion on nuclear supply chain socio-environmental conflicts in Soviet and post-Soviet contexts by bringing it together with nuclear peripheralization and environmental justice approaches. Descriptive statistics and qualitative coding were applied to 14 cases identified in the Global Atlas of Environmental Justice. Visible protests were first detected in 1976. The cases analysed comprise the whole nuclear supply chain; uranium mining bans, stopping nuclear reactors, and nuclear testing bans. Seven of the conflictive projects have been suspended by neighbours, citizens and communities, women, industrial workers, and Indigenous groups. However, nuclear projects remain of ongoing concern related to nuclear waste and potential nuclear accidents. Military violence intrinsic to nuclear power domination encounters anti-nuclear resistance in areas where nuclear socio-environmental legacies and current injustices are lived.

1. Introduction

After the fall of the Soviet Union in 1991, environmental dangers and harms from the nuclear supply chain – that is, uranium extraction, nuclear power production, nuclear weapons, and accumulated or newly produced waste – are a continuing concern (Malin, 2015; Uralbekov et al., 2011). This is the case for the Russian Federation but especially noticeable in its internal and external peripheries, such as Belarus, Lithuania, Kazakhstan, Ukraine, Kaliningrad oblast, as well as the Northern Indigenous lands and the Southern Ural Mountains of the Russian Federation. Nuclear development is 'designed' in such a way that the periphery suffers from economic, political and socio-environmental burdens (Abashin & Jenks, 2015; Nieto, 2011; Salmi, 2008).

The notion of Military Industrial Complex describes the relationship between a nation's military and the defence industry (Aspaturian, 1972; Fallows, 2002). It particularly applies to the nuclear industry. Military Industrial Complex was famously born in President Eisenhower's farewell address of 1961 and its application to the Soviet politics has been discussed (Aspaturian, 1972; Fallows, 2002).

In the light of Military Industrial Complex, this article examines the links between nuclear peripheralization and environmental justice in Soviet and post-Soviet countries. We study both the nuclear legacies and the novelties giving rise to nuclear conflicts. The term nuclear 'peripheralization' refers to spatial, economic, social and environmental marginality (Blowers, 2010, 1999) through which pro-nuclear actors, either state or private, repetitively target territories and lives of historically marginalised peoples in order to maintain hazardous nuclear production and waste disposal (Endres, 2009, p. 40 via Churchill, 1993; Runyan, 2018).

'Peripheries are the spatial effect of colonial state power at multiple scales and locations, which exceed the space and scale of the territorial state' (Akhter, 2017, p. 2). Thus, the concept of peripheralization applies to the periphery outside and inside the core zones (Grosfoguel, 2007). This form of coloniality is manifested in relations of exploitation between capital and labour; and relations of domination between metropolitan and peripheral states, including cultural, political, epistemic, and economic oppression of marginalised groups by dominant groups (Grosfoguel, 2007).

Russia colonised Siberia in the 16th century, and later on, the Caucasus and Central Asia (Tlostanova & Mignolo, 2009). Colonisation of the Russian Arctic also began in the 16th century. By 1870 the Arctic was a part of the Russian Empire. Under the Soviet time, the Arctic region was industrialised and exploited (Josephson, 2014).

Environmental justice (EJ) is a concept born from movements in the United States in the 1980s, referring to the struggle led by African-American, Asian, Latin, women, and Indigenous communities against environmental hazards and harms (Bullard & Chavis, 1996; Kojola & Pellow, 2020). EJ addresses how social and economic inequality, oppression, privilege, hierarchy, and practices lead to environmental injustices of historically marginalised people (Pellow, 2016). Environmental injustices are a social construct, in which, people who already suffer social, racial, gender, economic discrimination endure environmental harms (Bullard & Chavis, 1996; Pellow, 2016; Pellow & Brulle, 2005). EJ seeks to understand and make visible the forms these socio-environmental injustices take.

At the same time, EJ seeks to understand the struggles and responses of the people who oppose lived socio-environmental injustices and call for sustainability, solidarity, equity and justice (Pellow, 2016; Pellow & Brulle, 2005; Schlosberg, 2013). The topic of environmental justice in (post)-Soviet societies has been thoroughly analysed in a book edited by Agyeman and Ogneva-Himmelberger (2009). Compared to them, we emphasise environmental injustices only related to the nuclear supply chain.

People affected by nuclear projects often protest against and resist potential or actual contamination by radiation (Gordeev et al., 2002; Peluso & Watts, 2001). These are anti-nuclear conflicts, in which people confront and challenge nuclear power, and ultimately make visible the nuclear harms on their bodies, waters and lands (Malin, 2015; Marsh & Green, 2020). Studying such socio-environmental conflicts and environmental justice is important for understanding how economic, political, and environmental decisions impose negative environmental impacts on already marginalised and discriminated people (Pellow & Brulle, 2005; Schlosberg & Carruthers, 2010; Temper, 2019; Tonne et al., 2018).

For the purpose of this study, we understand the concept of environmental conflict (Martinez-Alier, 2002) as a resistance process related to the nuclear supply chain projects, such as uranium extraction, nuclear test sites, or nuclear power plant (NPP). Among the consequences that a nuclear project can have on people, their surrounding environment and their health are exposure to radiation; air, soil, and water contamination; displacement, migrations; and state repression. Opposition refers to a resistance against a nuclear project and its negative impacts on humans and the environment. On one hand, some protests might lead to a project cancellation. On the other hand, a project can remain in its operational stage, despite protests and oppositions (Scheidel et al., 2020); this is a more common outcome within the context of non-democratic political regimes.[1] Thus, the nexus of political regimes and environmental agenda is a highly important issue.

This paper contributes to this Special Issue through analysis of the nuclear supply chain projects and environmental injustice in post-Soviet autocracies (Russia, Belarus, and Kazakhstan), in semi-democracies (Kyrgyzstan and Ukraine) and in Lithuania (democracy). All these countries are former republics of the Union of Soviet Socialist Republics[2] and they all have nuclear legacies. We present the evidence of 14 nuclear conflict cases in these countries from the Global Atlas of Environmental Justice – the EJAtlas (Temper et al., 2018).

With the concept of 'nuclear peripheralization' and EJ we seek to contribute to the analysis of the historical and present conflicts on uranium extraction, NPP, nuclear weapon testing sites, nuclear power production and waste disposal issues. In doing so, in Section 2 we first trace the early 'enthusiasm' about nuclear power that Russia shared with the West from 1917 onwards. We briefly explain how nuclear power as a source of electricity and as part of the military arsenal became a feature of the Soviet industrial and geopolitical landscapes. Some conflicts are still linked to this historical legacy; some other conflicts are of post-Soviet origin, illustrating the links between military and civil nuclear power, and the relevance of energy technologies for politics. This leads to Section 3 on nuclear 'peripheralization' and to Section 4 on socio-environmental conflicts related to the nuclear chain. Section 5 applies the concepts of environmental justice to controversial nuclear projects that cause environmental conflicts. The Methodology follows in Section 6 introducing the 14 nuclear conflicts analysed. The Results are presented in Section 7 classifying the conflicts along the nuclear supply chain, the types of violence exercised and explaining further the significance of the nuclear 'peripheralization' notion. The Discussion in Section 8 presents the interrelations between historical and present nuclear chain conflicts, and comments on the links between participants and project outcomes. The last Section presents the conclusions pointing out that civil and military nuclear energy are technologies that go together, producing socio-environmental injustices across political regimes. However, environmental injustices are resisted by affected people all along the chain, both historically and presently.

2. The search for industrial and military nuclear energy

The biologist Vernadsky (1863–1945) is rightly acknowledged for his work on the geo-biochemical cycles, and the use of the concept of 'biosphere'. He developed a geo-engineering approach to the 'noosphere'. In the 1920s Vernadsky wrote influential pages on what one could call the 'anti-entropic energetics of life' (Vernadsky, 1926, 1924). We bring his views here because of his past and current stature in Russian and world science, and also because he represented the consensus on the virtues of nuclear power.

According to Kuzmin (2013), although Vernadsky was a biologist and not a nuclear physicist, 'one of the most interesting areas of Vernadsky's creativity and scientific management was connected to his works on radioactivity, search for its natural sources and practical applications of nuclear energy' (cf. Martinez-Alier, 1990, p. 226). Vernadsky recognised very early this new 'great' source of energy for humanity. He mentioned this at length in 1910 in a pre-Soviet speech, 'The urgent issues of radium': *'We watch a revelation of such a source of energy that will make negligible the power of steam, electricity, the power of explosive chemical processes [...], in the phenomenon of radioactivity we anticipate a source of nuclear energy which is millions of times greater than all energy sources that mankind was dreaming of.'*

Vernadsky held this favourable position to nuclear energy before and after 1917, in the periods of his life outside the Russian empire and inside the Soviet Union. According to Kuzmin (2013) Vernadsky collaborated in the 1930s and during World War II in the geological search for uranium in the Soviet Union. The pro-nuclear consensus that a revered scientist like Vernadsky expressed for years had many parallels in countries of the West.

After 1945, other scientists became openly alarmed at the apparent links between military and civil use of nuclear energy because the waste from 'civil' nuclear power became a raw material for bombs. Frederick Soddy was one of the critical nuclear scientists already in the 1940s. Lewis Mumford wrote at length on this already in the early 1950s (Mumford, 1956, p. 1147). We could trace similar worries in the Soviet Union much before 1990, in particular after the Kyshtym accident of 1957 that much later Zhores Medvedev made known to the world (EJAtlas, 2017). Thus, awareness of other nuclear accidents and damages particularly from nuclear testing was widespread in the Soviet Union and the West before 1990.

3. Nuclear peripheralization and resistance

The end of World War II signalled the expansion of nuclear age and nuclear weapons (Prăvălie, 2014, p. 729). During the Soviet period about 30–40% of the uranium needed for nuclear weapons was extracted from the Central Asian Republics of Kazakhstan, Kyrgyzstan, Tajikistan, and Uzbekistan. In fact, the uranium used for the first Soviet nuclear bomb was mined in Tajikistan. Today, the radioactive waste volumes associated with uranium mining in Kazakhstan, Kyrgyzstan, Tajikistan and Uzbekistan are estimated at 400 million tones (Salbu, 2013).

In the years following World War II, the Soviet Union but also the United States and Great Britain conducted many nuclear weapon tests at the expense of the environment and the people who lived far away from the nuclear powers but relatively near the chosen testing sites (Gordeev et al., 2002; Jacobs, 2013; Johansen, 2002).

In 1954, when nuclear fission technology was approved for commercial purposes, the first fully commercial nuclear power plant built by Westinghouse in the USA, was the Dresden Unit 1, with a production capacity of 250 megawatts (EIA, 2012). The first two Soviet commercial nuclear power plants began operating 10 years later in Beloyarsk (Urals) with a capacity of 100 megawatts and in Novovoronezh (Volga region) with 200 megawatts capacity (WNA, 2020). By 1990 the Soviet Union had a total capacity of about 18,000 megawatts of nuclear electricity (WNA, 2021).

Then, in 1986 the Chernobyl NPP 'meltdown' took place. In the late 1980 and early 1990s, political and economic instability marked the end of the Soviet Union and the Cold War. A crisis in the nuclear sector was not an exception (Kasperski, 2012, 2017). The ambitious programme to construct new and expand existing nuclear power capacity was put on hold (Marples, 1993).

In addition, only during the democratisation period of the 1980s-1990s, people of the contaminated places started openly to protest against officials responsible for the impacts of nuclear tests, accidents, and poor nuclear waste management risking the lives and the health of millions of Soviet citizens (Alexievich, 2006; Kasperski, 2012). For instance, in Belarus, commemorations of the Chernobyl victims were among the first public protests, where people expressed their concerns and opposition against radioactive contamination (Kasperski, 2012, 2019). At the same time, some formerly classified information on nuclear radiation harms became known to the public (Bauer et al., 2013; Johnston, 2007; Kasperski, 2012).

In 1989, the Nevada–Semipalatinsk Antinuclear Movement was formed in Kazakhstan (Bauer et al., 2013) against the Semipalatinsk nuclear weapons test site. The movement's largest demonstration with 50,000 participants was at the 44th anniversary of the nuclear attack on Hiroshima. In 1990, the Kazakhstan parliament passed a bill banning nuclear weapons testing in the whole country. The same year, the Semipalatinsk site was officially closed. The anti-nuclear movement was an important factor in the dismembering of the Soviet Union (UNESCO, 2005). These movements 'at the periphery' were helped by the independence of mass media that revolutionised the society across the vast territory of the USSR throughout the 1980s and 1990s.

Similarly, environmental movement 'Zelenyi Svit' in 1988 demanded from the Ukrainian government to declare a moratorium on any new nuclear reactors in the country (Marples, 1993; Sak, 1993). Finally, in 1995, the international Non-Proliferation of Nuclear Weapons Treaty was signed which ended the nuclear arms race and 'promised' to use nuclear energy only for 'peaceful purposes' (Magnarella, 2008; UN, 1995).

4. Nuclear supply chain-related socio-environmental conflicts

Nuclear power production and nuclear weapons are considered in this section since both are related issues. They are part of the Military Industrial Complex (Aspaturian, 1972; Fallows, 2002). According to Jacobs (2013), for the Soviet Union as well as for other nuclear powers (the UK, the USA, France, China), selecting a site for nuclear testing was not a process driven by scientific and military requirements alone. Rather, it was driven by relative scarcity of population. However, the sites were and still are populated (Jacobs, 2013; Turner, 1997). For instance, the Soviet Union performed nuclear testing in the Soviet Republic of Kazakhstan. It also tested in Novaya Zemlya – home to Indigenous people of the North (Jacobs, 2013; Khalturin et al., 2005). The 'Tsar Bomba' detonated in Novaya Zemlya in 1961 was the world's most powerful nuclear weapon ever detonated (see Khan, 2021).

Nuclear energy remains a key element in the political, institutional, and technological transformations of the post-Soviet industry (Kasperski, 2019, 2017). The industry pushes uranium extraction and waste disposal in Kazakhstan and Kyrgyzstan (Uralbekov et al., 2011). Further, the pro-nuclear lobby plays a major role in uranium mining, uranium enrichment, and nuclear plant constructions at the expense of thousands, if not millions, of people worldwide (Conde, 2017; Litmanen & Kojo, 2011).

Today, nuclear power plants (NPP) encounter opposition in post-Soviet neighbouring countries under the Espoo Convention – a treaty on Environmental Impact Assessment in a Transboundary Context signed in this city of Finland in 1991. A meeting of the Parties to the Espoo Convention decided that Belarus had violated the Convention in choosing a construction site for its new NPP Astravets so near to Vilnius (Lithuania) (Iržikevičius, 2019). Regarding the NPP in Kaliningrad oblast, the Rosatom considered the Espoo Convention even though Russia had not yet ratified the treaty. Further, a meeting of Parties to the Convention decided that Armenia violated its obligation by contemplating construction while the country has been asked to decommission the old Metsamor NPP reactor. A possible military threat against Metsamor was also raised by Azerbaijan (UNECE, 2020).

The EJAtlas database confirms that nuclear power in the former Soviet area is often synonymous with Rosatom – the Russian State Atomic Energy Corporation. The geopolitical power of the Soviet and now of the Russian Federation nuclear power industry extends inside the former Soviet countries but also outside. Like the French company Areva and its presence overseas, Rosatom has a conflictive presence in some cases in the Russian Federation and also in former Soviet republics, such as Armenia and Belarus.[3] Beyond these confines, already in Soviet times but now with renewed force, Rosatom is as well present in Finland, India, Turkey, South Africa, Tanzania, Jordan and Philippines.

Internally, however, uranium mining, nuclear power plant stations, and waste disposal – either new or the legacy from the Soviet time – still have negative environmental, social and health consequences (Petryna, 2002; Prăvălie, 2014). This 'invisible' and 'silenced' radiation (Nixon, 2011; Reich & Goto, 2015) is, however, made visible by people who live it and strongly oppose it (Dubuisson, 2020; Ziegler & Lyon, 2002). Protests against controversial uranium mines, NPPs, nuclear waste dumps, nuclear military installations, and nuclear accidents are present from Lithuania across Russia to Novaya Zemlya and the Urals.

5. The nuclear supply chain and environmental justice

Environmental justice scholarship has increasingly highlighted the need to put social justice struggles at the centre of struggles for environmental justice (Kojola & Pellow, 2020; Pellow & Brulle, 2005). For instance, exposure to radiation reveals intersecting patterns across social class, race, ethnicity, gender, abilities, ages and on different bodies, spaces, and ecosystems. Environmental justice struggles make visible the multiple axes at which social marginalisation, often based on colonial relations, lead to environmental injustice (Johnston, 2007; Marsh & Green, 2020; Pellow, 2016).

Present and historical hazardous nuclear-chain projects are implemented more often than not at internal or external 'peripheral' places, and harm ethnic and racialised people, including differences of gender, age, class, and their future generations (Endres, 2009; Fan, 2006; Malin & Ryder, 2018; Walker & Bulkeley, 2006). For the (post)-Soviet territories, for example, the Semipalatinsk test site not only exposed the local population and their future generations to radiation but also contributed to continuous psychological concerns for the people living with nuclear legacies (Bauer et al., 2013).

The nuclear-chain production is especially harmful to local inhabitants and future generations through water, air, and soil exposure (Bauer et al., 2013; Endres, 2009; Kyne & Bolin, 2016). This applies to both industrial and military uses (Malin, 2015; Prăvălie, 2014).

The state violence across the nuclear supply chain development is another aspect to be considered within the environmental justice framework (Marsh & Green, 2020; Pellow, 2016). Under the umbrella of nuclear defence and energy power, the militarised state brings violence to Indigenous groups, racially discriminated people and women (Johnston, 2007; Marsh & Green, 2020).These social groups have been repeatedly targeted to bear the burdens of nuclear tests, nuclear waste, and mine tailings (Kuletz, 2001). This was not the only characteristic of the (post)-Soviet nuclear geography (Johnston, 2007). It also happened in the United States, Australia, and Canada among others (Kyne & Bolin, 2016).

According to World Nuclear Association, over two-third of the world's *production* of uranium comes from mines in Kazakhstan. Canada follows in the production of uranium. In Canada 70% of uranium deposits are located on the traditional lands of First Nations (Graetz, 2014). In Australia, Aboriginal lands are assumed to be 'desert regions' or 'uninhabited', therefore targeted for uranium mining (Göcke, 2014). This is similar to Niger and Namibia where transnational companies, such as Areva and Rio Tinto operate (Conde & Kallis, 2012).

According to Atomic Archive, from 1945 until July 2020 the nuclear power countries, that is, the Soviet Union, the US, the UK, France, China, and North Korea conducted, in total, 1030 nuclear tests. US is the country with the highest number of nuclear tests, followed by the Soviet Union/Russian Federation, France, China, and the UK.

The places where the testing was performed include overseas or their internal colonised territories (Jacobs, 2013). For example, Lop Nor in China; Nevada in US and also in Bikini and Enewetak (Marshall Islands) (EJAtlas, 2018). France conducted its nuclear tests in Algeria and in Moruroa in the Pacific (EJAtlas, 2019); UK in Western Australia and the South Atlantic. Nuclear tests in Semipalatinsk (Kazakhstan) and Novaya Zemlya in the Arctic Russia were carried out by the Soviet Union, as also in Viliui (Sakha) where underground explosions took place to build dams for the diamond industry (Agyeman & Ogneva-Himmelberger, 2009, p. 194). India and Pakistan have carried some tests in internal 'desert' areas.

The same countries that performed most of the nuclear testing between 1945 and 2020, possess the highest number of operable nuclear reactors. Namely, the US, France, China, and the Russian Federation. Today, there are 442 operable nuclear reactors worldwide, out of which 95 are active in the US, 57 in France, 47 in China, 38 in the Russian Federation, 15 in Ukraine, and one in Belarus and one in Armenia (Statista, 2020).

6. Methodology

6.1. Data gathering

Socio-environmental conflicts in (post)-Soviet countries related to nuclear supply chain were gathered from the Global Atlas of Environmental Justice – the EJAtlas. The Atlas is a global database of socio-environmental conflicts and environmental justice struggles elaborated between academics and activists that facilitates research in comparative political ecology. It started in 2012 and reached 3360 cases by February 2021. It is described in Temper et al. (2018). Each entry in the EJAtlas has six pages, including a 500 to 1000 words description and over 80 variables. Recent peer-reviewed publications where the EJAtlas has been used include (Gobby et al., 2021; Martínez-Alier, 2021; Martinez-Alier et al., 2016; Scheidel et al., 2020; Temper et al., 2020). The EJAtlas is, however, not an exhaustive inventory of all existing environmental conflicts around the world, and therefore, some conflicts might have been left aside.

In January 2021, we identified seven existing nuclear cases in the Atlas. To enlarge the scope of this article, we have additionally written seven cases based on secondary sources. The newly uploaded cases were revised and moderate by editors of the Atlas and finally published. Thus, the 14 cases of nuclear supply chain-related conflicts in the countries appear in the Atlas when applying filters 'Country' AND 'Nuclear' OR 'Nuclear power plants' OR 'Nuclear waste storage' OR 'Uranium mining' (Appendix A).

6.2. Data analysis

Firstly, we used already established categories of the Atlas (Scheidel et al., 2020). Secondly, by following Gibbs (2004) qualitative bottom-up codification methods were applied, through which we identified new qualitative variables by reading cases description line by line. Both the established categories and the newly coded variables are listed in Appendix B.

In particular, we analyse anti-nuclear movements that build up social and environmental justice, that is, who are the social protagonists (which social class, gender, ethnic background); consequences and forms of resistance along the nuclear-chain supply; socio-environmental and health problems; the processes that have stopped or tried to stop different nuclear projects; state violence along the nuclear chain; radiation issues in localised communities and spaces. These variables were examined through *Degree* algorithm of the network analysis. Degree centrality assigns an importance score based on the number of coded links between variables (Golbeck, 2015).

Based on Blowers and Leroy (2006), Jacobs (2013), Marsh and Green (2020), Akhter (2017), and Pellow (2016), guiding concepts are 'nuclear peripheralization', 'environmental conflict', and 'environmental justice' in order to study how do people protest at the stages of the nuclear supply chain, in Soviet and post-Soviet countries (Appendix A). This article is thus a distillation of the information contained in the 14 cases in the EJAtlas.

7. Results

7.1. Nuclear supply chain peripheralization and socio-environmental conflicts

Figure 1 locates all the 14 cases according to their type in the historical and contemporary nuclear supply chain. Socio-environmental conflicts related to the Soviet nuclear testing and accumulated radioactive waste, born from the opposition from local people, are evident in both internal and external 'peripheries'. For instance, Novaya Zemlya remains a guarded military establishment on the Indigenous territories until the present time.

Conflicts against nuclear power plants including two nuclear explosions that lead to enormous socio-environmental and health consequences due to radiation, are situated in Chernobyl, Ukraine, and Mayak – a plutonium production site for nuclear weapons and nuclear fuel reprocessing plant. Mayak is located in the closed military City-40 (today Ozyorsk) near Chelyabinsk in the Russian Federation. In fact, Ozyorsk is the birthplace of the Soviet nuclear weapons program after World War II. The explosion of a nuclear reprocessing facility in Ozyorsk exposed 177,000 people to high levels of radiation. Still today, the city, its soils and waters are contaminated with radioactive waste due to uranium enrichment (Kyne & Bolin, 2016).

One of the most successful mass anti-nuclear protest movement – the Nevada-Semipalatinsk Anti-Nuclear movement (Kazakhstan) was active between 1989 and 1991. The movement achieved not only the closing down of the Semipalatinsk nuclear testing site, but a moratorium of all nuclear testing in the former Soviet Union, bringing thereby an alliance with the US anti-nuclear groups.

Conflicts on nuclear power plant are taking place in Armenia, Lithuania, Belarus, and Arctic Russia. Another two conflict cases related to NPPs are found in the Russian Federation (Bashkir and Sosnovy Bor, Leningrad Oblast). In the Lithuanian case, a referendum in 2012 ended plans for a new nuclear power plant after two large reactors at Ignalina had been stopped in 2004 and 2009 as well. There are now difficult issues regarding nuclear waste. In Belarus, a NPP has been built in Astrovets, not far from the border with Lithuania, despite many protests. Metsamor, the Armenian NPP, is ageing and the proximity of the plant to earthquake-prone areas makes it a most dangerous plant.

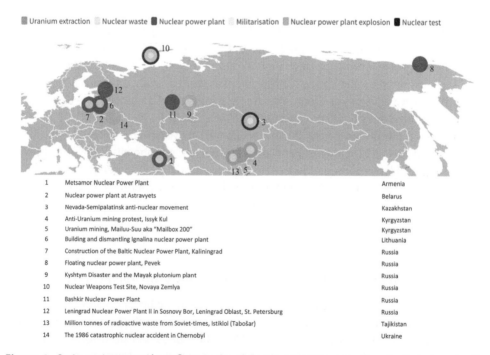

Figure 1. Socio-environmental conflicts in (post)-Soviet countries according to their type in the historical and contemporary nuclear supply chain.

Another dangerous floating nuclear power plant is placed in the Arctic town of Pevek, despite the opposition from socio-environmental groups.

Uranium extraction and tailings related conflicts are identified in Kyrgyzstan and Tajikistan. There are thousands of tons of radioactive waste accumulated in the town of Mailuu-Suu since the Soviet era, upstream in the Syr Darya river basin. Radioactive contamination of the environment and the people continue. In Kyrgyzstan further, people distrust the inappropriate waste management by national and international government bodies.

7.2. Characterisation of nuclear supply chain conflicts

Out of 14 nuclear-chain cases analysed in this article, nine are related to NPPs. There are six NPP conflicts in urban areas, and three cases identified in rural areas. Further, three cases on uranium extraction are only related to rural areas. Similarly, two nuclear tests took place in either rural or semi-urban areas. There are seven nuclear waste-related cases, five in rural areas and two in urban areas. However, nuclear waste cases overlap with conflicts on uranium extraction, electricity production and nuclear testing. (Figure 2).

In the analysed cases, further, there is a pattern of state violence which includes state secret classification projects (n = 7), militarisation and increase or the increase military presence (n = 5), arrests of people who peacefully protest in nuclear-chain conflicts (n = 4), and displacement of people from their territories where nuclear projects are either planned or already taking place (n = 2) (Figure 3).

Visible health consequences and nuclear accidents reported case include long-term health and psychological effects on people (n = 13), direct exposure to radiation (n = 12), occupational diseases (n = 6), direct deaths (n = 4) and accidents (n = 2) (Figure 4A). Potential health consequences are deemed to be occupational diseases (n = 4), deaths (n = 1), direct exposure to radiation (n = 1), and potential nuclear accidents are reported for 11 out of 14 cases (Figure 4B).

The most affected groups by nuclear-chain projects are neighbours and citizens (n = 14) (Figure 5); also industrial workers, women activists, Indigenous and traditional communities. Other social actors opposing nuclear projects are international and local environmental justice organisations (EJOs), local scientists and professionals as well as local governments and political parties.

Due to protests, four nuclear supply chain projects have been temporarily suspended and three completely stopped. iFive projects are still active or in operation and two projects are under construction (Figure 6). The earliest identified protest was in 1976 by the scientific community for the Kyshtym Disaster and the Mayak plutonium plant case. Civil society protests were identified for the Nevada-Semipalatinsk anti-nuclear movement in 1989. It is worth mentioning that Nevada-Semipalatinsk case is related to the Novaya Zemlya case (nuclear tests conducted between 1954 and 1990). Antinuclear activists opposed the 'Tsar bomba' test with their Arctic alliances in Novaya Zemlya. However, the Soviet Government secretly conduct the test on 24 October 1990. This was the last nuclear test to take place in the Soviet Union.

Figure 7 builds on Figure 6 and shows the period when a protest started (mobilisation stage) and the current situation of the project (status). For instance, in period of 1976-1989 in our data sample there are 3 mobilisations for reparations once nuclear impacts have been felt. Further, between 1990-1991and in the period of 2012-2017 there are protests in

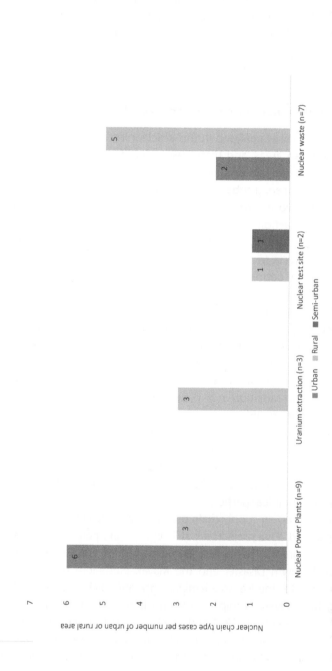

Figure 2. Nuclear supply chain conflicts (NPP, uranium extraction, and test sites) in urban, semi-urban or rural areas (n = 14). Nuclear waste conflicts (n = 7) are not mutually exclusive to other nuclear chain conflicts.

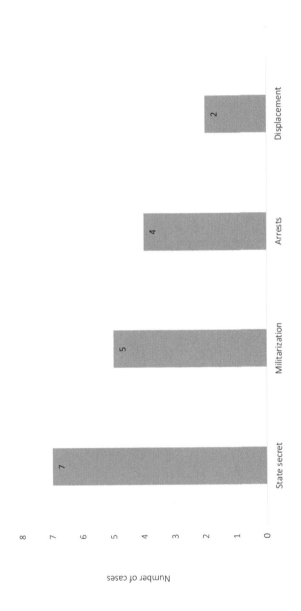

Figure 3. State violence in nuclear supply chain conflicts. Coded forms of violence are not mutually exclusive within analysed cases. N = 14.

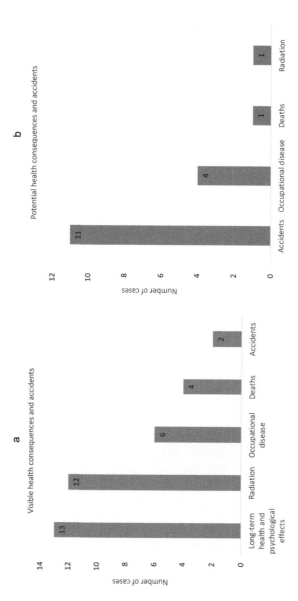

Figure 4. (A) Visible and (B) potential health consequences and accidents in the analysed cases. Variables are not mutually exclusive. N = 14.

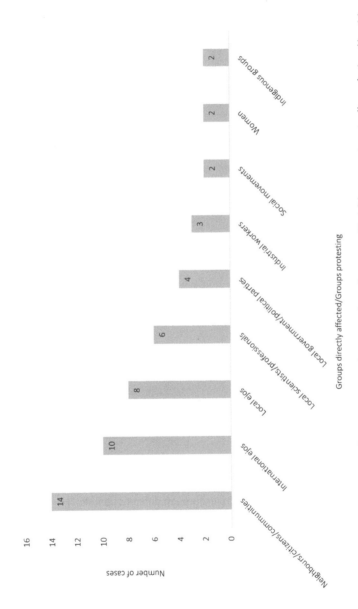

Figure 5. Social groups affected by nuclear supply chain projects and protagonists of protests. Variables are not mutually exclusive. N = 14.

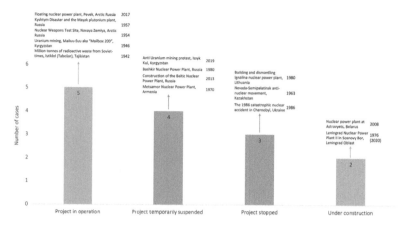

Figure 6. Start of the nuclear supply chain project (year) and current project status due to protests. Project in operation and under construction are considered as active projects (blue), while project temporary suspended and fully stopped are regarded as no-active projects (grey). N = 14.

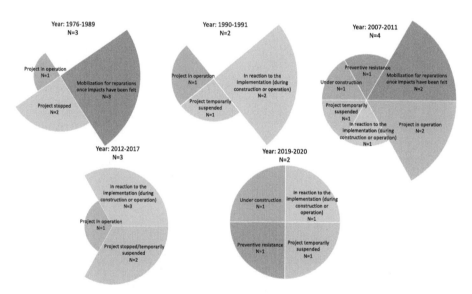

Figure 7. Mobilisation stage and project status through different periods. N = 14.

reaction to a project implementation. Preventive resistance first appears in 2007 and later in 2019–2020. In each of the periods at least one project has been suspended or fully stopped.

7.3. Interrelation between nuclear supply chain peripheralization, environmental justice struggles, and environmental conflict status

This section provides results of the interrelated process of nuclear peripheralization, environmental justice struggles by the people affected directly or indirectly by the nuclear supply chain, and environmental conflict status. Figure 8 is based on the codification

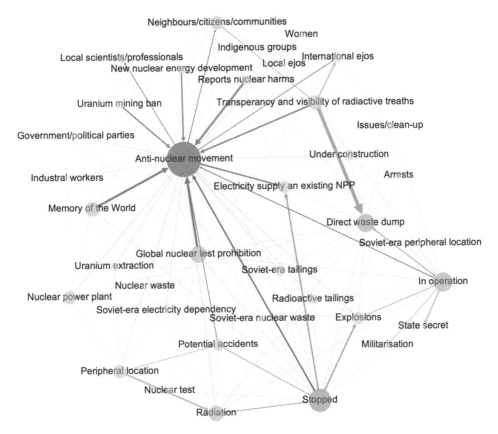

Figure 8. Nuclear peripheralization and resistance to it. Anti-nuclear movement is the central variable. The thicker the connecting line and the closer the variables, the stronger their relation. Data is based on the codification method and *Degree* algorithm of the network analysis.

methods and some established variables of the Atlas. Figure 8 illustrates the relations among such variables in a network based on the *Degree algorithm* (Golbeck, 2015). The central coded variable is the anti-nuclear movement against the nuclear peripheralization process.

Thus, nuclear peripheralization applies to the whole nuclear chain (Figure 8). For uranium extraction, nuclear peripheralization includes Soviet-era accumulated waste and its direct dump into the soils and water, where many Kyrgyz and Tajik people live. These cases are unsolved, and the projects are considered still as active or 'in operation'. These conflicts arise because accumulated and directly dumped nuclear waste still brings threats to the local people and their future generations. Groups protesting against uranium mining and tailings cases include Kyrgyz, Tajiks and Kazakh neighbours, citizens and local communities, local scientist and professionals, local government, and political parties but also international environmental justice organisations. Uranium tailings are frequently related to potential accidents of the waste overflow or soil run-off (Figure 8). The efforts and strong opposition by groups protesting led to an official uranium mining ban, for example. Still, nuclear waste issues conflicts remain although the uranium ban is officially declared.

Historical Soviet nuclear test cases in Kazakhstan and Novaya Zemlya presently still involve Soviet-era accumulated waste issues of the sites (Figure 8). People affected by direct radiations of the nuclear testing sites have successfully stopped the testing through anti-nuclear movement reaching thereby a global nuclear testing ban recognised as the Memory of the World by UNESCO in 2005. Groups involved in the anti-nuclear movement and finally nuclear disarmament of the Soviet Union include neighbours, citizens, and communities; international EJOs, local scientist and professionals, local government and political parties, women leaders, and Indigenous groups.

The accumulated nuclear waste and radiation issues due to testing are understood as projects in operation (Figure 8). These cases presently affect Indigenous groups and women leaders exercising resistance by openly speaking and protesting against nuclear harms done to their communities, bodies, and the surrounding environment. Further, these cases still involve militarisation of space and state secret classified information. The same was true for the nuclear testing stage before disarmament.

Nuclear power plant conflicts in operation show, again, nuclear waste management issues, explosions, and Soviet-era electricity dependency (Figure 8). Namely, in Ukraine, Belarus, Lithuania, Armenia, and Kaliningrad oblast. Internally to the Russian Federation, however, these places are the Russian Arctic region, the 'closed' military city of Ozyorsk, and Bashkiria in the Ural Mountains.

Potential accidents concerns are frequent for NPP cases either under construction or in operation (Figure 8). Nuclear waste issues due to explosions and electricity dependency, through which people living close to the project sites have felt radiation, are projects that have been stopped in terms of the operable NPP cycle. For stopped projects or projects under construction we observe the formation of the anti-nuclear movement, development of new nuclear energy laws, as well as decisions of not expanding new NPP capacity (sometimes because of excess capacity in the existing NPP).

Social actors for NPP projects in operation are neighbours, citizens, communities, women leaders, industrial workers, and international and local EJOs. The same is true for cases that have been stopped. Militarisation and state secret classified NPP project are, again, common for cases in operation; while arrests of people protesting occurred in the resistance process for projects that have been successfully stopped.

8. Discussion

This article examined 14 nuclear supply chain environmental conflicts by looking at the links between nuclear peripheralization and environmental justice struggles in both Soviet and post-Soviet times. Based on the results obtained, we discuss three main points. Namely, nuclear peripheralization and resistance to it; violence and transgenerational radiation effects; and geographical and political legacies of the nuclear industry.

8.1. Peripheralization, nuclear supply chain, and resistance

Our study confirms the concept of peripheralization as marked spaces of social marginalisation based on colonial state power relations, leading to environmental injustice (Johnston, 2007; Marsh & Green, 2020; Pellow, 2016; Akhter, 2017, p. 13). In line with Jacobs (2013), initially, nuclear testing resulted in a huge amount of space and bodies that were contaminated for military purposes, such as the Indigenous lands of Novaya Zemlya and Semipalatinsk site in Kazakhstan. Our results reveal further that related nuclear waste as well as contamination by radiation persist today over these large spaces. This is how nuclear peripheralization forms over time. These conflicts are ongoing.

Our results are similar to those reported by Endres (2009), which show how Indigenous people in the United States continue to resist nuclear projects and related waste storage located on their lands. Further, Fan (2006) indicates conflicts over the nuclear waste issues on Tribal lands in Taiwan as concerns for their cultural survival. Marsh and Green (2020) argue that uranium mines located on Aboriginal lands in Australia are grounded in a history of colonial oppression and the use of extractive violence, which desecrate Indigenous people and their traditional lands.

Our results further show that ongoing nuclear-chain conflicts occur in the same or nearby places where historically uranium mining and/or nuclear weapons test first took place. Accordingly, these are often militarised places where contamination by radiation persists through the Soviet-era uranium tailings, direct nuclear waste dumps from bombs, and presently, through nuclear power production. The cases, thus, can be considered as transgenerational environmental injustice (Kyne & Bolin, 2016) and a nuclear inheritance of the Military Industrial Complex (Aspaturian, 1972; Fallows, 2002) – embedded in social, historical, and political-economic complexity (Ishiyama, 2003).

Yet, the anti-nuclear movement both historically and presently play an important role in closing nuclear test sites and several NPP projects considered as potentially dangerous due to possible accidents. The military and the civilian use of nuclear energy cannot be seen as separate issues (Aspaturian, 1972; Fallows, 2002; Kuletz, 2001). In his early warnings against nuclear power Jungk (1979) highlighted that military and civilian usage of nuclear energy is inseparable. The author, further, argued how the risks of nuclear energy do not only threaten the environment, health, and well-being, but also democracy. This view had been anticipated by Mumford's (1970) notion of the 'Megamachine'.

In fact, it could be argued that civil and military nuclear energy are technologies whose effects are felt across political regimes. For instance, this can be mainly observed through the Kaliningrad oblast case, situated between Poland, Lithuania, and Belarus. A 'central' geostrategic importance of the oblast goes hand in hand not only with military deployments but also with developments in international relations (Nieto, 2011). However, the 2,400 MW NPP project in Kaliningrad oblast has been adjourned since 2011 because of the availability of natural gas to produce electricity, because of local resistance (Ecodefense Press-release, 2014), and because of geopolitical implications.

Consequences of uranium mining or nuclear weapons testing or NPP are far from over for the local inhabitants, confronting the radioactive legacies that seek socio-environmental justice for about eight decades (Johnston, 2007), thereby revealing the past and present nuclear supply chain issues. In that regard, resistance against nuclear supply chain cannot be seen as isolated episodes of struggle. These are persistent historical processes of what has been called 'nuclear' peripheralization (Akhter, 2017; Blowers, 2010, 1999), showing the role of political, military and economic powers in the nuclear supply chain, as well as histories of marginalised groups and their anti-nuclear struggles (Endres, 2009; Jacobs, 2013; Marsh & Green, 2020). Affected people confront these power relations, environmental and social degradation (Keeling & Sandlos, 2009). It is crucial to see through an environmental justice lens the role of the resistance that makes visible and confronts nuclear peripheralization, including prolongated exposure to radiation (Endres, 2009; Wiebe, 2016).

In this study, we observe the realities of many people who stand for socio-environmental justice to live in environments free of radioactive harms, state violence and militarisation (Fallows, 2002; Fan, 2006; Hanson et al., 2001; Pellow, 2016). Groups involved in protests include neighbours, citizens and communities, women, Indigenous and industrial workers, but also involve local scientists and international and local environmental justice organisations.

As observed through the cases under consideration, a vision of change towards socio-environmental justice is needed for building socially and environmentally just future for all (Pellow, 2016) – free of radioactive hazards and harms; challenging the power of state, military and corporate actors across the nuclear supply chain; reaching the different scales at which the chain is (radio)active over historical periods. These scales are USSR's military power and present day post-Soviet regional development and geopolitics (Nieto, 2011).

What started as a 'great new source of energy for the humanity' now takes the form of a renewable source, avoiding energy deficit and achieving development (Litmanen & Kojo, 2011). Often, nuclear power production discourse focuses on production of energy, while the nuclear waste that it brings along is downplayed by the nuclear lobby (Blowers, 2010). Against such views, the intersection of the discourses of nuclear peripheralization and environmental justice and the Military Industrial Complex expand the debate on resistance against historical nuclear military powers and contemporary nuclear extraction and production process; for the benefit of the nuclear centre power (Endres, 2009; Yelin & Miller, 2009) and at the expense of rural and urban inhabitants, the women, the industrial workers, and the Indigenous.

8.2. Violence and transgenerational radiation effects

State violence is manifested through nuclear projects as state secrets and militarisation processes. Violence and long-term consequences are manifested in health and psychological effects the projects have on the people, historical direct nuclear testing, projects taking place in large residential areas too, displacement of the people and sometimes violent targeting of people who protest. Exposure to radiation even at low doses (Alexievich, 2006; Lambert, 2001) increases the risk of cancer, as well as psychological uncertainties and implications of possible radiation exposure (Reich & Goto, 2015; Simon & Bouville, 2015). As shown throughout our analysis, indirect or 'slow' radiation violence (Navas et al., 2018; Nixon, 2011) cannot be overlooked. Long-term health and psychological effects are produced through violent nuclear environments (Peluso & Watts 2001). These adverse environmental, health and social impacts (Churchill, 1993; Endres, 2009; Kyne & Bolin, 2016) still arise from accumulated or newly produced waste, as well as from nuclear accidents or potential explosions analysed in the present article. As Alexievich (2006) puts it, *'people's stories reveal the fear, anger, and uncertainty with which they still live'*. We agree that there are active transgenerational nuclear socio-environmental issues lived through Soviet and post-Soviet times. Thus, nuclear peripheralization develops as a direct and indirect structural violence producing environmental injustice towards historically marginalised people (Ishiyama, 2003; Navas et al., 2018; Pellow, 2016).

8.3. Geographical and political legacies of the nuclear industry

This article has considered some socio-environmental conflicts born from the technological legacies of the nuclear industry in Soviet times that are still felt in post-Soviet times. Some conflicts, such as, the Rosatom-built new nuclear power plant (NPP) in Belarus not far from Vilnius, are post-Soviet. But many conflicts started in Soviet times and continue today under different political systems. For instance, those on uranium mining tailings waste in Kyrgyzstan.

Some conflicts were much more intense in Soviet times than today. This explains for instance, the movement against nuclear bomb testing in the Nevada-Semipalatinsk in Kazakhstan at the end of the Soviet regime in the 1980s. Research on post-Soviet nuclear power is a study not only of technological legacies but also of geographical and socio-political legacies (Izotov & Obydenkova, 2021; Libman & Obydenkova, 2021, 2019; Abrams & Auer, 2004). What remains of the 'secret' politics at the locations where military nuclear power was developed such as Ozyorsk (City 40) near Chelyabinsk and which suffered accidents? Which is the geopolitical legacy of Chernobyl, and its unacknowledged environmental liabilities? Which have been the phases of internal resistance to the controversial NPP of Metsamor in Armenia since the 1970s, and which actions have neighbouring countries threatened to take?

9. Conclusion

This article reveals resistance against nuclear supply chain peripheralization in Soviet and Post-Soviet context. This resistance arises from the dangers and risks of uranium extraction, nuclear power production, weapon test sites, accumulated or new waste disposal, leaks, dumps, and radiation. Nuclear peripheralization operates through *extraction-waste, nuclear testing-space-waste, production–waste–potential-accidents*; and finally is confronted by *struggles–visibility* against nuclear harms.

Thus, the long-lasting health and socio-environmental harms persist but so does affected people's resistance, making visible the invisible and challenging militarisation and pro-nuclear discourses. Based on the evidence of 14 conflicts over the period 1980–2020, we conclude that the outcomes of conflicts have been sometimes suspension or stopping projects. These cases are first and foremost the nuclear testing ban, followed by some uranium extraction bans, stopping some nuclear reactors; and in general, confronting power relation, direct and indirect violence of the nuclear power domination imposed through peripheralization where socio-environmental injustices and radiation effects are lived. However, not all conflict cases have successful outcomes from the point of view of environmental justice. Nuclear waste and potential accidents from NPP imply a continuous system of marginalisation against urban citizens and rural communities, industrial workers, women, and Indigenous communities.

We have made visible and analysed conflicts on uranium mining and NPP including large accidents. We have investigated the legacy of accumulated or newly produced nuclear waste, touching on the role of nuclear power conflicts in the dissolution of Soviet

Union and on some transboundary conflicts. The pattern and intensity of conflicts seems to have switched from the nuclear testing period and the big accidents (such as Chernobyl) in Soviet times to those born from civil nuclear power production in the post-Soviet times. However, there is persistence of conflicts on nuclear waste, radiation issues and impacts to health in both periods.

Aware of the link between the civil and military use of nuclear energy, we have focused on nuclear testing as an everlasting issue. Although stopped, it continues to the present time through accumulated nuclear waste. We conclude that civil and military nuclear energy are technologies that go together, and they are felt and resisted across political regimes.

Notes

1. (Fredriksson & Wollscheid, 2007; Obydenkova, 2008, pp. 2012, Obydenkova, Arpino, 2018).
2. These states are all marked with legacies of Communism likely to affect public opinion, attitudes, behaviour, public trust to political institutions, protests, and policy choices (Beissinger & Kotkin, 2014; Lankina et al., 2016; Pop-Eleches & Tucker, 2017).
3. Armenia and Belarus are member-states in all regional international organisations launched by Russia, but also member-states of the Eurasian Economic Union with only five states. Both Armenia and Belarus are the main benefactors of the EAEU (Libman & Obydenkova, 2018). It is plausible that in exchange for the economic benefits of this membership, they were suggested to host Rosatom.

Acknowledgments

We are grateful to anonymous referees for their invaluable comments and suggestions provided during the peer-review process. We would like to thank the editor of the special issue, Anastassia Obydenkova, for her support and encouragement. We would like to thank all individuals and activists who contributed to the nuclear-chain cases in the EJAtlas. We are also thankful to our EJAtlas Barcelona team, and especially to Daniela Del Bene for reading and moderating the cases and to Brototi Roy, Thiri May Aye, Sofía Avila, and Grettel Navas for comments and suggestion provided. This research benefited from financial support from the European Research Council (ERC) Advanced Grant ENVJUSTICE No. 695446.

Disclosure statement

No potential conflict of interest was reported by the author(s).

Funding

This work was supported by European Research Council [ENVJUSTICE 695446].

ORCID

Ksenija Hanaček http://orcid.org/0000-0001-5283-2309
Joan Martinez-Alier http://orcid.org/0000-0002-6124-539X

References

Abashin, S., & Jenks, A. (2015). Soviet Central Asia on the periphery. *Kritika: Explorations in Russian and Eurasian History, 16*(2), 359–374. https://doi.org/10.1353/kri.2015.0027

Abrams, J. P., & Auer, M. R. (2004). The disappearance of popular Environmental Activism in Post-Soviet Russia. In M.R Auer (Ed.) Restoring Cursed Earth: *Appraising environmental policy reforms in Eastern Europe and Russia*. Rowman & Littlefield Publishers.

Agyeman, J., & Ogneva-Himmelberger, Y. (2009). *Environmental justice and sustainability in the former Soviet Union*. MIT Press Cambridge.

Akhter, M. (2017). The proliferation of peripheries. *Progress in Human Geography*, 1–17. https://doi.org/10.1177/0309132517735697

Alexievich, S. (2006). *Voices from Chernobyl: The oral history of a nuclear disaster*. Picador.

Aspaturian, V. V. (1972). The Soviet military–industrial complex: Does it exist? *Journal of International Affairs, 26*(1), 1–28.

Bauer, S., Gusev, B., Belikhina, T., Moldagaliev, T., & Apsalikov, K. (2013). The Legacies of Soviet Nuclear testing in Kazakhstan. In D. Oughton, S. Hansson (Eds.) *Radioactivity in the environment (19) Social and Ethical Aspects of Radiation Risk Management* (pp. 241–258). Elsevier. https://doi.org/10.1016/B978-0-08-045015-5.00014-9

Beissinger, M., & Kotkin, S. (Eds.). (2014). *Historical legacies of communism in Russia and Eastern Europe*. Cambridge University Press.

Blowers, A. (1999). Nuclear waste and landscapes of risk. *Landscape Research, 24*(3), 241–264. https://doi.org/10.1080/01426399908706562

Blowers, A. (2010). Why dump on us? Power, pragmatism and the periphery in the siting of new nuclear reactors in the UK. *Journal of Integrative Environmental Sciences, 7*(3), 157–173. https://doi.org/10.1080/1943815X.2010.506488

Blowers, A., & LeRroy, P. (2007). Power, politics and environmental inequality: A theoretical and empirical analysis of the process of "peripheralisation". *Contemporary Environmental Politics 3*(2), 197-228 : From Margins to Mainstream . https://doi.org/10.1080/09644019408414139

Bullard, R., & Chavis, B. (1996). *Unequal protection: Environmental justice and communities of color*. Sierra Club Books.

Churchill, W. (1993). Radioactive colonization: A hidden holocaust in native North America. In M. Monroe (Ed.), *Struggle for the Land: Indigenous Resistance to Genocide, Ecocide, and Expropriation in Contemporary North America* (pp. 261–328). Common Courage Press.

Conde, M. (2017). Resistance to mining. A review. *Ecological Economics, 132*, 80–90. https://doi.org/10.1016/j.ecolecon.2016.08.025

Conde, M., & Kallis, G. (2012). The global uranium rush and its Africa frontier. Effects, reactions and social movements in Namibia. *Global Environmental Change, 22*(3), 596–610. https://doi.org/10.1016/j.gloenvcha.2012.03.007

Dubuisson, E. M. (2020). Whose world? Discourses of protection for land, environment, and natural resources in Kazakhstan. *Problems of Post-Communism*, 1–13. https://doi.org/10.1080/10758216.2020.1788398

Ecodefense Press-release (2014). Russian government declares Ecodefense a 'Foreign Agent' for resisting construction of nuclear power plant near Kaliningrad. Moscow, Kaliningrad.

Endres, D. (2009). The rhetoric of nuclear colonialism: Rhetorical exclusion of American Indian arguments in the Yucca Mountain Nuclear Waste Siting Decision. *Communication and Critical/Cultural Studies, 6*(1), 39–60. https://doi.org/10.1080/14791420802632103

Energy Information Administration U.S. (EIA). (2012). *Global generation capacity for nuclear power has grown to over 346 gigawatts since 1955*. https://www.eia.gov/todayinenergy/detail.php?id=6310#:~:text=Nuclear%20generating%20capacity%20additions%20began,the%20United%20States%20in%201951.

Fallows, B. J. (2002). The military-industrial complex. *Foreign Policy, 133*(133), 46–48. https://doi.org/10.2307/3183556

Fan, M. F. (2006). Nuclear waste facilities on Tribal Land: The Yami's struggles for environmental justice. *Local Environment, 11*(4), 433–444. https://doi.org/10.1080/13549830600785589

Fredriksson, P. G., & Wollscheid, J. R. (2007). Democratic institutions versus autocratic regimes: The case of environmental policy. *Public Choice, 130*(3–4), 381–393. https://doi.org/10.1007/s11127-006-9093-1

Gibbs, G. (2004). *Qualitative data analysis: Explorations with NVivo: Understanding social research.* Open University Press, Edmunsbury UK.

Gobby, J., Temper, L., Burke, M., & von Ellenrieder, N. (2021). Resistance as governance: Transformative strategies forged on the frontlines of extractivism in Canada. *Extractive Industries and Society,* 100919. https://doi.org/10.1016/j.exis.2021.100919

Göcke, K. (2014). Indigenous peoples in the nuclear age: Uranium mining on indigenous' lands. In J. L. Black-Branch, D. Fleck (Eds.) *Nuclear Non-Proliferation in International Law.* Springer. https://doi.org/10.1007/978-94-6265-020-6_8

Golbeck, J. (2015). Analyzing networks. In J. Golbeck, J.L. Klavans (Eds.) *Introduction to Social Media Investigation*:A Hands-on Approach. Elsevier . https://doi.org/10.1016/b978-0-12-801656-5.00021-4

Gordeev, K., Vasilenko, I., Lebedev, A., Bouville, A., Luckyanov, N., Simon, S., Stepanov, Y., Shinkarev, S., & Anspaugh, L. (2002). Fallout from nuclear tests: Dosimetry in Kazakhstan. *Radiation and Environmental Biophysics, 41*(1), 61–67. https://doi.org/10.1007/s00411-001-0139-y

Graetz, G. (2014). Uranium mining and First Peoples: The nuclear renaissance confronts historical legacies. *Journal of Cleaner Production, 84,* 339–347. https://doi.org/10.1016/j.jclepro.2014.03.055

Grosfoguel, R. (2007). The epistemic decolonial turn: Beyond political-economy paradigms. *Cultural Studies, 21*(2–3), 211–223. https://doi.org/10.1080/09502380601162514

Iržikevičius, R. (2019). Lithuania now has substantial legal arguments to deny access for electricity produced in the unsafe Astravyets Plant. *Lithuanian. Tribune*April 1, 2019. https://lithuaniatribune.com/lithuania-now-has-substantial-legal-arguments-to-deny-access-for-electricity-produced-in-the-unsafe-astravyets-plant/

Ishiyama, N. (2003). Environmental justice and American Indian Tribal Sovereignty: Case Study of a Land–Use Conflict in Skull Valley, Utah. *Antipode, 35*(1), 119–139. https://doi.org/10.1111/1467-8330.00305

Izotov, V., & Obydenkova, A. V. (2021). Geopolitical games in Eurasian regionalism: Ideational interactions and regional international organisations. *Post-Communist Economies, 33*(2–3), 150–174. https://doi.org/10.1080/14631377.2020.1793584

Jacobs, R. (2013). Nuclear conquistadors: Military colonialism in nuclear test site selection during the Cold War. *Asian Journal of Peacebuilding, 1*(2), 157–177. https://doi.org/10.18588/201311.000011

Johansen, B. E. (2002). The Inuit's Struggle with Dioxins and other organic pollutants. *The American Indian Quarterly, 26*(3), 479–490. https://doi.org/10.1353/aiq.2003.0041

Johnston, B. R. (2007). *Review of Half-Lives & Half-Truths: Confronting the Radioactive Legacies of the Cold War.* School for Advanced Research Press.

Josephson, P. R. (2014). *The conquest of the Russian Arctic.* Harvard University Press, London.

Jungk, R. (1979). *The nuclear state.* John Calder, London.

Kasperski, T. (2012). Chernobyl's aftermath in political symbols, monuments and rituals: Remembering the disaster in Belarus. *Anthropology of Eastern Europe Review, 30 (1),* 82–99.

Kasperski, T. (2017). Une transition vers plus de nucléaire? Analyse comparée des politiques énergétiques russe et ukrainienne. *Review International Politics Comparée, 24*(1-2), 101-125. https://doi.org/10.3917/ripc.241.0101

Kasperski, T. (2019). Children, nation and reactors: Imagining and promoting nuclear power in contemporary Ukraine. *Centaurus, 61*(1–2), 51–69. https://doi.org/10.1111/1600-0498.12226

Keeling, A., & Sandlos, J. (2009). Environmental justice goes underground? Historical notes from Canada's northern mining frontier. *Environmental Justice, 2*(3), 117–125. https://doi.org/10.1089/env.2009.0009

Khalturin, V. I., Rautian, T. G., Richards, P. G., & Leith, W. S. (2005). A review of nuclear testing by the Soviet Union at Novaya Zemlya, 1955–1990. *Science & Global Security, 13*(1–2), 1–42. https://doi.org/10.1080/08929880590961862

Khan, F. A. (2021). On Tsar Bomba —the most powerful nuclear weapon ever tested. *Physics Education, 56*(1), 013002. https://doi.org/10.1088/1361-6552/abbcbc

Kojola, E., & Pellow, D. N. (2020). New directions in environmental justice studies: Examining the state and violence. *Environmental Politics, 30*(1-2), 1–19. https://doi.org/10.1080/09644016.2020.1836898

Kuletz, V. (2001). Invisible spaces, Violent places: Cold War Nuclear and Militarized Landscapes. In N. L. Peluso & M. Watts (Eds.), *Violent environments,* 237-260. Cornell University Press.

Kuzmin, V. I. (2013). Vladimir I. Vernadsky and his role in resolution of challenges of nuclear energy utilization in Russia. *New Data on Minerals, 48,* 113–116. https://www.fmm.ru/images/4/40/NDM_2013_48_Kuzmin_eng.pdf

Kyne, D., & Bolin, B. (2016). Emerging environmental justice issues in nuclear power and radioactive contamination. *International Journal of Environmental Research and Public Health, 13*(7), 700. https://doi.org/10.3390/ijerph13070700

Lambert, B. (2001). *Radiation: Early warnings; late effects. in Late lessons from early warnings: The precautionary principle 1896-2000.* European Environment Agency Report No 22.

Lankina, T., Libman, A., Obydenkova, A. (2016). Authoritarian and democratic diffusion in post-communist regions. *Comparative Political Studies, 49*(12), 1599–1629. https://doi.org/10.1177/0010414016628270

Libman, A., & Obydenkova, A. (2019). Inequality and historical legacies: Evidence from post-communist regions. *Post-Communist Economies, 31*(6), 699–724. https://doi.org/10.1080/14631377.2019.1607440

Libman, A., & Obydenkova, A. (2021). *Historical legacies of communism: Modern politics, society, and economic development.* Cambridge University Press.

Libman, A., & Obydenkova, A. V. (2018). Understanding authoritarian regionalism. *Journal of Democracy, 29*(4), 151–165. https://doi.org/10.1353/jod.2018.0070

Litmanen, T., & Kojo, M. (2011). Not excluding nuclear power: The dynamics and stability of nuclear power policy arrangements in Finland. *Journal of Integrative Environmental Sciences, 8*(3), 171–194. https://doi.org/10.1080/1943815X.2011.585652

Magnarella, P. J. (2008). Attempts to reduce and eliminate nuclear weapons through the nuclear non-proliferation treaty and the creation of nuclear-weapon-free zones. *Peace & Change, 33*(4), 507–521. https://doi.org/10.1111/j.1468-0130.2008.00516.x

Malin, S. A. (2015). *The price of nuclear power: Uranium communities and environmental justice.* Rutgers University Press.

Malin, S. A., & Ryder, S. S. (2018). Developing deeply intersectional environmental justice scholarship. *Environmental Sociology, 4*(1), 1–7. https://doi.org/10.1080/23251042.2018.1446711

Marples, D. R. (1993). The post-Soviet nuclear power program. *Post-Soviet Geography, 34*(3), 172–184. https://doi.org/10.1080/10605851.1993.10640925

Marsh, J. K., & Green, J. (2020). First nations rights and colonising practices by the nuclear industry: An Australian battleground for environmental justice. *The Extractive Industries and Society, 7(3),* 870–881. https://doi.org/10.1016/j.exis.2019.01.010

Martinez-Alier, J. (1990). *Ecological economics: Energy, environment and society.* Blackwell.

Martinez-Alier, J. (2002). *The environmentalism of the poor: A study of ecological conflicts and valuation.* Edward Elgar Publishing.

Martínez-Alier, J. (2021). *Mapping ecological distribution conflicts: The EJAtlas.* The Extractive Industries and Society.

Martinez-Alier, J., Temper, L., Del Bene, D., & Scheidel, A. (2016). Is there a global environmental justice movement? *The Journal of Peasant Studies, 43*(3), 731–755. https://doi.org/10.1080/03066150.2016.1141198

Mumford, L. (1956). *Prospect in Thomas, W.L.ed. Man's Role in Changing the Face of the Earth.* University of Chicago Press, Chicago.

Mumford, L. (1970). *The myth of the machine: The Pentagon of Power.* Harcourt Brace Jovanovich.

Navas, G., Mingorria, S., & Aguilar-González, B. (2018). Violence in environmental conflicts: The need for a multidimensional approach. *Sustainability Science, 13*(3), 649–660. https://doi.org/10.1007/s11625-018-0551-8

Nieto, W. A. S. (2011). Assessing Kaliningrad's geostrategic role: The Russian periphery and a baltic concern. . *Journal of Baltic Studies*, *42*(4), 465–489. https://doi.org/10.1080/01629778.2011.621737

Nixon, R. (2011). *Slow violence and the environmentalism of the poor*. Harvard University Press.

Obydenkova, A. (2008). Regime transition in the regions of Russia: The freedom of mass media: Transnational impact on sub-national democratization? *European Journal of Political Research, 47* (2), 221–246. https://doi.org/10.1111/j.1475-6765.2007.00727.x

Obydenkova, A. V., and Arpino, B. (2018). Corruption and Trust in the European Union and National Institutions: Changes over the Great Recession across European States. *JCMS: Journal of Common Market Studies. 56* (3), 594–611. doi:10.1111/jcms.12646

Pellow, D. N. (2016). Toward a critical environmental justices studies. *Du Bois Review: Social Science Research on Race, 13*(2), 221–236. https://doi.org/10.1017/S1742058X1600014X

Pellow, D. N., & Brulle, R. J. (Eds.) (2005). *Power, justice, and the environment: A critical appraisal of the environmental justice movemen* (pp. 1–19). MIT Press.

Peluso, N. L., & Watts, M. (2001). *Violent environments*. Cornell University Press.

Petryna, A. (2002). *Life exposed: Biological Citizens after Chernobyl*. Princeton University Press.

Pop-Eleches, G., & Tucker, J. A. (2017). *Communism's shadow: Historical legacies and contemporary political attitudes*. Princeton University Press.

Prăvălie, R. (2014). Nuclear weapons tests and environmental consequences: A global perspective. *Ambio, 43*(6), 729–744. https://doi.org/10.1007/s13280-014-0491-1

Reich, M. R., & Goto, A. (2015). Towards long-term responses in Fukushima. *The Lancet, 386*(9992), 498–500. https://doi.org/10.1016/S0140-6736(15)61030-3

Runyan, A. S. (2018). Disposable waste, lands and bodies under Canada's gendered nuclear colonialism. *International Feminist Journal of Politics, 20*(1), 24–38. https://doi.org/10.1080/14616742.2017.1419824

Sak, P. B. (1993). Environmental Law in Ukraine: From the Roots to the Bud. *UCLA Journal of Environmental Law and Policy, 11,* 203-253. https://doi.org/10.5070/L5112018804

Salbu, B. (2013). Preface: Uranium mining legacy issue in Central Asia. *Journal of Environmental Radioactivity, 123,* 1–2. https://doi.org/10.1016/j.jenvrad.2011.12.010

Salmi, O. (2008). Drivers for adopting environmental management systems in the post-Soviet mining industry. *International Environmental Agreements: Politics, Law and Economics, 8*(1), 51–77. https://doi.org/10.1007/s10784-007-9046-2

Scheidel, A., Del Bene, D., Liu, J., Navas, G., Mingorría, S., Demaria, F., Avila, S., Roy, B., Ertör, I., Temper, L., & Martínez-Alier, J. (2020). Environmental conflicts and defenders: A global overview. *Global Environmental Change, 63,* 102104. https://doi.org/10.1016/j.gloenvcha.2020.102104

Schlosberg, D. (2013). Theorising environmental justice: The expanding sphere of a discourse. *Environmental Politics, 22*(1), 37–55. https://doi.org/10.1080/09644016.2013.755387

Schlosberg, D., & Carruthers, D. (2010). Indigenous struggles, environmental justice, and community capabilities. *Global Environmental Politics, 10*(4), 12–35. https://doi.org/10.1162/glep_a_00029

Simon, S. L., & Bouville, A. (2015). Health effects of nuclear weapons testing. *The Lancet, 386*(9992), 407–409. https://doi.org/10.1016/S0140-6736(15)61037-6

Statista. (2020). *Number of operable nuclear reactors worldwide as of May 2021, by country*. https://www.statista.com/statistics/267158/number-of-nuclear-reactors-in-operation-by-country/

Temper, L. (2019). Blocking pipelines, unsettling environmental justice: From rights of nature to responsibility to territory. *Local Environment, 24*(2), 94–112. https://doi.org/10.1080/13549839.2018.1536698

Temper, L., Avila, S., Bene, D. D., Gobby, J., Kosoy, N., Billon, P. L., Martinez-Alier, J., Perkins, P., Roy, B., Scheidel, A., & Walter, M. (2020). Movements shaping climate futures: A systematic mapping of protests against fossil fuel and low-carbon energy projects. *Environmental Research Letters, 15*(12), 123004. https://doi.org/10.1088/1748-9326/abc197

Temper, L., Del Bene, D., & Martinez-Alier, J. (2018). Mapping the frontiers and front lines of global environmental justice: The EJAtlas. *The Journal of Political Ecology, 22,* 255. https://doi.org/10.2458/v22i1.21108

Tlostanova, M. V., & Mignolo, W. D. (2009). Global coloniality and the decolonial option. *Kult, 6*, 130–147. http://www.postkolonial.dk/artikler/kult_6/MIGNOLO-TLOSTANOVA.pdf

Tonne, C., Milà, C., Fecht, D., Alvarez, M., Gulliver, J., Smith, J., Beevers, S., Ross Anderson, H., & Kelly, F. (2018). Socioeconomic and ethnic inequalities in exposure to air and noise pollution in London. *Environment International, 115*, 170–179. https://doi.org/10.1016/j.envint.2018.03.023

Turner, E. (1997). There are no peripheries to humanity: Northern Alaska nuclear dumping and the inupiat's search for redress. . *Anthropology Humanism, 22*(1), 95–109. https://doi.org/10.1525/ahu.1997.22.1.95

UNECE, (2020). *Meetings of the Parties to UNECE Treaties on Environmental Assessment mark thirty years of achievements under the Espoo Convention.* UN Sustainable Dev. Goals.

UNESCO, (2005). *Unesco Memory of the World: Audiovisual documents of the International antinuclear movement "Nevada-Semipalatinsk."*

United Nations [UN], (1995). *Treaty on the non-proliferation of nuclear weapons (NPT).*

Uralbekov, B. M., Smodis, B., & Burkitbayev, M. (2011). Uranium in natural waters sampled within former uranium mining sites in Kazakhstan and Kyrgyzstan. *Journal of Radioanalytical and Nuclear Chemistry, 289*(3), 805–810. https://doi.org/10.1007/s10967-011-1154-3

Vernadsky, V. (1924). *La Geóchimie.* Alcan.

Vernadsky, V. (1926). *La Biosphère.* Alcan.

Walker, G., & Bulkeley, H. (2006). Geographies of environmental justice. *Geoforum, 37*(5), 655–659. https://doi.org/10.1016/j.geoforum.2005.12.002

Wiebe, S. M. (2016). *Everyday Exposure: Indigenous mobilization and environmental justice in Canada's Chemical Valley.* UBC Press.

World Nuclear Association (WNA). (2020). Outline History of Nuclear Energy. Retrieved April 2, 2021, from https://www.world-nuclear.org/information-library/current-and-future-generation/outline-history-of-nuclear-energy.aspx#:~:text=The%20first%20nuclear%20reactor%20to,started%20up%20in%20December%201951.

World Nuclear Association (WNA), (2021). *Nuclear Power in Russia.* . Retrieved April 2, 2021, from https://www.world-nuclear.org/information-library/country-profiles/countries-o-s/russia-nuclear-power.aspx

Yelin, J. C., & Miller, D. S. (2009). A Brief History of Environmental Inequity and Military Colonialism on the Isle of Vieques, Puerto Rico. *Environmental Justice, 2*(3), 153–159. https://doi.org/10.1089/env.2009.0021

Ziegler, C. E., & Lyon, H. B. (2002). The politics of nuclear waste in Russia. *Problems of Post-Communism, 49*(4), 33–42. https://doi.org/10.1080/10758216.2002.11655994

Appendix A.

List of cases from the EJAtlas database analysed in this article

No.	Case	Country	Link to the EJAtlas with references to the sources of information
1	Metsamor Nuclear Power Plant	Armenia	Metsamor Nuclear Power Plant, EJAtlas
2	Nuclear power plant at Astravyets	Belarus	Nuclear power plant at Astravyets, EJAtlas
3	Nevada-Semipalatinsk anti-nuclear movement	Kazakhstan	Nevada-Semipalatinsk anti-nuclear movement, EJAtlas
4	Anti-Uranium mining protest, Issyk Kul	Kyrgyzstan	Anti-Uranium mining protest, Issyk Kul, EJAtlas
5	Uranium mining, Mailuu-Suu aka 'Mailbox 200'	Kyrgyzstan	Uranium mining, Mailuu-Suu aka "Mailbox 200", EJAtlas
6	Building and dismantling Ignalina nuclear power plant	Lithuania	Building and dismantling Ignalina nuclear power plant, EJAtlas
7	Construction of the Baltic Nuclear Power Plant, Kaliningrad	Russia	Construction of the Baltic Nuclear Power Plant, Kaliningrad, EJAtlas
8	Floating nuclear power plant, Pevek	Russia	Floating nuclear power plant, Pevek, EJAtlas
9	Kyshtym Disaster and the Mayak plutonium plant	Russia	Kyshtym Disaster and the Mayak plutonium plant, EJAtlas
10	Nuclear Weapons Test Site, Novaya Zemlya	Russia	Nuclear Weapons Test Site, Novaya Zemlya, EJAtlas
11	Bashkir Nuclear Power Plant	Russia	Bashkir Nuclear Power Plant, EJAtlas
12	Leningrad Nuclear Power Plant II in Sosnovy Bor, Leningrad Oblast	Russia	Leningrad Nuclear Power Plant II in Sosnovy Bor, Leningrad Oblast, EJAtlas
13	Million tonnes of radioactive waste from Soviet-times, Istiklol (Tabošar)	Tajikistan	Million tonnes of radioactive waste from Soviet-times, Istiklol (Tabošar), EJAtlas
14	The 1986 catastrophic nuclear accident in Chernobyl	Ukraine	The 1986 catastrophic nuclear accident in Chernobyl, EJAtlas

Appendix B.

Definitions used for nuclear supply chain conflicts codification based on Scheidel et al. (2020) of the EJAtlas categories; Churchill (1993), Endres (2009), Blowers and LeRoy (2006), Jacobs (2013), and Marsh and Green (2020), and Akhter (2017) for nuclear peripheralization applied for bottom-up qualitative codification of the cases description through EJ lens (Pellow, 2016)

Causes	Nuclear periphery	Consequences	Outcomes	Social actors
EJAtlas category: Conflict type first and second level	EJAtlas: Cases description text	EJAtlas: Social, economic, and health consequences (impacts) categories	EJAtlas: Project status category and cases description text	Groups mobilising
Nuclear (Level 1) Conflicts involving nuclear energy production and nuclear waste disposal **Nuclear (Level 2)** Uranium mining, nuclear testing, transportation, nuclear power plants, nuclear waste storage. **Please see** Scheidel et al. (2020).	**Nuclear periphery** Pro-nuclear actors dominate territories, spaces, bodies and lives of historically marginalised peoples in order to maintain nuclear production and nuclear waste disposals and their resistance (Jacobs, 2013; Blowers & LeRoy, 2006; Churchill, 1993; Endres, 2009; Akhter, 2017). **Bottom-up coding examples:** nuclear disarmament, Uranium mining ban, nuclear waste management, anti-nuclear movement etc. Intersectionality, multi-scalarity, state violence (Pellow, 2016).	**Environmental consequences** related to nuclear supply chain projects which may include Surface water pollution/ Decreasing water (physio-chemical, biological) quality; Groundwater pollution or depletion; Mine telling spills etc. **Health impacts** may include occupational disease and accidents, Infectious disease, Exposure to unknown or uncertain complex risks from **radiation**, and deaths. **Social impacts** may include militarisation and increased police presence, loss of livelihood, land dispossession, migration, displacement, loss of landscape and sense of place, Loss of traditional knowledge, practices, and culture etc.	**Suspension of the contentious project** due to protests and claims, or for financial and political reasons. The suspension can last days, months or even years. During the suspension, the project can be re-negotiated, and/or another environmental impact assessment can be carried out, or the project can be finally **stopped**. **Project in operation:** active status of the project development despite protest and oppositions Please see Scheidel et al. (2020). **Additional bottom-up coding: Achievements** regarding anti-nuclear protests.	**Indigenous communities and ethnic groups** that recognise themselves as Indigenous, tribal or traditional. Indigenous and tribal peoples are often known by national terms such as native peoples, aboriginal peoples, first nations, Adivasi, etc. Traditional communities include afro-descendent communities, such as quilombos, Garifuna, etc. **Women** collectives organisations playing a key role in the mobilisation against the contentious activity, either because they are affected by specific impacts (health, labour, household conditions, sexual exploitation, discrimination, or murder), or because they lead the main narratives of resistance and transformation. **Workers** of the nuclear supply chain (miners, industrial, informal workers)

(Continued)

(Continued).

Causes	Nuclear periphery	Consequences	Outcomes	Social actors
				Neighbours, citizens, communities Urban and rural community members defined by proximity or common interest for an EJ cause and mobilising together against a specific project that affects their immediate environment or interest. They include people not necessarily organised into formal collectives or associations. **Local environmental justice organisations (EJOs)** civil society organisations or informal collectives involved in the conflicts at a local scale. They frequently have a local profile when their scope and influence focus on a specific territory or can act on the country level. They include NGOs, associations and other grassroots organisations. **International EJOs** Transnational civil society organisations supporting resistance and counter-knowledge production in conflicts over resource extraction or waste disposal. They have an international profile (scope and influence beyond national borders) and include NGOs, coalitions, formal and informal activist networks, etc. **Social movements** or networks of a plurality of individuals, groups and/or organisations that recognise themselves as part of one movement, operating on the basis of shared collective identities or scopes. They may have existed before the conflict event or formed as a response to it **Please see** Scheidel et al. (2020).

Index

Note: Page numbers followed by "n" denote endnotes.

Abbott, K. W. 14
Acaravci, A. 113
Agyeman, J. 133
Akhter, M. 139
Alberta 88, 101, 102
Alexievich, S. 150
Al-mulali, U. 113
anti-nuclear movement 5, 8, 136, 139, 141, 147–149
Armenia 5, 69, 112, 116, 117, 119, 137, 138, 140, 148, 151
Australia 5, 88, 101, 103, 138, 149
authoritarian regimes 14, 39
autocracies 6, 7, 15, 30, 51
Azerbaijan 112, 115, 117, 137

Bae, J. H. 124
Bastola, U. 113
Beissinger, M. 63
Belarus 5, 112, 116, 117, 132, 134, 136–138, 140, 148, 149, 151
Blowers, A. 139
Breitung, J. 120
Bulgaria 112, 118
Buryj, O. V. 48
businesses 3, 7, 48, 51, 68, 84, 85, 88, 97, 102
Bychkova, A. 4

Cai, Y. 42
Canada 5, 7, 25, 29, 68, 88, 96, 98, 101, 103, 138
carbon border adjustment mechanism 85, 87, 103
carbon dioxide emissions 17, 21, 111, 113, 117–119, 124
carbon emissions 66, 111–114, 116–118, 124, 125
carbon offsets 5, 82, 102, 104
carbon price 83–88, 96, 99–104
carbon pricing 4, 5, 83, 87, 88, 96, 101–104; design 100
carbon regulation 84, 86, 99–101, 103, 104

carbon tax 68, 74, 83, 88, 96, 97, 99–103
case selection, motivation 40–41
causality test 120
causal relationship 111–114, 116, 120, 122
Cheng, X.-M. 113
Chernetsky, V. 64
China 3, 7, 15–17, 21, 25–30, 40, 41, 43, 45, 51, 113, 138
Cieślik, A. 115
civil nuclear power 134, 135
clean energy 23, 24, 27; initiatives 23–24
Clean Energy Ministerial (CEM) 3, 15, 20–26, 28–30; initiatives 21, 25–29
climate change 4, 13, 19, 20, 61, 62, 64–69, 73, 75, 82, 111; governance 14, 30; and green economy 68–70; and international cooperation 70–72; and national strength 65–68; policies 7, 19, 62, 65, 75, 76
climate clubs 6, 13–15, 20, 22, 23, 30, 31
climate governance 14, 15, 23
CO_2 emissions 99, 101, 110–117, 119, 122–125
conflicts 37–43, 47–49, 134, 141, 149, 151, 152
Croatia 112, 118
Czech Republic 112, 118, 125

Danilova, N. 68
data gathering 138
Dellink, R. 111
Demchuk, A. L. 5, 7
democratisation 5, 6, 38, 45, 124, 125
dependent variables 22, 116, 118
diffusion 5–7, 23, 103
Downs, A. 45
Dubuisson, E. M. 63, 73
Dumitrescu, E.-I. 120

economic growth 17, 20, 82, 84, 87, 103, 104, 111–115, 117, 123, 124
EJAtlas (Global Atlas of Environmental Justice) 134, 135, 138, 139

INDEX

emissions 4–7, 66, 70, 82, 85, 87, 96, 101–103, 113, 125; profiles 16–20
emissions trading scheme (ETS) 65
empirical analysis 24, 30, 39, 113
Endres, D. 149
energy 15, 16, 21, 22, 62, 69, 88, 96, 100, 102, 111, 113, 123, 135, 150; consumption 5, 18, 25, 83, 111–114, 122, 124; efficiency 17, 25, 27, 29, 60, 68, 69; governance 3, 13–15, 17, 22; policy 18, 20, 27, 84; sector 21, 30, 83, 98, 99, 101, 104, 115; transitions 86, 103; use 104, 111, 113–115, 119, 122–124
energy-exporting countries 5, 84, 87, 88, 102
environmental activists 40, 42, 43, 48, 49
environmental authoritarianism 41, 42, 51
environmental challenges 5, 6, 8, 52, 82, 124
environmental conflicts 3, 5, 37–43, 45, 47–51; management 3, 37–52
environmental degradation 3, 17, 40, 41, 47, 50, 111, 116
environmental impact assessment (EIA) 49, 50, 135
environmental injustices 133, 134, 137, 148, 149
environmental issues 3, 38–40, 43, 45, 47, 64, 66, 115, 122
environmental justice (EJ) 38, 132–152
environmental movements 3, 6–8, 38–41, 46, 48, 49, 52
environmental politics 7, 38, 74
environmental protests 39, 41, 43, 48
Essandoh, O. K. 117
Estonia 112, 118, 119

Fan, M. F. 149
Finland 19, 25, 27, 137
foreign capital inflows 116, 119
foreign direct investment (FDI) 5, 7, 110–112, 114, 116, 117, 119, 123
fossil fuel combustion 98, 99
fossil fuels exporting countries 82–104
Fredriksson, P. G. 76n8

Gibbs, G. 139
global climate change 22, 110
Goczek, Ł. 115
Green, J. 139, 149
green economy 60, 65, 67, 68, 70; aspirations 60–76
greenhouse gas emissions (GHGs) 15, 16, 65, 66, 68–70, 75, 84, 85, 87, 98, 101; regulation 82–104

Hakimi, A. 116
Hamdi, H. 116
Hanaèek, K. 7
Haug, A. A. 116
He, F. 116

Heathershaw, J. 63
Henderson, J. 18
Hofstede, G. 39, 41
Horvath, R. 115
Hotak, S. 117
Huggan, G. 63
Hungary 112, 118
Hurlin, C. 120
Hussain, J. 114

IEA 60, 86, 101
Im, K. S. 120
independent variables 119
international agenda 60–76
international cooperation 20, 22, 30, 65, 70
international trade 38, 116, 117, 123
Isaeva, A. 7
Isaksen, K. A. 74

Jacobs, R. 136, 139, 148
Jungk, R. 149

Kao, C. 121
Kashem, M. A. 113
Kazakhstan 4, 5, 7, 60–64, 66–73, 75, 115, 118, 136; climate change policy 60–76; vulnerabilities 61, 62
Kemberling, M. 43
Khan, Z. 116
Kropp, S 50
Kuzmin, V. I. 135
Kyoto Protocol 6, 13, 15, 21, 66, 84
Kyrgyz Republic 112, 118, 119
Kyrgyzstan 115, 116, 134–136, 141, 151

land use, land-use change and forestry (LULUCF) 85
Lang, G. 43
Latvia 19, 112, 118
leadership 13–31
LeRroy, P. 139
Levin, A. 120
Li, R. 119
Li, X. 52n4
Li, Y. 43
Libman, A. 52n3, 76n8
Lithuania 112, 118, 132, 134, 137, 140, 148, 149
Lopez, L. 120
Lora-Wainwright, A. 42

Maddala, G. S. 120
Makarov, A. A. 86
Makarov, I. A. 7, 86
Marsh, J. K. 139, 149
Martinez-Alier, J. 7
Medvedev, Dmitry 15, 20
Melnikov, Y. 21

military nuclear energy 134–135
Mitrova, T. 18, 21
Mol, A. P. J. 52n8
Moldova 112, 118, 119
Mumford, L. 149

Nathaniel, S. 114
national actors 3, 51
national strength 60, 65, 67, 68; climate change and 65–68
nation-states 3, 4
negative emissions technologies 23, 27
Neumayer, E. 76n8
non-state actors 13, 14
Normee Che Sab, C. 113
Norway 5, 7, 88, 96, 98, 103
nuclear chain 4–7, 134, 139, 147
nuclear energy 26, 70, 98, 134–136, 149, 152
nuclear peripheralization 133–136, 139, 146–151
nuclear power 24, 27, 29, 133–137, 151
nuclear supply chain 132–152; conflicts 141–146; peripheralization 139–141, 146, 151
nuclear supply chain-related socio-environmental conflicts 136–137

Obydenkova, A. V. 52n3, 76n8
Ogneva-Himmelberger, Y. 133
Omri, A. 114
Ostrom, E. 14, 50
Ozturk, I. 113

panel unit-root test 120
Pao, H.-T. 113
Pedroni, P. 120
Pedroni's cointegration 120, 121
Pellow, D. N. 139
peripheralization 133, 134, 148, 151
Peszko, G. 86
Petrović-Ranđelović, M. 114
Plantan, E. 42
Poberezhskaya, M. 4, 68
Poland 24, 112, 118, 149
political discourse analysis (PDA) 64
political economy analysis 102
political legacies 148, 151
post-Soviet economies 112, 114, 117, 122–125
primary energy consumption 88, 98

radiation 133, 134, 137, 138, 140, 141, 148–151
radioactive waste 140, 141
Rahman, M. M. 113
renewable energy 18, 21, 25–27, 29, 69
resistance 45, 134, 135, 139, 148–151
Rinscheid, A. 30
Roberts, J. T. 43

Romania 112, 118
Russia 3, 6, 15, 19, 21, 22, 25–27, 29, 41, 45, 46, 49, 51, 84–87, 102; carbon pricing design in 100; climate policy 84–86; economy 84, 99, 101; environmental conflicts and vertical of power 45–50; GHG emissions in 85, 98; opportunities and challenges for 82–104
Russian Federation 47, 50, 84, 112, 115, 118, 119, 125, 132, 137, 138, 140
Russian government 18, 19, 28–30, 48

Sadikov, A. 114, 119, 122
Saidi, K. 114
Salahodjaev, R. 7, 76n8
Sapkota, P. 113
Schatz, E. 74
Schuhmann, J. 50
Shakhanova, G. 63
Shyrokykh, K. 3, 6
Slovak Republic 112, 118
Slovenia 112, 118
social groups 51, 64, 88, 100, 103, 138
socio-environmental conflicts 5, 133, 134, 138, 139, 151
socio-environmental justice 149, 150
Soviet Union 45, 62, 118, 122, 132, 134–136, 138, 141, 148
Sprinz, D. F. 20
state secrets 148, 150
state violence 138, 139, 141, 150
Stepanov, I. A. 7
Stokke, K. 74
Stone, R. W. 22
sustainable development goals 38, 72

Tajikistan 115, 135, 141
Temper, L. 139
Tosun, J. 3, 6, 30
trade 5, 7, 73, 111, 112, 116, 117, 119, 122–124; openness 112, 114, 124
transgenerational radiation effects 148, 150
transition countries 117, 124, 125
Turkmenistan 69, 112, 115, 118, 119

Ucal, M. 116
Ukraine 5, 112, 118, 132, 134, 138, 140, 148
Umurzakov, U. 114
United Nations Framework Convention on Climate Change (UNFCCC) 61
uranium 135, 136, 138
Uzbekistan 62, 115, 135

Van Dijk, T. A. 64
variables 113, 114, 116, 119–122, 124, 139, 147
Vinogradov, M. 47

violence 134, 138, 150–151; *see also* state violence
Vogel, D. 38
vulnerable industries 100, 103

Watters, K. 76n4
Weber, S. 120
Weinthal, E. 76n4
Weischer, L. 23
Wollscheid, J. R. 76n8

World Nuclear Association 138
Wu, S. 120

Xu, Y. 43

Yanitsky, O. N. 50
Young, M. C. 63

Zeynalov, A. 115
Zhang, X.-P. 113